MODERN PERL PROGRAMMING

MICHAEL SALTZMAN

Prentice Hall PTR
Upper Saddle River, NJ 07458
www.phptr.com

ISBN 0-13-008965-6

90000

9 780130 089656

Library of Congress Cataloging-in-Publication Data

CIP data available

Production Supervisor: Wil Mara
Executive Editor: Jill Harry
Editorial Assistant: Sarah Hand
Marketing Manager: Dan DePasquale
Buyer: Maura Zaldivar
Cover Designer: Talar Boorujy
Composition: Sean Donahue

 © 2002 Prentice Hall PTR
A Division of Pearson Education, Inc.
Upper Saddle River, NJ 07458

The publisher offers discounts on this book when ordered in bulk quantities. For more information contact: Corporate Sales Department, Prentice Hall PTR, One Lake Street, Upper Saddle River, NJ 07458. Phone: 800-382-3419; FAX: 201-236-7141; E-mail: corpsales@prenhall.com.

Printed in the United States of America

10 9 8 7 6 5 4 3 2 1

ISBN 0-13-008965-6

Pearson Education LTD.
Pearson Education Australia PTY, Limited
Pearson Education Singapore, Pte. Ltd
Pearson Education North Asia Ltd
Pearson Education Canada, Ltd.
Pearson Educación de Mexico, S.A. de C.V.
Pearson Education—Japan
Pearson Education Malaysia, Pte. Ltd
Pearson Education, Upper Saddle River, New Jersey

TABLE OF CONTENTS

CHAPTER 1

A TUTORIAL INTRODUCTION TO PERL...........1

CHAPTER 2

INPUT AND OUTPUT IN PERL. 29

CHAPTER 3

OPERATORS IN PERL 49

CHAPTER 4

ARRAYS AND ARRAY FUNCTIONS 69

CHAPTER 5

HASHES 87

CHAPTER 6

REGULAR EXPRESSIONS 105

CHAPTER 7

SUBPROGRAMS 125

CHAPTER 8

GENERATING REPORTS IN PERL 147

CHAPTER 9

ACCESSING SYSTEM RESOURCES 159

CHAPTER 10

PERL REFERENCES 175

CHAPTER 11

OBJECT-ORIENTED PROGRAMMING 201

CHAPTER 12

CLIENT/SERVER APPLICATIONS. 217

CHAPTER 13

CGI PROGRAMMING WITH PERL 231

CHAPTER 14

GRAPHICAL USER INTERFACES
WITH THE Tk.PM MODULE 253

CHAPTER 15

ACCESSING REAL DATABASES IN PERL 287

CHAPTER 16

DEBUGGING PERL SCRIPTS 307

PREFACE

Welcome to the world of Perl programming. I know that few of you enjoy reading the preface, but it may help to at least browse through it to make the reading of the actual text a little easier. In this section I will tell you a little about Perl and a lot about conventions used in this book. But first, I have a few questions to answer.

What Is Perl?

Perl is a programming language that was created by Larry Wall in the early 1980s. The language has gained widespread popularity over the last few decades. In the beginning, Perl was used by a small group of Unix system administrators who needed a language, superior to the Unix shell, to do various system administration tasks. With the exponential growth of the Internet and the popularity of the World Wide Web's Common Gateway Interface (CGI) programming paradigm, the number of Perl programmers has also grown exponentially.

Why program in Perl?

Being familiar with many programming languages, I'm in a good position to judge them. I have had my favorite languages throughout the years: Fortran, PL/1, C, C++, Java, and of course, Perl. Too many people argue about which language is the best. No language can be all things to all people. Each language has its strengths and weaknesses. However, no language that I know has the expressive capability and ease of use of Perl. You, of course, can decide for yourself when you finish reading this book.

Why did I write this book?

I have been an instructor of computer programming languages for more than three decades. In that time, I have had the occasion to learn many languages. My typical approach would be to buy a book on the subject, plow through it, and write as many programs as I could to test out various features of the language.

I'm very critical of textbooks. Most of the textbooks that I've read never seem to be at the correct level. Half of them seemed too elementary; the other half seemed too advanced. I always wanted one that was right in the middle. I've tried to write this book for the intermediate audience because I think I can save people in that category a lot of time and research.

Who should read this book?

This is a book about Perl programming, so anybody who is interested in writing Perl programs should read this book. Since Perl is a programming language, you would think this means only programmers should read it. Currently, however, there is a blur over who is a programmer. Many Web-sters who maintain Web pages also write CGI scripts. System administrators need to write scripts to support users. Managers periodically want to write scripts to create reports for various staff members above and below them in the corporate hierarchy. All these groups would profit from reading this book.

Overview of the Book

The book is organized in three sections: beginning, intermediate, and advanced. In the beginning section, you will see topics such as: input and output, operators, arrays, control structures, and data types. In the intermediate section, you will see topics such as: associative arrays, regular expressions, subroutines, report writing, and accessing system resources. The advanced section includes topics such as: references, object-oriented programming, client/server programming, CGI programming, graphical user interfaces (GUIs) with the Tk module, accessing real databases in Perl, and debugging.

Chapter Summaries

Chapter 1: A Perl Tutorial

… demonstrates many fundamental Perl features so that you can start writing Perl programs quickly. Subsequent chapters will drill more deeply into each of the topics presented here.

Chapter 2: Simple I/O

… looks more deeply into reading and writing files. Some of Perl's operators for determining the type of a file are explored. Finally, this chapter looks at how you can determine information about files.

Chapter 3: Perl Operators

… examines the Perl operators. A Perl expression is a syntactically correct combination of operators and operands. Perl has a plethora of operators. Many of them originated with the

C language and some of them are particular to Perl. In this chapter, we will explore all of the operators, including those used for bit manipulation, string manipulation, and regular expressions.

Chapter 4: Arrays and Array Functions

… takes an in-depth look at arrays in Perl. All programming languages use arrays heavily and Perl is no exception. However, you will see that Perl arrays are dynamic and are supported by a wide variety of functions. We will take a look at some of the nice features of Perl arrays. Finally, we will look at many of the more common array functions used by Perl programmers.

Chapter 5: Hashes

… looks at a common scenario in programming languages: paired data. Associative arrays, also called hashes, provide an efficient way to search for values by their keys. In this chapter, we will show how hashes may be used to efficiently solve a wide variety of commonly encountered problems.

Chapter 6: Regular Expressions

… refers to patterns that are expressed with characters armed with special meanings. These patterns may be compared to strings to see if the strings match the patterns. These regular expressions make it easy for Perl to validate data, make substitutions, or pick out portions of a match.

Chapter 7: Subprograms

… investigates the wide gamut of possibilities when you write your own functions. This chapter examines all of the principles having to do with subroutines in Perl. Some languages refer to these blocks as functions, while others refer to them as subroutines, and still others refer to them as procedures. In Perl, they are referred to as either subroutines or functions. Perl does not differentiate between these two terms.

Chapter 8: Generating Reports in Perl

… demonstrates Perl's report writing capabilities. Reports are typically written by system administrators to summarize user and file activity. You can have Perl automatically generate headers and body formats. This chapter gives the details of the rudimentary report writing capabilities of Perl.

Chapter 9: Accessing System Resources

… reveals the many system calls that are available via Perl. There is a strong Unix flavor to these functions. However, many of them have been implemented on Windows so that they have a consistent behavior regardless of the operating system.

Chapter 10: Perl References

… moves the reader along into slightly advanced concepts. This chapter concentrates on a thorough treatment of references, Perl's version of pointers. References are used for almost all advanced Perl topics.

Chapter 11: Object-Oriented Programming

… gives the details on how to write Perl programs that use objects and methods. This important chapter is the basis of many of the Perl modules found at various Perl repositories on the Internet.

Chapter 12: Client/Server Applications

… explores the possibilities of writing network applications with Perl. After reviewing some networking fundamentals, we'll give some examples of writing clients that connect to real servers. Then we will write a few servers of our own.

Chapter 13: CGI Applications

… explores the topics of writing back-end programs invoked by Web servers to process front-end fill-in forms. This style of programming, called CGI scripting, is largely responsible for the exponential growth of Perl.

Chapter 14: Graphical User Interfaces with the `Tk.pm` Module

… gives a great many details about writing GUIs in Perl using the `Tk.pm` module. This is a great undertaking as this is a vast body of knowledge. This chapter demonstrates many `Tk` capabilities, but at a high level. All the methods in this section take many options. We will only show a few for each and leave the rest for a book that specializes in writing GUIs in Perl using the `Tk` module. Our approach in this section will be to introduce a few widgets and build a program in pieces. At the conclusion of this section, we will have built a GUI with an application behind it.

Chapter 15: Accessing Real Databases in Perl

… shows how to integrate SQL commands within your Perl scripts so that real databases may be accessed. To remain vendor-neutral, we will use the MySQL database, which can be downloaded at www.mysql.com. With this database, we will demonstrate the principles of accessing all databases in Perl, regardless of whether the actual database is Oracle, Sybase, Access, etc.

Chapter 16: Debugging Perl Scripts

… explores many of the possibilities of debugging your Perl code. Debugging a piece of software is a difficult task in any programming language. Since Perl is so permissive, there is much room for error. This chapter shows many techniques for finding errors, including the use of the Perl debugger itself.

Conventions Used in this Book

Spelling

In any technical field, a new vocabulary is introduced. These new words may cause spelling debates. To no small degree, this applies to any subject matter concerned with software. Here are a few words and the spellings we will use:

A filehandle refers to a name within a Perl program that is connected to an actual disk file. We will spell this word as filehandle, not file handle.

A database is a set of data that is connected together in some form. We will spell this word as database, not data base.

A filename is the name given to a file. We will spell this as filename, not file name.

A newline character is the character generated when you press the Enter key. We will spell this as newline, not new line.

The word "builtin" will be used to indicate that certain items are built into the language. For example, we might say that the length function is a builtin Perl function.

Fonts

Various fonts will be used in this book to emphasize certain components of the book. All Perl keywords, variable names, reserved words, and code will be set in the Courier font. For example:

The following code illustrates the push and print functions in Perl:

```
push(@values,10);
print "@values \n";
```

Unix vs. Windows

Perl programs run in many environments, though the two major operating systems in the marketplace of 2002 are Unix and Windows (and their variants). As you will see, there is a slight difference between executing a Perl program in these two environments. To normalize the way a Perl program is executed in this book, we will always use the % symbol as the system prompt. If you are using Unix, the first line of every script needs to be:

```
#!/usr/bin/perl
```

where the first two characters are #! and the rest of the line is the complete pathname for the Perl executable. We used /usr/bin/perl, where it is located on Linux, but it may be different on your system.

We will simply give the name of a Perl program to execute it, although on Windows, you'll need to put the word "perl" in front of the executable file. On Unix, you will want to make each file executable by using the chmod command. We will not show the chmod command being executed each time. We will simply show the execution of Perl scripts as follows:

```
% countfiles.pl
There are 10 files in the current directory
%
```

Filenames for Perl scripts

In the Perl world, there is no restriction on the naming of Perl executable files. Despite this lack of restriction, we will always name our example scripts with the .pl extension.

User input

When a program requires user input, it will always be in boldface font, as shown in the following example:

```
% addinput.pl
Enter first number 25
Enter second number 50
Sum is 75
%
```

Displaying programs

Whenever we display a program file, it will always have the same format. The first four lines will be comments. The first line will have the name of the Perl executable used to execute the script. There will also be ample comments to describe what each program is doing. Comments in Perl begin with the # character and are terminated with an end of line. Here is an example program file:

```
#!/usr/bin/perl
#
#   length.pl
#
while ( 1 )                          # always true
{   print "-> ";                     # issue a prompt
    $line = <STDIN>;                 # read a line
    chomp($line);                    # nix the newline
    $len = length($line);            # comp line length
    print "$len is length of $line";
}
```

Standard input and standard output redirections

Perl matured on Unix. On those systems, there is a common notion of two popular files—the standard input file (the keyboard) and the standard output file (the display). This nomenclature has been adopted by the Windows world as well. Thus, we will often speak of a program that reads from the standard input, and we will also speak of a program that writes to the standard output. The following program is one of them:

```
% addinput.pl
Enter first number 25
Enter second number 50
Sum is 75
%
```

The < symbol may be used to redirect the standard input so that the data can come from a disk file. The > symbol may be used to redirect the standard output to a disk file. We will use these notations whenever necessary. For example, the following demonstrates how to read from a disk file and write to another disk file:

```
% printlines.pl < inputfile > outputfile
```

Because of the < symbol, the program takes its input from the file named inputfile rather than from the keyboard. Likewise, the program directs its output to the disk file named outputfile rather than to the display.

The newline character

If you are a Unix user, you are familiar with the newline character. It is generated when the user presses the Return (or Enter) key. Perl scripts honor this convention regardless of the operating system.

Writing style

In writing a book about a programming language, the author is faced with many different decisions. Since this book contains many complete code examples, I must show you the code and explain it. This leads to two inevitable choices: show the code and then write about it, or write about it and then show the code. There are drawbacks and advantages to each choice. For the most part, I have given the code first and then given the explanation. When you become frustrated reading some of the code, have a little patience, for the explanation will surely follow.

Displaying files

Occasionally, you may need to display a few data files so you can interpret the results of programs. On Unix systems, this is usually accomplished with the `cat` command; on Windows, this is usually accomplished with the `type` command. To stay neutral, we will use a mythical `display` command as follows:

```
% display datafile
Michael   Saltzman   Columbia          Maryland
Susan     Saltzman   Charleston        South Carolina
Erin      Flanagan   Annapolis         Maryland
Patti     Ordonez    Columbia          Maryland
Maria     Gonzalez   Pikesville        Maryland
Dave      Flanagan   Bowie             Maryland
Bob       Knox       Ft. Lauderdale    Florida
%
```

Source files

All of the code found in the examples is available online, as well as the solutions to the exercises that appear in each chapter. Please go to **www.phptr.com/saltzman/** to retrieve this material.

Acknowledgments

There are those that I wish to thank for this work. Robert Oberg originally put me in touch with the folks at Prentice Hall. Without him, this work would never have happened. I also want to thank Michael DaConta and Scott Meyers. Each of them may not know it, but they inspired me to become an author. I also want to thank the /training/etc staff, who aided me in various ways as this book went from an idea to a publication. They are Bob Knox, Erin Flanagan, Patti Ordonez, Dave Flanagan, Maria Gonzales, and last, but certainly not least, Susan Saltzman, my partner at work and at home.

1

A TUTORIAL
INTRODUCTION TO PERL

The goal in this chapter is to demonstrate many fundamental Perl features so that you may start writing Perl programs quickly. Subsequent chapters will drill more deeply into each of the topics presented here.

1.1   Getting Started

Programming languages come in all shapes and sizes. There are many ways of categorizing them. Some are considered high-level and some are considered low-level. The basic difference between these characterizations is the amount of code you need to write to express an idea. The less code you need to write, the higher the level of the language. Perl is a high-level programming language. Sometimes it is compiled and sometimes it is interpreted.

Perl was written in the early 1980s by a modern-day Renaissance man named Larry Wall. Perl combines the best features of the Unix shells, C language, and some of the more famous Unix utilities such as awk, grep, and sed. Once you are familiar with Perl, you will probably choose Perl over any of the shells, if management gives you a choice.

Perl is often referred to as a scripting language. Likewise, Perl programs are often called Perl scripts, but this distinction is largely irrelevant. Perl is currently used in a wide variety of domains, including system administration, client/server and CGI applications, text and file processing, database retrievals, biomedical processing, and many other domains.

Perl is extremely easy to learn even though there are some notational learning curves to be conquered in certain advanced features of the language.

You can download Perl freeware at the site www.activestate.com. This site has versions of Perl for most major platforms, including Windows variants, Unix variants, and Microsoft.net. For the Macintosh, you can visit www.macperl.com. For any and all information about Perl, visit www.perl.com.

Similar to other pieces of software, Perl has undergone quite a transformation since the first version was released in January 1988. Perl 2.0 was released in June 1988 and Perl 3.0 was released in October 1989. However, the most important releases are the Perl 4 release

in March 1991 and the Perl 5 release in October 1994. A new version of Perl, Perl 5.6, was
released in early 2001.

We will assume that you have installed Perl on your machine and that you are ready to
write Perl programs.

1.1.1 The first Perl program

Here's a simple Perl program:

```
#!/usr/bin/perl
#
#     first.pl
#
print "Please enter your name ";
$name = <STDIN>;
chomp ($name);
print "Your name is $name";
```

Perl programs are written using your favorite text editor. Once you have typed your code
into a file, there is no need to compile it—you simply execute it.

The # is a special character in Perl. Anything that follows this character is interpreted as
a comment. A comment is terminated by the end of a line. Thus, the first four lines above
are comments. (Actually, the top line is treated in a special way on Unix systems—we will
see this later.)

Note that all Perl statements end in a semicolon. The `print` statement places data on
the standard output file, the display. In this case, a prompt is displayed requesting that the
user enter a name. Let's assume for now that the data that is printed needs to be wrapped in
double quotes.

The next line reads a line typed by the user on the keyboard. The data will be stored
inside the Perl variable `$name`. This data includes the newline character. In Perl, all variable names have some punctuation associated with them. The `$` signifies that this variable
can hold one value. This one value could be a number, a string, or something else. In any
case, it will be treated as a single value. In this case, the string typed in by the user is held
there. Variables that begin with `$` are referred to as scalar variables. We will have more to
say about these variables later.

`<STDIN>` is the Perl operator for reading a line from the standard input file, the keyboard. A line is defined as all of the characters up to and including the newline character.
This character is generated when you press the Return (or Enter) key. Thus, the following
code reads a line from the user at the keyboard:

```
$name = <STDIN>;
```

chomp is a Perl function that discards the last character in a variable only if it is a new-line. Thus, the newline is discarded from $name. Finally, another print is used to print the value of the variable $name. Incidentally, there is another function, named chop, which unconditionally eliminates the last character of a variable.

Before we show how first.pl is executed, we need to make a slight diversion and mention a few differences between running your Perl scripts on a Unix system vs. running scripts on a Windows system. On Unix, the first line of every Perl script must appear as:

```
#!/usr/bin/perl
```

Unix shell programmers may recognize this. The first two characters are interpreted as special by any of the Unix shells. These two characters, #!, tell the Unix shell to use the command /usr/bin/perl to execute this script. So if you are on a Unix system, change the first line of your scripts to the complete pathname of the Perl executable, which in our case is #!/usr/bin/perl.

On Unix, after you have prepared your script, it should be made executable using the chmod command. We'll use the % as the system prompt for all of our examples:

```
% chmod 755 first.pl
```

Now you can simply execute the program as follows:

```
% first.pl
```

On a Windows machine, the easiest way to proceed is to open a DOS window and type the following to execute first.pl. On Windows, the #! line is treated as a comment.

```
% perl first.pl
Please enter your name Michael
Your name is Michael
%
```

Here's an example of how to execute this program on Unix:

```
% first.pl
Please enter your name Michael
Your name is Michael
%
```

Note that throughout the book, what the user types will be in bold letters. You can also see that all non-comment lines end with the semicolon character. Syntactically, the semicolon is a statement separator, not a statement terminator; thus, the last statement in a script, or the last statement of any block (statements delimited by curly braces ({ })), does not have to be terminated with a semicolon. However, it is good practice to place one there since you may later add some Perl code to the end of the script.

1.1.2   Some elementary I/O

Thus far, we have seen the `print` function used several times. We now would like to explore how a Perl program performs elementary input and output. Whenever you wish to place some information on the user's display, you use the `print` function. By default, your data will be sent to the standard output file, the display. Perl programs understand the concept of a filehandle, a name that is associated with a file. Perl defines a few builtin filehandles, one of which is `STDOUT`. If you wish, you may use a filehandle in the `print` function to explicitly specify the destination for the data to be printed. The following two lines are therefore functionally identical to one another:

```
print STDOUT "this string gets sent to the display";
print "this string gets sent to the display";
```

You may also create your own filehandle by using the `open` function. This function associates a filehandle with an actual disk file. `open` contains two arguments, the first of which is a filehandle and the second of which contains the name of the file to be created and the mode (input or output) of the file. The access mode is given as a punctuation symbol. The following `open` function associates the file named `mydata` with the filehandle `OUTPUT`. The > punctuation symbol specifies that the file will be used as an output file. Be careful here. If the file already exists, its data will be truncated.

The name `OUTPUT` is one of our choosing. We could have called it `OUT` or anything else. When you create a filehandle, use a naming convention that is mnemonically sound.

Here's a sample program, `iodemo.pl`, that creates a file and sends some data to the file associated with the filehandle and to the display:

```
#!/usr/bin/perl
#
#   iodemo.pl
#
open(OUTPUT,"> mydata");
print STDOUT "Welcome to the Perl language\n";
print OUTPUT "This data goes to a file\n";
print STDOUT "I think you will enjoy it\n";
print OUTPUT "Likewise this goes to a file also\n";
```

When you execute the above program, you'll only see two lines on the display. The other two lines have been sent to the file named mydata. Note that we've also placed the newline character, \n, at the end of each line. Without this character, both strings end up on the same physical output line. This is a good place to do some testing of your own. If you load a copy of iotest.pl, you may remove the newline characters, run the program again, and observe the results.

Notice that this program created a file named mydata. If you want to see the two lines in that file, you may use whichever utility comes with your system to display them (e.g., cat on Unix or type with Windows).

```
% iodemo.pl
Welcome to the Perl language
I think you will enjoy it
% display mydata
This data goes to a file
Likewise this goes to a file also
%
```

The next example will demonstrate how to open a file for input. Ultimately, we will also need to know how to handle errors produced by open, but we will delay that until later.

You may open a file for input simply by using the < symbol at the beginning of the second argument to the open function. Of course, the file should exist or an attempt to open it will cause an error. If you do not specify any punctuation with the second argument, then the file is opened for input by default. Thus, the following lines are equivalent:

```
open(INPUT, "< input");
open(INPUT, "input");
```

Now that you have created the association between the filehandle and an actual disk file, you may use the <> operator to read from the file.

```
$line = <INPUT>;
```

$line is a scalar variable used to store the line that is entered by the user. We saw something close to this earlier when we read a line from the standard input with:

```
$line = <STDIN>;
```

The difference between the previous two lines of code is that INPUT is a filehandle created in the Perl program, whereas STDIN is a filehandle predefined in the Perl language.

The snippet of code below reads the only two lines from the file `mydata` created above and sends them to the display:

```
open(INPUTFILE, "< mydata");
$firstline = <INPUTFILE>;
print "$firstline";
$firstline = <INPUTFILE>;
print "$firstline";
```

Each line of the form:

```
$variable = <SOME_FILE_HANDLE>;
```

reads the next line from the file associated with:

```
SOME_FILE_HANDLE
```

There's also a predefined filehandle, named `ARGV`, which is used to step through a group of files named on the command line. We will see more information about this and other filehandles later.

1.2   Perl Variables

Perl does not have a strict type system, although there is a distinction between three different kinds of variables. A scalar variable must begin with $. A scalar may hold a single value. An array variable must begin with @. An array is a collection of scalars. A hash variable must begin with %. A hash, sometimes called an associative array, holds pairs of values.

Perl variables are case-sensitive. They may be composed of any number of characters. It is also allowable, albeit confusing to programmers, to have a scalar variable with the same name as an array variable, both of which have the same name as a hash. In other words, each of the following is a different variable:

```
$names      scalar named names
@names      array named names
%names      hash named names
```

1.2.1 Scalars

Depending on the language with which you are most familiar, the following Perl code may seem a little strange to you, since the same variable, $data, is used to store an integer value and then a string value.

```
#!/usr/bin/perl
#
#    scalars.pl
#
print "input a number ";
$data = <STDIN>;
chomp($data);
print "$data * $data is ";
print  $data * $data;
print "\n";
print "input your name ";
$data = <STDIN>;
print "Your name is $data\n";
% scalars.pl
input a number 25
25 * 25 is 625
input your name Michael
your name is Michael
%
```

This is not a problem in Perl because $data is a scalar and as such may contain any single value. That value may be a string or any kind of number. In any expression concerning $data, it is the operator which determines how to treat the value held in the variable, that is, as a string or as a number. For now, the important item is that $data is a scalar and thus may hold a single value.

1.2.2 Arrays

An array is an ordered list of elements typically separated by commas. Here are a few examples of arrays:

```
@names = (Mike, "Susan Smyth", "Erin\nFlanagan");
@bas = (.324, .298, .245);
@record = ("Mike", 27, .324, "Columbia, Md");
$data = 6;                        # a scalar
@numbers = (1,2,3,4,5, $data);    # an array
```

The @numbers array contains a series of numbers. The @names array contains a series of strings. If any of these strings contains a blank, a newline, or a tab, it needs to be protected by using quotes. Note also that an array, such as @record, may contain disparate types since each of them is a scalar. The important thing is that an array is a list of scalars. If you need to know the size of an array, simply assign the array to a scalar.

```
$size = @record;        # size = 4
$size = @numbers        # size = 6
$size = @names;         # size = 3
```

An important property of Perl arrays is that they are dynamic. This is a departure from other languages, but it is a very useful feature.

```
@numbers = (80, @numbers, 90);
$size = @numbers;              # size = 8
```

If you need to access a particular scalar in an array, then you must index the element with a subscript using square bracket notation, [ ]. Perl indices begin with 0. Here are a few examples:

```
@record = ("Mike", 27, .324, "Columbia, Md");
print "$record[0]\n";      #  Mike
print "$record[1]\n";      #  27
```

An entire array can be printed by placing double quotes around the array's name. This prints each element of the array with a space separating the elements. This is generally the way you will want to see array values displayed:

```
print "@record\n";         # mike 27 .324 Columbia, Md
```

If you want the array elements adjacent to one another, simply omit the quotes:

```
print @record;             # mike27.324Columbia, Md
```

Note also that anything in single quotes will print literally::

```
print '@record';           # @record
```

The simple program below, `arrays.pl`, demonstrates these introductory concepts about arrays:

```perl
#!/usr/bin/perl
#
#       arrays.pl
#
@values = (10, 20, 15);
$size = @values;
print 'For @values array', "\n";
print "Size is $size\n";
print "Elements (with spaces) are @values\n";
print "Elements (no spaces) are ";
print  @values;
print "\nElements one by one\n";
print "$values[0]\n";
print "$values[1]\n";
print "$values[2]\n";

% arrays.pl
For @values array
Size is 3
Elements (with spaces) are 10 20 15
Elements (no spaces) are 102015
Elements one by one
10
20
15
%
```

1.2.3   Array functions

Perl contains many array functions. Some of the more common ones are shown here. `pop` returns the last element of an array and also removes this element from the array.

```perl
@values = ( 1,2,8,14 );
$result = pop(@values);       # result = 14
print "@values \n";           # 1 2 8
print pop(@values),"\n";      # 8
print "@values\n";            # 1 2
```

`push` pushes a value onto the bottom of an array. You may push as many elements onto an array as you wish.

```
push(@values,10);                # 1 2 10
print "@values \n";              # 1 2 10
push(@values, 11,8);             # 1 2 10 11 8
push(@values, @values);          # 1 2 10 11 8 1 2 10 11 8
```

The shift and unshift functions behave like pop and push, except that they operate on the beginning of an array, not the end of an array.

```
shift(@values);                  # 2 10 11 8 1 2 10 11 8
unshift(@values, 1, 15)          # 1 15 2 10 11 8 1 2 10 11 8
```

reverse returns a list in reverse order, leaving the original list unchanged.

```
@back = reverse(@values);
print "@back\n";                 # 8 11 10 2 1 8 11 10 2 15 1
print "@values\n";               # 1 15 2 10 11 8 1 2 10 11 8
```

sort sorts a list in dictionary order, returning the sorted list and leaving the original list
unchanged.

```
@names = (Jo, Pete, Bill, Bob, Zeke, Al);
@sorted = sort(@names);
print "@names\n";        # Jo Pete Bill Bob Zeke Al
print "@sorted\n";       # Al Bill Bob Jo Pete Zeke
```

join takes a separator string and an array and produces a scalar consisting of all array
elements with the separator between them. split is the opposite of join. It takes a string
and splits it into an array based on a delimiter given as the first argument. Here is an example to demonstrate split and join:

```
#!/usr/bin/perl
#
#   splitjoin.pl
#
print "enter your favorite colors ";
$colors = <STDIN>;
@colors = split(" ", $colors);
$size = @colors;
print "You entered $size colors\n";
$colors = join("&", @colors);
print "They are:\n$colors\n";
```

continued...

```
% splitjoin.pl
enter your favorite colors red green blue orange
You entered 4 colors
They are:
red&green&blue&orange
%
```

The program prompts you for your favorite colors. When you respond, the program splits your answers into an array and then determines the size of the array, which is the number of colors. Then these colors are joined into a single scalar separated by the & character.

1.2.4   Arrays and STDIN

Recall that the following code reads a line from the standard input:

```
$name = <STDIN>;
```

If the variable above had been an array rather than a scalar, then Perl would have read the entire file into the array. Each line of the file would have become the next element of the array.

```
@data = <STDIN>;            # read entire file
```

This makes copying a file (STDIN to STDOUT) as easy as:

```
@data = <STDIN>;            # read all lines from STDIN
print @data;                # print each element (i.e. each line)
```

Of course, the key issue here is the fact that the variable at the left of the = is an array. Thus, we could read all the lines from any file as long as we have a filehandle associated with that file.

```
open(INPUT, "< mydata");     # open file named 'mydata'
@lines = <INPUT>;            # read all lines from file
```

Many files have header information in the first line and the actual data in succeeding lines. Using the concept in this section, we can use the script justdata.pl to read such a file.

```
#!/usr/bin/perl
#
#       jastdata.pl
#
open(DATAFILE, "< datafile");    # open file
$head = <DATAFILE>;              # read first line
@remainder = <DATAFILE>;         # read rest of lines
print @remainder;
```

The first line of code opens the file `datafile`. The next line of Perl code reads the first line of `datafile`. Since the next line of Perl code has an array on the left of the assignment operator, all the remaining lines of the `datafile` are read.

1.2.5 Associative arrays

An associative array is a collection of pairs where the first element of the pair is called the key and the second element of each pair is called the value associated with the key. The idea behind associative arrays is that the key can be used to retrieve the value. Associative arrays are often called hashes. This data type is used to implement table lookups. There are many problems that can be solved using hashes. The key is usually string data. Thus, you could look up a capital city by its state or you could look up a bank balance by the name of the account. Associative arrays save the programmer the actual programming of the lookup. If you need to define an associative array, remember that its name must begin with the % symbol. Beyond that, the pairs must be specified.

```
%accounts = (    Mike  => 100,
                 Sue   => 200,
                 Erin  => 150,
                 Patti => 250,
);
```

The symbol `=>` can be used to make the associations clear. However, the following notation may be used as well. In this case, the associations are made in terms of the orderings; that is, the first two entries represent the first pair, the next two elements represent the second pair, etc.

```
%accounts = (Mike, 100, Sue, 200, Erin, 50, Patti, 250);
```

Since an associative array and a regular array may have the same name, to extract a particular value from an associative array, you must use the curly brace form of the subscript operator. The key that acts as the subscript may be quoted or not. Of course, if the key contains embedded blanks, then the key must be quoted.

```
$accounts{Mike}              #           yields  100
$accounts{Sue}               #           yields  200
```

Here's a small example of declaring an associative array and then seeing if a value entered by the user is present in the array:

```
#!/usr/bin/perl
#
#   hash.pl
#
%accounts = (    Mike => 100,
                 Sue => 200,
                 Erin => 150,
                 Patti => 250
                 );
print "enter a name ";
$name = <STDIN>;          # read a name
chomp($name);             # remove newline character
print "$name has balance: $accounts{$name}\n";

% hash.pl
enter a name Mike
Mike has balance: 100
%
```

Besides using a key to retrieve a value, a common activity on hashes is to get a list of all the keys or a list of all the values. These last two activities are accomplished through the use of two functions: keys and values. The keys function returns a list of keys and the values function returns a list of values.

```
@allthekeys = keys(%accounts);
@allthevalues = values(%accounts);
```

Like normal arrays, associative arrays are also dynamic, and thus it is a simple matter to add or delete pairs. The delete function deletes a (key, value) pair.

```
delete $accounts{Mike};
```

You may grow an associative array by adding elements as shown here:

```
$accounts{Maria} = 100;
$accounts{Dave} = 100;
```

Hashes are extremely important in Perl; thus, we will devote an entire chapter to them later in this book. Just remember that a hash is a collection of names, value pairs, and that a value may be retrieved by its key. Any attempt to add an already seen key with a new value will replace the original value for the key.

1.3   Control Flow Constructs

We will now take a rapid trip through all of the Perl control flow constructs. Most of these constructs are taken directly from the C language, although there are some minor differences.

1.3.1   if, else, elsif

An `if` structure is how decisions are made in Perl. An `if` has a condition and a code body. If the condition evaluates to non-zero (true), then all the statements in the body of the `if` are executed. If the condition evaluates to zero (false), then the statements in the body of the `if` are not executed. The curly braces are required in Perl even when the code body contains only one statement.

```
if ( $a > $max)
{
    $max = $a;
}
```

The `if, else` allows for two-way control flow. If the tested condition is true, the code immediately beneath the `if` is executed; if the tested condition is false, the code beneath the `else` is executed.

```
if ( $a > $b)
{
    $max = $a;
}
else
{
    $max = $b
}
```

Perl also has an `elsif` construct, which provides a multi-way branch.

```
print "Enter your grade ";
$grade = <STDIN>;
if ( $grade < 70 )              # < is the less than operator
{
    print "You get a D\n";
```

continued...

```
}
elsif ( $grade < 80 )
{
    print "You get a C\n";
}
elsif ( $grade < 90)
{
    print "You get a B\n";
}
else
{
    print "You get an A\n";
}
print "end of construct\n";
```

Each of these conditions is tested in turn. If one of them is true, then the code body for that condition is executed. The next line to be executed is the line of code beneath the entire construction (`print`, in this case). The final `else` is optional and is executed if all the conditions are false.

1.3.2   `unless`

The `unless` construct has the exact opposite logic of the `if` construct; that is, if the tested condition is false, then the code body is executed. `unless` is not used often except in error checking, as you will see later.

```
unless ( $a == $b )                  # == is the equality operator
{
    print "this stuff executes when\n";
    print '$a is not equal to $b\n';
}
```

1.3.3   `while`

The `while` construct is a looping construct. As long as the loop control condition is non-zero, the loop is repeated. When the loop control condition evaluates to false, the loop test fails and the code beyond the `while` construct is executed. As a side issue here, when Perl encounters a variable that it has not formerly seen, it proceeds as if the value of that variable is zero. Thus, `$i` does not have to be formally initialized in the loop below:

```
$i = 0;
while ( $i <= 10)                           # while $i <= 10
{
    print "$i\n";
    $i = $i + 1;
}
print "code beneath the loop\n";
```

You can use a `while` loop to implement an endless loop. Usually, endless loops represent buggy code, but that is not always the case. Here is a common programming idiom:

```
#!/usr/bin/perl
#
#   length.pl
#
while ( 1 )                         # always true
{
    print "-> ";                    # issue a prompt
    $line = <STDIN>;                # read a line
    chomp($line);                   # nix the newline
    $len = length($line);           # compute line length
    print "$len is length of $line";
}
```

The above code waits for the user to enter a line whereupon both the length of the line and the line itself are printed. Then the process is repeated forever. Of course, this type of program needs a way of terminating. Simply type the `control-C` sequence.

1.3.4 until

The `until` construct loops until the tested condition is true. When the tested condition becomes true, then the code beyond the `until` is executed. Most developers prefer `while` to `until` because its logic seems to be slightly more straightforward.

```
$i = 1;
until ( $i > 10)
{                                   #   prints 1
    print "$i\n";                   #   through 10
    $i = $i + 1;                    #
}
```

1.3.5 for

A `for` loop is yet another way of looping. This construct has two parts: the `for` statement and the code body. The `for` statement itself has three parts separated by semicolons: the initialization, the test, and the modification. First, the initialization takes place. Next, the condition is tested. If the condition is true, then the code body is executed, after which the modification step is executed. The loop continues with a retesting of the condition, etc.

```
for ( $i = 1; $i <= 10; $i = $i + 1)
{
    $s =  $s + $i;              #       compute sum of
}                               #       first 10 integers
```

1.3.6   foreach

The `foreach` loop is similar to a `for` loop except that the number of iterations of this style of loop is determined by a set of list elements in the `foreach` statement. Here is a `foreach` loop that totals the elements in an array:

```
@list = (1, 2, 3, 4, 5, 6, 7, 8, 9, 10);
foreach $item (@list)
{
    $sum = $sum + $item;
}
```

Each item in the `@list` array is bound to the loop variable, `$item` in this code, which in turn is added to `$sum`. It is important to know that inside a `foreach` loop, the control variable is an alias for the element in the list to which it is currently bound. Because of this, a change to the control variable is, in effect, a change to the list element. We can use this concept to change each array element.

```
foreach $ref (@list)
{
        $ref = $ref * 2;                    # double each item
}
```

Each iteration above doubles the element to which `$ref` is bound. Thus, at the end of the loop, all of the elements in the `@list` array have been doubled.

1.3.7   Statement modifiers

Unlike other languages, Perl always requires the open and close curly braces when your code uses the keywords `unless`, `until`, `while`, `if`, `for`, and `foreach`. This is true even if your control flow construct only has one statement in it. Thus, each of the following generates an error in translation:

```
if ( $a > $b )                           # error: no curly braces
    print "$a > $b\n";
unless ($a > $b)                         # error: no curly braces
    print "$a <= $b\n";
```

However, for those cases in which there is only one statement inside the control structure, Perl allows a shorter form called the modifier form. This form may be used with if, unless, while, and until. To use this form, simply code one statement before the control structure.

```
$x = 50;
$y = 10;
$name = "Mike";
print "$name\n" if $x > $y;
print "$name\n" unless $x < $y;
print "$name\n" while $y++ < $x;        # ++ to be explained later
print "$name\n" until $x > $y++;        # ++ to be explained later
```

Keep in mind the control structure is still evaluated first, so any statement execution still depends on the truth of the test. When you use this form, the set of parentheses that delimits the condition is not required.

1.3.8   What is true and what is false?

In many of the control structures above, a test must be made to determine if the body of the control structure is executed. When an expression is tested for true or false, Perl only cares about whether the expression has the value zero or not. Zero is considered false and anything else is considered true. There are different versions of zero, however! Each of the following is considered to be zero: "", "0", 0, and 0.0.

1.4   Altering Loop Control Flow

Often, the programmer needs to alter the usual behavior of loop iteration. Each of the following works equally well with any of Perl's looping constructs:

```
next
redo
last
```

1.4.1   last

The Perl keyword last breaks the loop and causes control to be thrown to the first statement following the loop. For example, suppose we wanted to find the index of the first negative element in an array.

```perl
#!/usr/bin/perl
#
#   negative.pl
#
print "Enter some numbers ";
$input = <STDIN>;
@n = split(" ", $input);
for ( $i = 0; $i < @n; $i = $i + 1 )
{
    if ( $n[$i] < 0 )
    {
        last;
    }
}
if ($i != @n)
{
    print "$n[$i] found at position $i in @n\n";
}
else
{
    print "no negatives found in @n";
}

% negative.pl
Enter some numbers 2 4 11 -5 8 10
-5 found at position 3 in 2 4 11 -5 8 10
%
```

In the above code, several numbers are entered by the user and they are split into the array @n. Next, each one is tested to see if it is less than zero. If it is, `last` takes control of the program to the first statement beneath the loop.

There are two paths in the program that may bring program control to the second `if` statement: either a negative value is found in the array or we cycle through the loop exhaustively without finding any negatives. In the latter case, the value of `$i` will be the same as the number of elements in the array. Otherwise, it will be different. Thus, we need to determine which case this is. The statement that controls the second `if`:

```perl
($i != @n)
```

appears to compare a scalar to an array. Whenever this is the case in Perl, the array is said to be evaluated in a scalar context. This always produces the number of elements in the array. Actually, the second part of the `for` loop uses a similar construction, which also causes Perl to evaluate @n in a scalar context.

```perl
$i < @n
```

1.4.2 next

The Perl next statement causes control of the program to jump to the next iteration of the loop. One way to think of this is that when next is executed, loop control drops to the final curly brace of the loop and then normal control is resumed. For example, to add all the positive even elements of an array, we might code as follows:

```
for ( $i = 0; $i < @n; $i = $i + 1 )
{
    if ( $n[$i] <  0 )
    {
        next;
    }
    if ( $n[$i] % 2 == 1 )    # Note:  % is the mod operator
    {
        next
    }
    $sum = $sum + $n[$i];
}
```

Note here that we have also used the modulus (or remainder) operator, the % symbol. This operator takes two integers and produces the remainder of dividing the first operand by the second operand. Thus, 10 % 2 is zero and 11 % 2 is one. This is one way of determining whether a number is odd or even.

1.4.3 redo

The redo statement is not used often, but it is quite useful when the need arises. redo redoes the current loop without modifying the control variable.

1.4.4 Labeled blocks

Occasionally, you will need to break out of a loop that is nested inside one or more other loops. For this reason, Perl provides a labeled block. When last is used with a label, control flows to the first statement beyond the labeled block.

```
OUT:    for ( $i = 0;   $i < 5; $i = $i + 1)
        {
            for ( $j = 0;   $j < 5; $j = $j + 1)
            {
                if ($j == $i)
                {
                    last OUT;
                }
            }
        }
        print "first statement after loops\n";
```

You can also use labels in connection with `next` or `redo`. With `next`, control flows to the next iteration of the labeled block. With `redo`, the loop of the labeled block is redone.

1.5   A Few Special Perl Variables

As you become more familiar with Perl, you will see many predefined names. Some of these names are filehandles, others are functions, while still others are arrays and variables. A few of these are used so often that we wanted to introduce them early in the book.

1.5.1 $_

The predefined variable `$_` has many different uses in Perl. Often it is a default string for various operations. For example, the following code reads lines from a file until the end of the file is reached:

```
while($line = <STDIN>)
{
    print $line;
}
```

You may write this code more succinctly by relying on the default variable, `$_`. That is, if you do not specify the variable that receives the line being read, then it is as though you have coded as follows:

```
while($_ = <STDIN>)
{
    print $_;
}
```

Of course, there's no need to code as above, since the following is equivalent:

```
while(<STDIN>)
{
    print $_;
}
```

`$_` can also be the default variable to be printed. Thus, the above may be written as:

```
while(<STDIN>)
{
    print;
}
```

Finally, we could use the modifier form:

```
print $_ while(<STDIN>);
```

There are also a host of functions that operate on $_ by default. Thus:

```
chop            is the same as              chop($_)
chomp;          is the same as              chomp($_)
split("")       is the same as              split("" , $_)
```

1.5.2 $.

Another special variable is $., the input line number. Here's a simple example that uses $. to print the line and line number of all lines read from <STDIN>:

```
print "$.\t$_" while(<STDIN>);
```

The \t is the tab character. Along with the \n (newline) and other escape sequences, it must be enclosed within double quotes to yield its intended meaning. Here is another simple example that prints the number of lines in a file:

```
while(<STDIN>)
{
}
print "$.\n";
```

1.6   Regular Expressions

Perl is rich with capabilities. Probably the two most important features of Perl are hashes and regular expressions, each of which is described further in a separate chapter. In this section, we will introduce regular expressions and give a few simple examples. A regular expression is a set of characters used to express a pattern. This pattern is then used to determine if a string matches it. Once a pattern is matched, it may be stored, printed, replaced, or some action can be taken as a result of the match.

1.6.1   Pattern matching

It is a recurring theme that a program needs to verify that some input is an integer or that some input is composed of alphabetic characters. It should be noted that there are many other well-known patterns such as e-mail addresses, phone numbers, etc.

Pattern matching may be used to verify input. Although there are many issues with regard to regular expressions and pattern matching, our intent is to show a few simple examples and postpone the details until later.

In the simplest case, a regular expression is enclosed in forward slashes and is matched against $_. Thus, the following program prints all lines that match the pattern mike, that is, the lines contain the consecutive characters "m," "i," "k," and "e":

```
while(<STDIN>)
{
    print if ( /mike/ );
}
```

Of course this is different than the question "Does $line equal the string mike?" This latter question is coded as:

```
if ($line eq "mike" )
{
    print $line;
}
```

There are many regular expression metacharacters, that is, characters that do not represent themselves, but have special meanings. For example, the period means "any character"; therefore, the following program prints any line if it matches any three-letter pattern beginning with "r" and ending with "t":

```
while(<STDIN>)
{
    print if ( /r.t/ );
}
```

This would include lines containing "rat," "rot," "rut," and also "strut" and "rotation." It would not match "rt3" or "rt." In other words, the period must match a single character regardless of what it is. You can use ^ and $ to anchor the pattern to the beginning or end of a string, respectively. You may also match against any string, not just $_, but in doing so, you need to use the operator =~. The following example illustrates these points:

```
while($line = <STDIN>)
{
    print "$line" if ($line =~ /^r.t/ );
}
```

The above example prints all lines if they begin with "r," then have "any character," and end with "t." Case-sensitivity is always honored with regular expressions. To ignore case, just place an "i" after the pattern.

```
while($line = <STDIN>)
{
    print "$line" if ($line =~ /r.t$/i );
}
```

The above code prints those lines that end with "r," "any character," "t," regardless of case. Keep in mind that regular expressions are with respect to strings and not lines, even though the examples thus far have all dealt with lines.

1.6.2 Substitutions

Another reason for doing a pattern match is to make a substitution if there is a match. Perl uses the s operator for this action. The following code will print each line entered on the standard output with Michael replacing Mike:

```
while(<STDIN>)
{
    s/Mike/Michael/g;
    print;
}
```

The substitution operator automatically operates on $_. If you omit the "g," then the substitution only occurs on the first occurrence of the pattern on each line. In either case, the match is made against $_, unless a specific variable is named. If you need to name the variable, you may code it as shown here:

```
while($line = <STDIN>)
{
    $line =~ s/Mike/Michael/g;
    print $line;
}
```

1.7 Writing Your Own Functions

Functions in a programming language serve two important purposes. They allow you to reuse code and they serve to generalize an algorithm that can be used on different data. Perl has several hundred builtin functions. We've seen a few thus far: print, open, chomp, push, pop, etc. In this section of the tutorial, you will learn how to write your own functions.

Functions are typically written once and stored in a library so that they can be used in a wide variety of programs. Later in the book, we will demonstrate how that can be done. For now, we will assume that any function you write will be coded at the beginning of the file in which you wish to use the function. Perl functions are defined with the word "sub", followed by the name of the function, followed by a pair of curly braces that enclose the body of the function.

```
sub functionname
{
    body of function
}
```

To invoke a Perl function, give the name of the function preceded by the & symbol. If the function has arguments, list them within a set of parentheses following the function name. Inside the function, the arguments are accessed through the special Perl builtin array named @_. Here's an example that demonstrates a function that sums the elements of the array passed to it. Note that we've just given the bare essentials of writing your own functions. Later, we will have much more to say about this topic.

```
#!/usr/bin/perl
#
#   function.pl
#
sub total
{
    $sum = 0;
    foreach $item (@_)
    {
      $sum += $item;                              # add $item to $sum
    }
    return $sum;
}
@data1 = (1,2,3,4);
$result = total(@data1);
print "Sum of @data1 is $result\n";
@data2 = (1,2,3,4,5);
$result = total(@data2);
print "Sum of @data2 is $result\n";
$result = total(@data1, @data2);
print "Sum of @data1 and @data2 is $result\n";

% functions.pl
Sum of 1 2 3 4 is 10
Sum of 1 2 3 4 5 is 15
Sum of 1 2 3 4 and 1 2 3 4 5 is 25
%
```

The function treats all arguments sent to it as one array. Thus, you can send an actual array, a list of values, or combinations of these. Inside the function, there is simply a loop that traverses the builtin parameter array, @_. We will give the full details about arguments, parameters, and local variables in a later chapter.

Perl functions are versatile. They may return scalars, arrays, hashes, or just about anything else, but they all return something. Of course, if you must, you can disregard the returned value. If you want to return a value from a function, then you can either use the return statement or you can rely on the fact that the last expression that is evaluated inside the function will be returned. Thus, the above function could have been written as:

```
sub total
{
    $sum = 0;
    foreach $item (@_)
    {
            $sum += $item;
    }
    $sum;        # last expression evaluated
}
```

Do not fall into the following trap by coding the function as follows:

```
sub total
{
    $sum = 0;
    foreach $item (@_)
    {
            $sum += $item;
    }
}
```

It may appear that the last expression evaluated is the statement inside the loop, but this is not the case. To terminate the foreach loop, Perl had to evaluate the elements in the list to determine that the loop was finished.

Exercises

1. Write a Perl script to print the lines of a file in reverse order, last line to first line.
2. Using the associative array shown below, ask the user to enter a course number such as 100. Your program should print the course title. Repeat this process five times.

```
%courses = (
            "100", "C Language Programming",
            "101", "C++ Programming",
            "102", "Perl Programming",
            103", "Java Programming",
            );
```

3. Use the push and pop functions to reverse a set of numbers given by a user. Have the numbers entered on the same line and use split to create an array of them. Then, pop each element off the array and push it onto a second array.
4. Write a subroutine that returns the largest number from a list of numbers.
5. You enter your favorite store with $74.87. Your favorite items cost $4.21, $4.51, and $4.63, respectively. You spend all of your money and you buy exactly 17 items. How many of each item did you buy?

INPUT AND OUTPUT IN PERL

In this chapter, we will look more deeply into reading and writing files. Next, we will look at some of Perl's operators for determining the type of a file. Finally, we will look at how you can determine information about files.

2.1 Filehandles

To perform any input or output in Perl, you need to associate the name of a disk file with a name in your program. The name in your program is called a filehandle and the mapping is accomplished through the `open` function.

2.1.1 Builtin filehandles

Some filehandles in Perl are built into the language. The more commonly used builtin file-handles are:

```
STDIN       connected to the user's keyboard
STDOUT      connected to the user's display
STDERR      connected to the user's display
```

When `STDOUT` is used with the `print` function, the data to be printed ends up on the user's console. If no filehandle is specified, `STDOUT` is assumed. Thus, the following two `print` statements are identical:

```
print "hello there\n";
print STDOUT "hello there\n";
```

29

Error messages should be sent to STDERR.

```
print STDERR "Cannot open this file\n":
print STDERR "too many arguments\n";
```

When STDERR is used with the print function, the data is also displayed on the user's console. However, there is a difference between STDOUT and STDERR, as demonstrated by the following program:

```
#!/usr/bin/perl
#
#   printing.pl
#
print STDOUT "good output # 1\n";
print STDOUT "good output # 2\n";
print STDERR "error output # 1\n";
print STDERR "error output # 2\n";
```

When the above program is executed, the results are as follows:

```
% printing.pl
good output # 1
good output # 2
error output # 1
error output # 2
%
```

Note that regardless of the filehandle used, all of the output is shown on the console.

However, if your operating system allows you to redirect the standard output or to send the standard output through a pipe to another command, then only data targeted for STDOUT will be redirected or piped.

```
% printing.pl > output
error output # 1
error output # 2
%
```

In the above example, the data sent to STDOUT has been redirected to the file named output. On Unix, you can also redirect STDERR, but exactly how you do that depends on which shell you are using. For example, in the Korn or Bourne shells, you can code:

```
% printing.pl 2> errs
good output # 1
good output # 2
%
```

In this case, the error output is saved to the file named `errs`. It is safe to say that normally, the error output should not be redirected because its purpose is to be seen by the user.

2.1.2 The `print` function

The `print` function prints a comma-separated list of expressions to the file whose handle is specified immediately after the `print` function. The following program prints a table of Fahrenheit and Celsius temperatures in the range and step size requested by the user:

```
% convert.pl
enter start temperature 0
enter end temperature 100
enter increment -2
increment must be positive
%
% convert.pl
enter start temperature 0
enter end temperature 80
enter increment 20
CELSIUS    FAHRENHEIT
0    32
20   68
40   104
60   140
80   176
%

#!/usr/bin/perl
#
#   comvert.pl
#
print "enter start temperature ";
$start = <STDIN>;
chop($start);
print "enter end temperature ";
$end = <STDIN>;
print "enter increment ";
$inc = <STDIN>;
if ( $end <= $start )
{
    print STDERR "start <= end\n";
```

continued...

```
    exit(0);
}
if ( $inc <= 0 )
{
    print STDERR "increment must be positive\n";
    exit(1);
}
print "CELSIUS\tFAHRENHEIT\n";
for ($i = $start; $i <= $end; $i += $inc)
{
    $faren = $i * 1.8 + 32;
    print STDOUT "$i\t$fahren\n";
}
```

In each of the `print` statements above, there is only one item to be printed, but this is not always the case. Examine the following example:

```
#!/usr/bin/perl
#
#   prlist.pl
#
print "enter a number ";
chomp($f = <STDIN>);
print "enter another ";
chomp($s = <STDIN>);
print "$f * $s = ", $f * $s, "\n";
print "$f + $s = ", $f + $s, "\n";
% prlist.pl
enter a number 10
enter a number 20
10 * 20 = 200
10 + 20 = 30
%
```

Each of the `print` functions above has several items to display. In this case, a comma-separated list must be used for each item. Finally, if there are any Perl operators within a quoted string, they are not treated as an operator, but rather they are treated like any other character and thus printed literally. Note also that the sequence of reading a line and chomping away the newline character is so common that the following idiom is often used:

```
chomp($s = <STDIN>);
```

2.1.3 The `printf` function

You may have noticed that there is no control over the output when you are using `print`. That's fine for development or debugging, but not for production. If you need finer control over your output, you can use the `printf` function. The first argument to this function is a string containing text characters to be printed literally and format characters that describe succeeding arguments. The format characters are introduced by the % symbol and are terminated with a letter of the alphabet that signifies integer (%d), octal (%o), hexadecimal (%x), floating point (%f), or string data (%s). Between the beginning and ending format characters, you can have a modifier that specifies the field width or alignment. Here are some examples to illustrate `printf`:

```perl
#!/usr/bin/perl
#
#   printf.pl
#
$a = 5;
printf "|%d|\n", $a;
printf "|%5d|\n", $a;
printf "|%10d|\n", $a;
printf "|%-d|\n", $a;
printf "|%-5d|\n", $a;
printf "|%-10d|\n", $a;
$b = "hello";
printf "|%5s|\n", $b;
printf "|%10s|\n", $b;
printf "|%20s|\n", $b;
printf "|%-5s|\n", $b;
printf "|%-10s|\n", $b;
printf "|%-20s|\n", $b;
$c = 99.537;
printf "|%10.2f|\n", $c;
printf "|%20.2f|\n", $c;
printf "|%-10.2f|\n", $c;
printf "|%-20.2f|\n", $c;
```

The output from the code above is shown on the next page. It is informative to try to match the output with the code that produced it. Within any format item, the number suggests the field width. A – character within the format implies left adjustment. Thus, the following format:

```
%-20s
```

means to format the data item as a left-adjusted string within a field width of 20 positions.

```
% printf.pl
|5|
|    5|
|         5|
|5|
|5    |
```

continued...

```
|5         |
|hello|
|     hello|
|                 hello|
|hello|
|hello    |
|hello              |
|     99.54|
|           99.54|
|99.54     |
|99.54              |
%
```

printf is often used when a table with columns needs to be printed.

```
for ($i = 40; $i <= 200; $i += 20)
{
    printf "%9d%9d%9d\n", $i, $i * $i, $i * $i * $i;
}
        40     1600     64000
        60     3600    216000
        80     6400    512000
       100    10000   1000000
       120    14400   1728000
       140    19600   2744000
       160    25600   4096000
       180    32400   5832000
       200    40000   8000000
```

2.1.4 sprintf

Perl also has a sprintf function that behaves exactly like printf except that the data is sent to a string rather than to the display.

```
$i = 20;
$f = 10.568;
$s = "hello";
$output = sprintf "%-10s%5d%10.2f\n", $s, $i, $f;
print length($output), "|$output\n";
```

Executing the code above would produce the line shown below:

```
26|hello        20      10.57
```

The first value output from above is the length of the string returned by the `sprintf` function. The string `hello` is printed with a `-10s` format. This means to left-adjust it in a field width of ten. The value `$i` is printed with a `%5d` format. This means to display this value in a field of five, right-adjusted. The variable `$f` is formatted with the `%10.2f` specification. This means to display it within a field of ten characters with two digits to the right of the decimal point. Note also that this value is rounded.

2.2   Creating Your Own Filehandles

When a program needs to perform some disk input or output, it needs to make an association between a file in the filesystem and a name in the program. As we have seen, there are some pre-existing filehandles: `STDIN`, `STDOUT`, and `STDERR`. In Perl, this mapping is accomplished through the `open` function.

2.2.1   open

This function takes two arguments: a filehandle that the programmer creates and the name of a disk file with some punctuation indicating the access mode. Access modes allow a file to be opened for reading, writing, both reading and writing, or appending. The `open` function may also be used to associate a filehandle with a process if your operating system allows this. You may also associate a filehandle with a process on a different machine. Here are several examples of opening a file for output:

```
$filename=sortedfile;
open(OUTPUT,"> outputfile");
open(DATAFILE,"> $filename");
```

and a few for input:

```
$filename=sortedfile;
open(OUTPUT,"< outputfile");
open(DATAFILE,"$filename");
```

In the last case above, notice that if there is no punctuation, the file is opened implicitly for reading. Once you have the handles, you can perform operations on the files. Here's a program that gets the filenames from the user and then copies one file to the other:

```
#!/usr/bin/perl
#
#   copy.pl
#
print "enter input filename ";
chomp($input = <STDIN>);
```

continued...

```
print "enter input output filename ";
chomp($output = <STDIN>);
open(INPUT, "< $input");
open(OUTPUT, "> $output");
while($line = <INPUT>)
{
    print OUTPUT $line;
}
% copy.pl
enter input filename input
enter output filename output
%
```

Note the loop above could have been written more succinctly if we relied on $_:

```
while(<INPUT>)
{
    print OUTPUT;
}
```

or it could have been more terse if we used the modifier form of while:

```
print OUTPUT while(<INPUT>);
```

In any case, you do not see any results on the display when you run this program because all of the output is sent to the file named output.

You may open a file for appending by using the >> notation:

```
open(ADDRECORDS, ">> myfile");
```

Finally, you may open a file for both reading and writing:

```
open(HANDLE1,"+< $filename");      # no recreate
open(HANDLE2,"+> $filename");      # truncates
```

The first of the two above lines should be used if you plan on doing reads and writes on an existing file. This is a common situation for applications that need to update files. The latter of the above lines should be used if you intend to do reads and writes on a file that will be created in your application. This is less likely, but still possible. In Chapter 8, we will see an example of updating a file.

Any use of the open function with the > symbol will automatically destroy an existing file. This mode is really for the creation of a file, so beware of the last open shown above.

Sometimes it is necessary to determine if a file already exists to know the correct mode to use in the `open` function.

2.2.2 `die`

All of the examples thus far have neglected the situation when the file open fails. This may happen for many reasons:

- lack of proper permission
- per user file table is full
- system wide file table is full
- too many inodes open (Unix)
- open for read and no file exists

To cope with these and other errors, the `die` function may be used to terminate a program when an `open` failure occurs. This function is usually coded as follows:

```
open(INPUT, "< myfile") || die;
```

The `||` symbols represent the `logical or` operator. If the `open` succeeds, a non-zero value is returned and thus the second part of the `||` is not executed. However, if the `open` fails, it returns the value 0 and the second part of the `||` is evaluated. The purpose of the `die` function is to terminate your program with an error message. You may want to rely on the default error message from `die`, which is:

```
Died at ./filename linenumber
```

If you don't like the default error message, you may add your own.

```
open(INPUT, "< file1") || die "can't open myfile";
```

However, the default error message will still appear. You may omit the default error message by simply adding a newline to your own error string.

```
open(INPUT, "< file1") || die "can't open myfile\n";
```

Finally, if you use the special Perl variable `$!`, the operating system error message is displayed. Here are the various forms of `die`:

```
open(AFILE, "< badname") || die;
open(AFILE, "< badname") || die "message";
open(AFILE, "< badname") || die "message\n";
open(AFILE, "< badname") || die "some message $!";
open(AFILE, "< badname") || die "some message $!\n";
```

2.2.3 Closing files

Each process has a fixed number of files that may be opened concurrently. When you are finished processing a file, it is still in an open state. It still occupies a slot in an operating system table. This slot becomes available for use by another file only when the process executes the `close` function.

```
close(filehandle);
```

2.2.4 Pipes

Pipes were one of the creations of Unix. However, they may also be used on Windows platforms, albeit to a limited degree. For those of you unfamiliar with pipes, we will present a very short description of them. The Unix operating system provides a plethora of commands, each of which does a simple job very efficiently. Power comes from the ability to chain some of these commands together. The pipe mechanism takes the output of one command and feeds this data to another command. Here is an example:

The command `wc -l` counts lines in a file and reports the output on the display. The `who` command displays one line of output for each user currently using your Unix system. Thus, to count the number of users on your system, you can arrange to have the output of the `who` command sent directly to the `wc -l` command. On the Unix command line, the | symbol tells the Unix shell to funnel the data required for the pipe. The command would look like this:

```
% who | wc -l
```

2.2.4.1 Opening pipe files.   Within a Perl program, you can easily send data to or receive data from a pipe. To do this, you must associate a filehandle with a process via a pipe, then either read or write on the pipe, and finally close the association. Pipes are a Unix feature, and thus code segments such as the following may not work on all systems:

```perl
#!/usr/bin/perl
#
#        mysort.pl
#
print "enter input filename ";
chomp($fn = <STDIN>);
open(INPUT, "< $fn") || die "Can't open $fn\n";
open(SORT, "| sort") || die "can't open sort\n";
while(<INPUT>)
{
        print SORT;
}
```

continued...

```
close(SORT);
close(INPUT);

% mysort.pl
enter input filename mysort.pl
        print SORT;
#
#
#       mysort.pl
#!/usr/bin/perl
{
}
chomp($fn = <STDIN>);
close(INPUT);
close(SORT);
open(INPUT, "< $fn") || die "Can't open $fn\n";
open(SORT, "| sort") || die "can't open sort\n";
print "enter input filename ";
while(<INPUT>)
```

The program asks the user for the name of the file to be sorted. In this example, we use the source file mycopy.pl as the input file. Next, a pipe handle is created and mapped to your system's sort utility.

```
open(SORT, "| sort") || die "can't open sort\n";
```

Any data sent to SORT ends up being sent to the system's sort utility. To do this correctly, we placed the | symbol in front of the process name. Then, when the program prints on the SORT handle, the data is sent to the sort process. The sort process terminates when close is executed on the pipe handle.

```
close(SORT);
```

When you want your Perl program to receive data from a process rather than writing to the process, the | symbol must be placed after the process name. The program below uses the utility name find to find all files recursively under the current directory. Of those, a regular expression is used to print any file whose name does not begin with a dot. Since the dot is a special character, we had to use the sequence \. to nullify its special meaning. If your system does not have a find command, then the program below will die. If this is the case, you might try using DIR instead of find.

```
#!/usr/bin/perl
#
#  find.pl
#
open(FIND,"find . |")|| die "can't start find\n";while(<FIND>)
{
    print if ( $_ !~ /^\./ );
}
```

When the above program executes, the following line:

```
while(<FIND>)
```

will read line after line from the find process. On a Unix system, the find command will yield all the files recursively under the directory specified in the find command.

In the above open function, we specified the current directory, that is, the file whose name is dot (.). Once again, if you are using Windows, you may have limited capability with pipe handles in Perl.

2.3   File Operators

Many applications, particularly system administration utilities, must be able to determine the type of a file. Perl has many operators to yield information about a file. Some of this information is: file type, whether the file is readable and/or writeable, whether it is a directory or not, and other pieces of information. Below is a partial list of these operators. Some of this information may be useful only on Unix systems.

```
-r     file is readable
-w     file is writeable
-x     file is executable
-f     file is a plain file
-d     file is a directory
-e     file exists
-B     file is a binary file
-T     file is a text file
-M     age of file in days
-A     age since last accessed
```

Here is an example of how to use a few of these operators. In each case, we will assume that $file contains the name of a file.

To determine if a file is a directory:

```
print "$file is a file\n" if ( -d $file );
```

To determine if a file is a text file:

```
print "$file is a text file\n" if ( -T $file );
```

To track the number of days since a file was last modified:

```
$lastmod = -M $file
```

2.4 The stat Function

Many programs are interested in the data of a file. However, a separate class of programs is interested in data about files. Sometimes the information is about the type of a file, while other times it relates to the size of a file or the modification date of a file. Perl uses the stat function to retrieve information about a file. Some of this information may only be useful on a Unix operating system. The stat function takes a filename or filehandle and returns an array of 13 elements. Table 2.1 summarizes this information:

Table 2.1   Return Values from the stat Function

Index	Meaning
0	device of the file
1	inode number
2	mode of the file
3	number of links
4	user ID of the owner
5	group ID of the owner
6	raw device
7	size of the file
8	file access time
9	file modification time
10	file creation time
11	block size for the filesystem
12	number of data blocks

Here's an example of using the `stat` function:

```
#!/usr/bin/perl
#
#    stat.pl
#
while(1)
{   print "enter a filename ";
    chomp($fn = <STDIN>);
    last if ($fn eq "quit");
    if (! -e $fn)
    {
       print STDERR "$fn does not exist\n";
       next;
    }
    @info = stat($fn);
    print "$fn has size $info[7]\n";
}
```

2.5   Other Filehandles

In addition to the predefined filehandles STDOUT, STDERR, and STDIN, there are a few other filehandles to know about.

2.5.1   The ARGV filehandle

 This special handle allows Perl scripts to easily read files whose names are given as arguments on the command line. Try running this program:

```
#!/usr/bin/perl
#
#    readargs.pl
#
while(<ARGV>)
{
    print "$.\t$_";
}
```

This is a tiny program by measurement, but it is extremely powerful. If there are arguments on the command line, Perl treats each one as a file and reads from them one line at a time. If there are no arguments, the program reads the standard input.

Recall also that $. is a special Perl variable that gives the current line number of a file. Essentially, the above program simply prints all the lines and line numbers from the files whose names appear on the command line. You can find the files sprintf.pl and readargs.pl among the downloaded files.

```
% readargs.pl  sprintf.pl  readargs.pl
1   #!/usr/bin/perl
2   #
3   #          sprintf.pl
4   #
5   $int = 20;
6   $float = 10.56;
7   $string = "hello";
8   $output = sprintf "%-10s%10d%10f.2\n", $string, $int, $float;
9   print "$output\n";
10  #!/usr/bin/perl
11  #
12  #          readargs.pl
13  #
14  while(<ARGV>)
15  {
16      print "$.\t$_";
17  }
%
```

If you examine the execution of the program, you will see that the line numbers do not recycle when the next file on the command line is processed. If you want that behavior, you need to detect when the end of each file is reached.

2.5.1.1 The eof function.   The eof function detects when you are at the end of the file you are reading. You can also give a filehandle as an argument to this function, in which case, it will detect if you are at the end of that file.

We may modify the above example so that when we detect the end of the file, we then close the file. The close has the effect of resetting the $. variable. In the program below, we also print the name of the file when we reach its end. The name of the file is held in the special Perl variable named $ARGV.

```
#!/usr/bin/perl
#
#   eof.pl
#
while(<ARGV>)
{
    print "$.\t$_";
    if ( eof )
    {
        print "EOF on $ARGV\n\n";
        close ARGV;
```

continued...

```
        }
}

% eof.pl  table.pl table.pl
1   #!/usr/bin/perl
2   #
3   #      table.pl
4   #
5   for ($i = 20; $i <= 200; $i+= 20)
6   {
7          printf "%9d%9d%9d\n", $i, $i * $i, $i * $i * $i;
8   }
EOF on table.pl
1   #!/usr/bin/perl
2   #
3   #      table.pl
4   #
5   for ($i = 20; $i <= 200; $i+= 20)
6   {
7          printf "%9d%9d%9d\n", $i, $i * $i, $i * $i * $i;
8   }
EOF on table.pl
%
```

2.5.2   The `null` filehandle: `<>`

Perl also has a filehandle known as the null filehandle. It is represented by the usual angled
brackets, `<>`, but with nothing inside them. Be careful because even a blank inside them
will cause an error. `<>` behaves exactly like the `ARGV` filehandle.

```
#!/usr/bin/perl
#
#   null.pl
#
while(<>)
{
    print;
}
% null.pl null.pl
#
#   null.pl
#
while(<>)
{
    print;

}
```

continued...

```
% null.pl
This is from the
This is from the
keyboard
keyboard
%
```

2.5.3   The DATA filehandle

The DATA filehandle is convenient for debugging Perl programs. This filehandle is used in connection with the special keyword __END__. If any Perl script contains only those characters left-adjusted on a line, then the Perl script will not process any Perl code beneath that line. Instead, you may place data behind that line and use the <DATA> filehandle to read it. Examine the file testdata.pl shown below:

```
#!/usr/bin/perl
#
#   testdata.pl
#
while(<DATA>)
{
    @words = split;
    $tot += @words;
}

print "Total words = $tot\n";
__END__
This is the data file that you can read
by using the DATA filehandle.  You must
have the END line coded properly as above.
%
% testdata.pl
Total words = 24
%
```

Exercises

1. Write a Perl script to print the numbers from 1 to 100 in three fields labeled DEC, OCT, and HEX, respectively.
2. Write a Perl program that reads the `/etc/passwd` file and `printf`s the output as neatly as that shown below. If you're not using a Unix derivative, use the file called `passwd` provided with the downloaded files.

```
LOGIN NAME   USER_ID   SHELL_PROGRAM
Mike         123       /bin/ksh
soozie       124       /bin/sh
alan         125       /bin/csh
```

3. Write a program that gets the first and last lines of a file and places them in a file called `hat` (headers and trailers). Get the input file from the command line. (To get the last line, you may read all the lines into an array or use the Unix `tail -1` command with a pipe handle.)
4. Wrap a loop around Exercise 3 so that each file named on the command line is processed.
5. Only if on Unix: Write a Perl script that opens two pipes. The first pipe should perform an ls –l and pipe the results to your Perl program.
   The second pipe should open a sort (by file size) and sort the output generated from lines read from the first pipe.
6. Use the `stat` function to print the sizes of all the files in the current directory. To do this, you will need some way to generate the names of all the files in that directory. If on Unix, use either `ls` or `find`; if on Windows, use `DIR`.

OPERATORS IN PERL

A Perl expression is a syntactically correct combination of operators and operands. Perl has a plethora of operators. Many of them originated with the C language and some of them are particular to Perl. In this chapter, we will explore all of the operators, including those used for bit manipulation, string manipulation, and regular expressions.

3.1   Perl Operators

Perl has an abundance of operators. Many of them come from the C programming language, some come from Unix shells, and others are strictly particular to Perl. Before we see the complete set of Perl operators, we need to explain some preliminary concepts.

Operator precedence defines the order in which operators are executed. Operator associativity defines the order when there are ties in the precedence. For example, most languages define multiplication to be higher in precedence than addition, and thus the following evaluates to 17, not 21:

```
$x = 2 + 5 * 3;
```

But what if an expression involves operators of the same precedence?

```
$x = 200 / 5 * 10;
```

The precedence here does not tell us anything because / and * are at the same level in the hierarchy. To evaluate this expression, we need to know the associativity of these operators. Is it left to right or right to left?

As it turns out, the associativity of these particular operators is left to right. Therefore, the above expression has the value 400. To ensure that the multiplication was executed first, you could use a set of parentheses as follows:

```
$x = 200 / (5 * 10);
```

The above expression now has a value of 4 because whatever is in parentheses is evaluated first. In the case of nested parentheses, the innermost set is evaluated first.

Knowing about operators in Perl is very important because often it is the operators that determine how a variable will be treated. For example, in the following expression:

```
$x = "20abc" + "3xyz"
```

it appears as though we are attempting to add two strings. The + operator tells Perl to treat the strings as numbers. Perl does the best it can since the strings are not really representations of numbers. The result in $x is 23. However, if we use the Perl concatenation operator, the dot, the expression below evaluates to the string "20abc3xyz."

```
$x = "20abc" . "3xyz"
```

Table 3.1 lists the hierarchy of Perl operators. Operators on Level 1 have the highest precedence;. Level 2 operators have the next highest precedence, etc. The first column lists the level of precedence, the second column gives the names of the operators on this level, and the third column gives a brief description of the operators on this level.

Operators on Levels 3, 4, and 18 associate right to left. Operators on Levels 2, 9, 10, 11, and 16 do not have any associativity. All other levels associate left to right.

Table 3.1   Operators, Precedence, and Associativity

Level	Operator	Description
1	( )	function call
	[ ]	subscript
	{ }	block
2	++	auto increment
	--	auto decrement
3	!, not	logical not
	~	bitwise not
	-	unary minus
4	**	exponentiation
5	=~	pattern match
	!~	no pattern match

continued...

Table 3.1   Operators, Precedence, and Associativity (CONTINUED)

Level	Operator	Description
6	*	multiplication
	/	division
	%	modulus
	x	repeat
7	+	addition
	-	subtraction
	.	concatenation
8	<<	left shift
	>>	right shift
9	-d, -f, etc.	file test operators
10	<	numeric greater than
	<=	numeric less than or equal
	>	numeric greater than
	>=	numeric greater than or equal
	gt	string greater than
	le	string less than or equal
	gt	string greater than
	ge	string greater than or equal
11	==	numeric equality
	!=	numeric inequality
	<=>	numeric signed comparison
	eq	string equality
	ne	string inequality
	cmp	numeric signed comparison
12	&	bitwise logical AND
13	|	bitwise or
	^	exclusive or
14	&&, and	logical AND
15	||, or	logical OR
16	..	range operator
17	?:	conditional expression
18	=, +=, etc.	assignment operators
19	,	comma operator

3.1.1   Assignment operators

Most operators are binary in nature. This means they have two operands. For example, the addition operator is binary. In the line of code below, $y and $z are the two operands:

```
$x = $y + $z;
```

Any binary operator can be written using the assignment operator rather than using the longer and more traditional approach. Here are some traditional assignment statements using some simple arithmetic operators:

```
$x = $x + 5;              # addition
$x = $x / 2;              # division
$x = $x * 2;              # multiplication
$x = $x ** 5;             # exponentiation
```

Perl has a set of operators that is collectively referred to as the assignment operators. These operators consist of any binary operator followed by the assignment symbol. Here are a few examples of assignment operators. Each statement below is functionally equivalent to the respective statement above:

```
$x += 5;                  # addition
$x /= 2;                  # division
$x *= 2;                  # multiplication
$x **= 5;                 # exponentiation
```

These operators may save you some typing and therefore save you some errors. For example, compare the following two statements. Which is easier to type?

```
$table[$index] = $table[$index] + $increment;
$table[$index] += $increment;
```

3.1.2   Increment and decrement operators

Since adding and subtracting one to a variable are two very common constructions, Perl allows you to use some special operators, the auto-increment and auto-decrement operators, to perform these operations. These operators can also save you from some typing errors. The expression:

```
$x++
```

adds one to the scalar $x. Likewise, the following expression also adds one to $x:

```
++$x
```

Thus, the two above expressions appear to be the same as is evidenced by the following program segment:

```
$x = 10;                       # $x = 10
$x++;                          # $x = 11
++$x;                          # $x = 12
print "$x\n";                  # 12 is printed
```

You may see Perl code written in either of the following two equivalent ways:

```
for ($ct = 0; $ct < 10; $ct++)
{
}

for ($ct = 0; $ct < 10; ++$ct)
{
}
```

In all of the above cases, each ++ causes the variable to which it is applied to be increased by one. However, there is a distinction between applying the ++ before the variable, a pre-increment, or after the variable, a post-increment. A pre-increment first increments the variable and then uses the incremented value. A post-increment uses the value of the variable before it is incremented. If either of these increments are part of a larger expression, you must be careful about whether you want the pre- or post-version of the operator.

```
#!/usr/bin/perl
#
#   prepost.pl
#
$x = 10;
$y = 20;
print $x++, "\n"; # prints $x, then increments $x
print ++$y, "\n"; # increments $y, then prints it
$c = $x++ + ++$y; # increment $y, do $x + $y, increment $x
print "$c\n";

% prepost.pl
10
21
33
%
```

In the last expression above, $y is incremented before it is used and $x is incremented after it is used. The pre- and post-decrement operators work similarly. Be careful not to put the ++ operators inside quotes in expressions such as the following. They will be treated literally rather than being treated as an operator.

```
$x = 12;
print "$x++\n";              # prints 12++
```

3.1.3   Modulus (remainder) operator

The modulus operator, %, gives you the remainder when you divide one number by another. This can be used in a variety of problems. For example, to determine if a number is divisible by 10, you might code as shown below:

```
print "$num divisible by 10\n" if (( $num % 10 ) == 0);
```

Here, the remainder of dividing $num by 10 is compared against 0. Incidentally, the precedence of the % operator is higher than the precedence of the numerical equality operator, ==, and thus you might have coded the above as:

```
print "$num divisible by 10\n" if ( $num % 10  == 0);
```

Finally, since we are using the modifier form of if, the parentheses surrounding the if conditional are also unnecessary.

```
print "$num divisible by 10\n" if  $num % 10  == 0;
```

3.1.4   Conditional expression

Another notational convenience is the conditional expression. This operator can be used to express the same idea expressed in an if statement. This operator has three operands: the first operand is tested for true or false in the same way that the if condition is tested; the other two operands represent the value of the operation when the first operand evaluates to true or false, respectively. Notice the following two cases:

```
1)
   $y = 20;
   if ( $x > $y )
   {
```

continued...

```
    $max = $x;
}
else
{
    $max = $y;
}

2)
  $max = $x > $y ? $x : $y;
```

In the second case, $x > $y is evaluated. If true, the expression between ? and : gets assigned to $max. Otherwise, the expression to the right of : gets assigned to $max. Thus, the conditional expression is of the form:

```
e1 ? e2 : e3
```

The value of this expression is either e2 or e3 depending on whether e1 is true or false, respectively. Here are some other uses of this expression:

```
$ans = 120;
$ans = $x % 2  == 0 ? "even" : "odd";    # $ans = "even"
$ans = $x % 2 ? "odd" : "even";          # $ans = "even"
$ans = $x ? "not zero" : "zero";         # $ans = "not zero"
```

3.1.5 Range operator

The range operator is a pair of dots (. .). It has many uses in Perl. Perhaps the most useful is to create a sequence of elements to fill an array. The code below sums the numbers in the range 1 to 100:

```
@numbers = (1..100); # the numbers 1, 2, 3,... ,100
foreach $item (@numbers)
{
    $sum += $item;
}
```

Rather than explicitly writing out the values in a particular sequence, the range operator generates them for you. This operator can be used with numbers or with characters. The code below prints upper- and lowercase characters:

```
foreach $item (a..z, A..Z);
{
    print "$item";
}
```

3.1.6   String operators

Perl is very good at string manipulation. Toward that end, there are many string operators
that we need to present. There are also many string functions that we will discuss. We will
look at the operators first.

The concatenation operator is the dot (.). If you have some strings to glue together, it is
a routine matter. Here's an example that reads lines from the standard input, strips out the
blanks, and glues all the lines together:

```perl
#!/usr/bin/perl
#
#   glue.pl
#
while(<STDIN>)
{
    s/ //g;              # substitute nothing for each space
    $tot = $tot . $_; # concatenate each line to $tot
}
print length($tot), "\n";
print "$tot\n";          # print the long string

% glue.pl
this is it
so is this
and this
26
thisisit
soisthis
andthis
%
```

It's hard to tell from the output, but only one string has been printed. This string is the
concatenation of the strings typed by the user. It appears as though several strings have been
printed. That's because each line contains a newline character. We printed the length of the
string to prove that only one string was printed. It is easy to see that the blanks have been
suppressed by the substitution.

There's also a replication operator, x, which is used to repeat a string a given number of
times. Here's some code to demonstrate how this operator works:

```perl
#!/usr/bin/perl
#
#   repeat.pl
#
print "enter a string and a repeat factor ";
$input = <STDIN>;
($str, $factor) = split(" ", $input);
```

continued...

```
$repeat = $str x $factor;
print "$str repeated $factor times is $repeat\n";
if ($repeat =~ /^[0-9]/ )
{
    $repeat *= 2;
     print "Notice what happened: $repeat\n";
}


% repeat.pl
enter a string and a repeat factor today 3
today repeated 3 times is todaytodaytoday
% repeat.pl
enter a string and a repeat factor 123 2
123 repeated 2 times is 123123
Notice what happened: 246246
%
```

In the above example, the replication operator is used to repeat the input string. The program tests to see if the string begins with a digit. If so, the string is multiplied by two. Remember that a scalar may be treated as a string or a number depending on the operator processing it.

3.1.7   Relational operators

We've already used some relational operators without giving any specific details. Relational operators have two different flavors: numeric and string. Table 3.2 summarizes the operators used for string comparisons and the operators used for numerical comparisons:

Table 3.2   Relational Operators

Meaning	*Numeric*	*String*
Greater than	>	gt
Greater than or equal	>=	ge
Less than	<	lt
Less than or equal	<=	le
Equal	==	eq
Not equal	!=	ne
Signed equality	<=>	cmp

Most of the operators should be familiar to you with the exception of the == and the operators in the last row. As you can see, the == operator is used for numeric equality, whereas eq is used for string equality. cmp and < = > are similar in nature to the C language strcmp function in that they return −1 if the left operand is lower than the right operand, 1 if the opposite condition is true, and 0 if the operands are equal.

The example below instructs the user to enter some numbers. The program uses a regular expression to ensure that only digits were entered. A message is printed if this is not the case. The program sums all the numeric entries. The user should enter the string quit to terminate the input.

Here's the running of the program followed by the source code. Notice the comparison to terminate the program correctly uses eq rather than == .

```perl
#!/usr/bin/perl
#
#      totals.pl
#
print "enter some numbers\nor 'quit' to exit\n";
while(1)
{
    print "enter ";
    $in = <STDIN>;
    chomp($in);
    last if ( $in eq "quit");
    if ($in !~ /^[0-9]+$/ )
    {
        print "$in not a number\n";
        next;
    }
    $sum += $in;
}
print "sum is $sum\n";

% totals.pl
enter some numbers
or "quit" to exit
enter 243
enter 123
enter hello
hello not a number
enter 34
enter quit
sum is 400
%
```

3.1.8   Logical operators

Logical operators operate on compound conditions. In Perl, these are "short-circuit" operators; that is, they stop evaluating when they have determined the truth condition. The logical operators are:

```
Logical not             !
Logical and             &&
Logical or              ||
```

You may also use the English words not, and, and or as respective synonyms for the above operators.

Short-circuit operators add efficiency to programs. For example, if $x has the value zero, then it would be inefficient to evaluate the second and third comparisons of the compound condition below:

```
if ( $x == 0 || $y == 0 || $z == 0)
{
    # something
}
```

Sometimes this can make a difference in the flow of data through your program. For example, in the code below, a line will be read only if $x does not have the value zero:

```
if ($x == 0 || ($y = <STDIN>) )
{
    # do something
}
```

In this particular example, the inner parentheses are necessary. To understand why this is the case, first notice that there are three operators in the evaluated condition. Without the inner parentheses, they will be evaluated in the order ==, ||, and =, as if the condition had been parenthesized as:

```
if ((($a == 0) || $b ) = <STDIN> )
```

Now you can see the problem! The evaluation of the || is either true or false, thus generating a one or a zero. In either case, this constant value cannot be the recipient of the line input with <STDIN>.

Here are a few examples of the use of logical operators:

```
print "$a is between 0 and 9" if ( $a >= 0 && $a <= 9);
print "$a is between 0 and 9" if ( $a >= 0 and $a <= 9);

print  "$a is not a digit" if ( ! ($a >= 0 && $a <= 9));
print  "$a is not a digit" if ( not ($a >= 0 && $a <= 9));

print  "$a is zero or one" if ( $a == 0 || $a == 1);
print  "$a is zero or one" if ( $a == 0 or $a == 1);
```

3.1.9 Bit manipulation operators

A programmer can spend many years writing software before running into a problem where the manipulation of bits is needed. On the other hand, if you are a systems programmer, then you have undoubtedly run into many situations where these techniques are needed. Perl uses the same bit manipulation operators that C uses:

```
bitwise logical not                 ~
bitwise logical and                 &
bitwise logical or                  |
bitwise exclusive or                ^
shift right                         >>
shift left                          <<
```

Here are a few examples of rudimentary bit manipulation operations. You can represent octal and hexadecimal constants in Perl by using a leading 0 or leading 0x, respectively, in front of a number. These constants are used in bit manipulation problems. Here are a few elementary bit operations:

```
$x = 0555;              #    ..000 101 101 101
$z = ~$x                #    ..111 010 010 010
$a = 045;               #    ..000 000 100 101
$b = 066;               #    ..000 000 110 110
$c = $a | $b            #    ..000 000 110 111
$d = $a & $b            #    ..000 000 100 100
$d = $d << 1            #     000 001 001 000
```

The above lines of code are intentionally mechanical so that you can see the results of various bit manipulation operations. For completeness, we offer a function that computes the number of bits that are set in a variable:

```
sub countbits
{
    $count = 0;
    $value = $_[0];        # first argument to function
    while($value != 0)     # is the value zero
    {                      # No
        #     add 1 to count if rightmost bit
        #     is set, i.e. is a one
        $count++ if ($value & 01);
        $value >>= 1;   # right-shift all bits by one
    }
    return $count;
}
```

The value sent to the function is tucked away in the variable $value. As long as it is not zero, the bit on the extreme right is tested to see if it is a one. If it is, it is counted. In either case, $value is shifted one bit to the right and the process is repeated.

```
#!/usr/bin/perl
#
#     bits.pl
#
while(1)
{
    print "enter a number ";
    $in = <STDIN>;
    chomp($in);
    last if ( $in eq "quit");
    $bits = countbits($in);
    print "$in contains [$bits] 1 bits\n";
}
```

3.1.10 Regular expression operators

Recall from Chapter 1 that regular expressions are a set of metacharacters that forms patterns that are used to match strings. Every string either matches a particular regular expression or it doesn't. There are two regular expression operators that match a string: the match operator, m, and the substitution operator, s.

The regular expression must be enclosed in forward slashes, number signs, exclamation points, or a few other characters. However, when you use slashes, the m operator is unnecessary. Thus, the following are equivalent:

```
/^[0-9]+$/
m/^[0-9]+$/
m#^[0-9]+$#
m!^[0-9]+$!
```

You might use a set of delimiters other than slashes when the regular expression contains a slash.

To replace one string with another, the s operator is mandatory. However, you may still use the same sets of delimiters as described above.

```
s/January/February/
s#/January#February#
s!January!February!
```

3.1.11   Some string functions

We've already discussed the concatenation and replication operators. In reality, these are the only string operators. However, there are many string functions whose use is closely related to the string operators; therefore, we present them here.

The length function returns the length of a string.

```
$string="Susan\tis\tthe\npresident\tof\tthe\ncompany\n";
$len = length($string);       # length = 38
```

Remember that the "\t" sequence represents the tab character and the "\n" sequence represents the newline character. Thus, each of these sequences counts as a single character in the code above.

The index function returns the first position (zero-based) within a string where a second string is found or −1 if the second string is not found. index can also have a third argument: an integer specifying how much to skip in the first string before you start indexing.

```
$s = "if you don't succeed, try try again";
$pos1 = index($s,"try");                  # pos = 22
$pos2 = index($s, "Try");                 # pos = -1
$pos3 = index($s, "try", $pos1 + 1);      # pos = 26
```

The rindex function behaves like index, but returns the index of the last occurrence of the second string.

```
$s = "He had had had where she had had had had";
$pos = rindex($s, "had");                 # pos = 37
```

The substr function returns a portion of a string starting at a specified position for a specified length. If the length is not given, the entire string from the specified beginning position is returned.

```
$var = "HOME=/users/home";
$where = index($var, "=");
$name = substr($var, 0, $where);
$val = substr($var, $where + 1);          # HOME
print "$name\n$val\n";                    # /users/home
```

The `substr` function may also be used to alter a string. That is, it can be used on the left-hand side of an assignment:

```
#!/usr/bin/perl
#
#   substr.pl
#
$test = "Java is inferior";
substr($test, 8, 5) = "super";
print "$test\n";
substr($test, 0, 4) = "Perl";
print "$test\n";
substr($test, 0, 0) = "My My: ";
print "$test\n";
```

The first `substr` above changes `infer` to `super`. Next, `Java` is changed to `Perl`. And finally, `"My  My: "` is prepended to the phrase.

```
% substr.pl
Java is superior
Perl is superior
My My: Perl is superior
%
```

The functions `lc` and `uc` return the lowercase and uppercase versions of the argument strings, respectively. The functions `lcfirst` and `ucfirst` return the argument strings with only the first character changed to the appropriate case.

```
#!/usr/bin/perl
#
#   cases.pl
#
print "Enter a string: ";
$string = <STDIN>;
print "LOWERCASE: ", lc($string);
print "FIRST CHAR: ", lcfirst($string), "\n";
print "UPPERCASE: ", uc($string);
print "FIRST CHAR: ", ucfirst($string);
```

continued...

```
% cases.pl
Enter a string: a SIMPLE string
LOWERCASE: a simple string
FIRST CHAR: a simple string

UPPERCASE: A SIMPLE STRING
FIRST CHAR: A simple string
%
```

3.1.12   The comma operator

Perl has a comma operator, the , symbol. There is little need for this operator, but we include it both for completeness and to assure that you understand a few Perl idioms.

In Perl, the semicolon is a statement separator. However, the same statement may have many comma-separated assignments. For example, the following sequence of statements:

```
$a = 10;
$b = 20;
$c = $a + $b;
```

may be written as:

```
$a = 10, $b = 20, $c = $a + $b;
```

although there is no particular advantage to doing so. Since you may use this technique in any place where you might code a Perl statement, the following is also possible:

```
for ($i = low, $j = high; $i < $j; $i++, $j--)
{
    # do something
}
```

You may also use the comma operator in any conditional, but beware how this is evaluated.

```
while($a = <STDIN>, $a ne "quit\n")
{
    print $a;
}
```

In this context, the comma operator's value is strictly the value of the last expression in the series. Actually, the above expression is somewhat useful.

Later, we will present information to allow you to extract an array slice, that is, an array that is composed of selected array elements. Using this technique, you will need to know about the comma operator. Here is a preview:

```
@list = (2,4,6,8,10);
$first = $list[0];    # retrieve the first element
$last  = $list[4];    # retrieve the last element
@both = @list[0,4];   # retrieve both elements
@both = $list[0,4];   # You probably didn't mean this
```

The last two lines above attempt to use an array slice, but only one of them is correct. To obtain a slice, you need to use @ notation. Thus, only the first statement below is correct, and therefore the comma operator is evaluated in an array context yielding elements 0 and 4:

```
@both = @list[0,4];    # retrieve both elements
@both = $list[0,4];    # You probably didn't mean this
```

The latter statement above uses $ rather than @. Thus, the comma operator is evaluated in a scalar context and evaluates to the value 4, the last of the comma-separated items.

Exercises

1. Write a Perl program that reads in three numbers and checks to see if the last one is an odd number between the first two.
2. Write a program that displays the sum of the following integers (use the range operator at least once):

```
1,2,3,...100,201,202,203...300.
```

3. Write some code that prompts the user for a string. Then prompt for a second string. Print the position number within the first string where the second instance of the second string occurred (within the first string).Here is an example of the execution of the program.% program

```
enter string -> hello there, this is a string
enter next string -> th
the second occurrence of (th) in the first string
is at position 13
%
```

4. Write a program that reads a positive number and then prints the binary pattern of the number.

```
% prog
enter a number 58
58 in decimal is 111010 in binary
%
```

ARRAYS AND ARRAY FUNCTIONS

All programming languages rely heavily on arrays, and Perl is no exception. However, you will see that Perl arrays are dynamic and are supported by a wide variety of functions. We will take a look at some of the nice features of Perl arrays. Finally, we will look at many of the more common array functions used by Perl programmers.

4.1 Introduction

An array is an ordered list of items, each of which is a scalar, such that each scalar element can be retrieved by an index. In Perl, an array is identified by a variable whose name begins with the @ character. Here are a few examples of array names:

```
@names        @days_of_the_week        @months
```

4.1.1 Arrays are dynamic

Perl arrays are not of fixed length. An array can grow or shrink as a result of the requirements of a program in execution. This is usually referred to as dynamic storage allocation. In some languages, the programmer is responsible for managing this dynamic storage, but in Perl, this burden is taken from you. Each of the following creates an array:

```
@numbers = (10,11,12,13,14,15,16,17,18,19);
@names = (al, pete, jane, "john smith", joe);
@ranges = (1..10, 20..30, 40..50);
```

An array may also be created dynamically by a series of assignments.

```
$data[3] = 5;            # @data array now has 4 elements
$data[5] = 10;           # now it has 6;
```

Even though the above code only accesses two elements of the @data array, the size of the array is six. The unreferenced elements of the array contain the special value undef. The following program may help you understand these concepts:

```perl
#!/usr/bin/perl
#
#   sparse.pl
#
$data[5] = 20;
$data[3] = 5;
foreach $value (@data)
{
        $sparse = 0;
        $sparse = 1 if $value eq undef;
        $num++;
        print "$num\t|$sparse|$value|\n";
}


% sparse.pl
1    |1||
2    |1||
3    |1||
4    |0|5|
5    |1||
6    |0|20|
%
```

The program loops through all the elements of the array and lists the element at each position. The program also tests for the value undef and prints a 1 if the test is true or a 0 if it is false.

You may assign one array to another regardless of the sizes of the arrays. If they do not have the same number of elements originally, the array on the left either grows or shrinks to accommodate its new size.

```
@a = (1,2,3);            # 3 elements
@b = (8,9,10,11,12);     # 5 elements
@c = (1..100);           # 100 elements
@a = @b;                 # @a = (8,9,10,11,12);
@c = @a;                 # @c = (8,9,10,11,12);
```

4.1.2   Treating an array in a scalar context

You will have many occasions to determine the size of an array. You can obtain this simply by assigning the array to a scalar.

```
@date = (1,3,2,4,10,20);
$size = @data;                     # $size = 6
```

In the last assignment above, the array is said to be treated in a scalar context. There are many instances when an array in Perl is treated this way. The following examples show how you can use this feature to control loops:

```
for ($ct = 0; $ct < @data; $ct++)
{
    print $data[$ct];
}
while(@data > 0 )
{
    print pop(@data);
}
```

In both cases above, each array is compared with a scalar using a relational operator. In these contexts, Perl uses the number of elements in the array for the comparison.

If you try to compare two arrays using arithmetic equality, keep in mind that you are treating both arrays in a scalar context and thus you will be determining if they have the same size. If you actually want to compare their contents, you must loop through both arrays, testing each element for equality.

```
@data = (1,2,3);
@vals = (4,5,6);
if ( @data == @vals)        # true if they have the same size
{
}
```

4.1.3   Selecting an element from an array

On the many occasions when you want to select an element from an array, you must use the subscript operator, a set of square brackets that encloses an index. The index selects the element of the array.

Since an array is a group of scalars, you must also place a $ in front of each selection. As you examine the examples below, note that subscripts in Perl begin with 0:

```
@data = (2, 5, 8, 12, 11, 15, 7);
print $data[0];          # The first element, i.e., 2
print $data[1];          # prints 5
```

Every array also has a scalar associated with it whose name is $#arrayname. For the array @data, this variable is named $#data. The value of this variable is the highest subscript in the array. Thus, for @data, $#data has the value 6. You may use this fact to retrieve the last element of an array.

```
print $data[$#data];      # prints 7
```

Perl also lets you subscript an array from the bottom element simply by using negative subscripts.

```
print $data[-1];          # prints 7
print $data[-2];          # prints 15
```

4.1.4 Arrays and lists

A list is a set of elements enclosed in parentheses. Thus, an array is really a named list. As you have seen, you can assign one array to another:

```
@vals = @data;
```

You may also assign an array to a list:

```
($a, $b, $c) = @data;
```

The assignment saves you the trouble of coding the following:

```
$a = $data[0];
$b = $data[1];
$c = $data[2];
```

Here are a few other examples of arrays and lists:

```
($a, $b) = ($b, $a);      # exchange $a, $b
($first, @a) = @a;        # $first = shift(@a);
```

4.1.5   Array slices

Any portion of an array may be selected rather than selecting just a single element. This is called an array slice.

```
@numbers = (1..9);              # the numbers 1 through 9
($low, $high) = @numbers[0,8];# $low = 1, $high = 9
```

Be aware of the difference between the following two expressions: one has a $, which means it refers to one item; the other has a @, which means it is an array. In the latter case, you may recall from the comma operator that the subscript [0,8] is evaluated in a scalar context, yielding the last element in the comma-separated list.

```
@numbers[0,8];                  # $numbers[0], $numbers[8]
$numbers[0,8];                  # $numbers[8]
```

Array slices are useful in extracting elements from functions that return arrays. Here's a code snippet that extracts the lowest and highest alphabetic strings from a list:

```
#!/usr/bin/perl
#
#   slices.pl
#
@a = (Bo, Al, Jo, Mike, Zeke, Sue );
($low, $high) = (sort(@a))[0,-1];
print "$low, $high";

% slices.pl
Al, Zeke
%
```

Or to obtain the size of a file, you could code the following:

```
$size = (stat("myfile"))[7];
```

Recall here that the stat function returns a 13-element array, the seventh element of which is the size of the array. In cases where we desire a slice from a function returning an array, we need to use an extra set of parentheses to satisfy the precedence of the operators.

4.2   The @ARGV Array

Perl contains a few arrays that are built into the language. One of these is named @ARGV. This array holds the arguments sent to the program from the command line. For example, if you execute a command as follows:

```
% findfiles here size 100
```

the @ARGV array will contain the three elements here, size, and 100. You may use @ARGV the way you use any other array in Perl. Since most Perl commands are executed from the command line, various items involving @ARGV can be very useful. Here's a program to demonstrate some information about @ARGV:

```
#!/usr/bin/perl
#
#   raise.pl
#
die "$0: base expo\n" unless $#ARGV == 1;
die "$0: base must be an integer\n"
unless $ARGV[0] =~ /^[0-9]+$/ ;
die "$0: power must be an integer\n"
unless $ARGV[1] =~ /^[0-9]+$/;
print $ARGV[0] ** $ARGV[1];, "\n"

% raise.pl
raise.pl: base exponent
% raise.pl 2 a
raise.pl: power must be an integer
% raise.pl a 2
raise.pl: base must be an integer
% raise.pl 2 10
1024
%
```

Besides using @ARGV in various ways, the above program shows a typical use of unless in error checking. The program also demonstrates the special variable $0, the command name.

4.3   Array Functions

Perl has a plethora of functions that operate on arrays. We will give examples of some common array functions here.

push and pop allow for stack operations. push and shift allow for queue operations. push, pop, shift, and unshift allow for deque operations. join and split are exact opposites, the latter creating an array from a scalar and the former creating a scalar from an array. grep performs various tests on array elements.

4.3.1   push **and** pop

To get familiar with the push and pop functions, we'll write some code to reverse an array. This is accomplished by popping off the top element of one array and pushing it onto another array.

```perl
#!/usr/bin/perl
#
#   reverse.pl
#
@data = (10,30,20,40);
while(@data)
{
    push(@newdata, pop(@data));
}
print "@newdata\n";
```

Each iteration of the loop pops an element from the @data array and pushes it onto the @newdata array. Eventually, the @data array becomes empty and the while loop terminates.

With a single function call, you may push as many items onto an array as you wish. For example, the following pushes one array and two other values onto another array:

```perl
@data = (1,2,3,4);
@items = (10,20,30,40);
push (@data, @items, 100, 200);
print "@data";           # 1,2,3,4,10,20,30,40,100,200
```

4.3.2   shift **and** unshift

shift removes the top element of an array. It is often used to process command-line arguments.

```perl
#!/usr/bin/perl
#
#   argcount.pl
#
$ct = 1;
while(@ARGV)
{   print "arg $ct:\t $ARGV[0]\n";
    shift(@ARGV);
    $ct++;
}
```

If the shift function has no arguments, then by default, it is @ARGV that is shifted. This is true unless you are in a subroutine, in which case, it is @_ that is shifted by default. You will see later that @_ is a builtin Perl array that holds the parameters sent to any function.

```
% argcount.pl one two three
arg 1:      one
arg 2:      two
arg 3:      three
%
```

The unshift function adds elements to the beginning of an array. One or more elements may be added.

```perl
@names = (Mike, Sue, Erin);
unshift(@names, Maria, Patti, Dave);
print "@names\n";        # Maria Patti Dave Mike Sue Erin
```

4.3.3 reverse

In Chapter 1, we introduced the reverse function. It returns an array without changing the contents of the array you pass to it. To have this function place the reversed values in a new array, you may code the following:

```perl
@names = (me, you, him, her, us);
@reversed = reverse(@names)
print "@names\n";# me you him her us
print "@reversed\n";# us her him you me
```

To reverse the values in the same array, you may code the following:

```perl
@names = (me you him her us);
@names = reverse(@names);
```

reverse can also take a scalar and reverse the characters within it:

```
$name = Michael;
$reversed = reverse($name);
$name = reverse($name); # $name = leahciM
```

4.3.4 split

split takes a delimiter and a string as its two arguments and returns the list of values in the string separated by the delimiter. There are a variety of ways in which split can be used. Without any arguments, split splits $_ on whitespace. If you omit the second argument, split automatically splits $_. split can also take a third argument that defines the number of elements in the returned list.

The program below reads each line of a file having colon-separated fields. The program splits each line into its various fields and then prints those lines whose third field is greater than the value given as the first command-line argument. Here is the input file:

```
% display data
Mike:1:50000:6812 Caravan Court
Susan:2:45000:9748 Basket Ring Road
Erin:3:70000:111 Main Street
Sally:4:50000:345 Flower Drum Drive
Patti:5:60000:247 Creekside Row
%
```

And here is the program, split.pl:

```
#!/usr/bin/perl
#
#   split.pl
#
print "enter input file ";
chomp($in = <STDIN>);
open(INPUT, "< $in") || die "can't open $in\n";
while(<INPUT>)
{
    @info = split(":");
    print if ($info[2] > $ARGV[0] );
}
% split.pl 55000
enter input file data
Erin:3:70000:111 Main Street
Patti:5:60000:247 Creekside Row
%
```

split also has the little known property of splitting a string into single characters. To do this, use the empty string, " ", as the first argument.

```
$_ = "Hi there how are you.";
@chars = split("");
print "First character is $chars[0]\n"; # prints 'H'
```

The first argument to split may be any regular expression. For example, to extract all the data surrounded by sets of digits, you might use the following:

```
$_ = "Mike2345is45789from12345Columbia";
@info = split(/[0-9]+/);
print "@info\n";                # Mike is from Columbia
```

4.3.5 join

join is the inverse of split. join takes an expression and a list and creates a string consisting of each element in the list with the expression as a delimiter.

```
@a = (10, 20, 30);
$x = join(".",@a);        # $x ="10.20.30";
```

join is very useful in problems such as when you want to print the reverse of an array such as the following:

```
@data = (Al, Joe, Pete, Alice, Mike, Sam, Ed);
print reverse(@data);
```

Here, the output will obscure the results. All the names will be run together because the array produced by the reverse function is not double quoted.

```
EdSamMikeAlicePeteJoeAl
```

You might be tempted to place the function in double quotes:

```
print "reverse(@data)";
```

so that the resultant array that is printed has spaces between its elements. If you try this, here is what you will see printed:

```
reverse(Al Joe Pete Alice Mike Sam Ed)
```

print does not recognize function names within quotes. This is where the `join` function can help:

```
print join(" ", reverse(@data));
```

Now the output is readable:

```
Ed Sam Mike Alice Pete Joe Al
```

4.3.6   `sort`

There are many variations of sorting algorithms. Each variation, however, has two different phases: the comparison phase and the exchange phase. If the two items being compared are out of order, then they are exchanged. The Perl `sort` function compares items using dictionary order as the means of comparison.

```
@names = (Mike, Alan, Roger, Dave);
@sorted = sort(@names);
print "@sorted\n";              # Alan Dave Mike Roger
```

If you want a different comparison behavior, you must first create this function and then pass it to `sort` as an extra argument. If, for example, you want to sort numerically, then you must supply a special comparison subroutine. The only restriction on this subroutine is that when it compares two items, it must return −1, 0, or +1, depending upon how the two items compare.

When you supply this function as an argument to the `sort` function, you are in effect telling `sort` to call your subroutine whenever it must compare two items. `sort` expects the logic in your subroutine to use two special Perl variables: $a and $b. Here is a user-supplied comparison function that allows you to sort items numerically:

```
sub numcmp
{
   if ( $a < $b )
   {
      return -1
   }
   elsif ( $a == $b )
{
      return 0;
   }
   return 1;
}
```

Of course, you could rewrite this using the `<=>` operator. This operator returns −1, 0, or +1, depending on the result of the comparisons.

```perl
sub numcmp
{
    $a <=> $b
}
```

Then you execute `sort` as follows:

```perl
numbers = (10,20,40,30,-5,100);
@res =  sort numcmp (@numbers);
```

Here's an extended example to demonstrate this technique:

```perl
#!/usr/bin/perl
#
#   sorts.pl
#
sub numcmp
{
    return $a <=> $b;
}
sub revcmp
{
    return $b <=> $a;
}
print "first draw 10 random numbers\n";
srand(time);# seed the random number generator
foreach $i (1..5)
{
    push(@numbers, int (rand(100)));
    push(@numbers, int (rand(1000)));
}
print "Random numbers: @numbers\n\n";
print "Sort as chars:   ";
print join(" ", sort(@numbers)), "\n\n";
print "Sort numeric:    ";
print join(" ", sort numcmp(@numbers)), "\n\n";
print "Reverse numeric:";
print join(" ", sort revcmp(@numbers)), "\n";

% sorts.pl
first draw 10 random numbers
Random numbers: 51 661 56 456 70 484 5 681 13 249

Sort as chars:   13 249 456 484 5 51 56 661 681 70
```

continued...

```
Sort numeric:     5 13 51 56 70 249 456 484 661 681

Reverse numeric:681 661 484 456 249 70 56 51 13 5
%
```

As you can see, ten random numbers are drawn: five are between 0 and 100 and the other five are between 0 and 1000. Before the random numbers are created, the `srand` function is executed to seed the random number generator, `rand`. `rand` returns a floating point number between 0 and its first argument. The `time` function is used as the seed for the `srand` function. The `int` function truncates each floating point number to an integer.

```
foreach $i (1..5)
{
    push(@numbers, int (rand(100)));
    push(@numbers, int (rand(1000)));
}
```

Various sorts are performed on the numbers, which are printed after each sort. You can see that the "bare" `sort` will sort them alphabetically, and thus it takes a special `sort` to sort them numerically.

Incidentally, the invocation of the `sort` function may be written as follows, that is, with the `sort` code in a block:

```
@res = sort { $a <=> $b } (@numbers);
```

If you are not sure of the purpose of $a, and $b, think about what happens when the `sort` is executed. It compares two items by calling the function that you supply. It then either swaps the two items or not based on the value that your function returns. $a and $b hold these two items! You might get a better idea of how this works if you print the values sent to the supplied function as follows:

```
#!/usr/bin/perl
#
#   debug.pl
#
srand(time);
sub numcmp
{
    $ct++;
    print "comparing ($a,$b)\n";
    return $a <=> $b;
}
foreach $i (1..5)
```

continued...

```
    {
        push(@numbers, int (rand(100)));
        push(@numbers, int (rand(1000)));
    }
    print "@numbers\n";
    print join(" ", sort numcmp(@numbers)), "\n";
    print "$ct comparisons\n";
% debug.pl
77 380 19 403 53 260 21 987 10 932
comparing (403,53)
comparing (53,260)
comparing (403,260)
comparing (19,260)
comparing (380,260)
comparing (260,21)
comparing (77,260)
comparing (260,987)
comparing (260,10)
comparing (260,932)
comparing (987,380)
comparing (403,987)
comparing (403,380)
comparing (932,987)
comparing (932,403)
comparing (21,77)
comparing (19,77)
comparing (19,21)
comparing (53,77)
comparing (53,21)
comparing (10,77)
comparing (10,53)
comparing (10,21)
comparing (10,19)
10 19 21 53 77 260 380 403 932 987
24 comparisons
%
```

4.3.7 grep

The grep function pattern matches an expression against each element of a list and returns a list of all the elements that matched the pattern. In the two uses of grep below, the matched lines are returned, that is, those that begin with a number:

```
@lines=<STDIN>;                    # read entire file
@hits=grep(/^[0-9]/,@lines);       # the strings
print "@hits\n";
$hits=grep(/^[0-9]/,@lines);       # the number of strings
print "$hits\n";
```

In one case, the lines themselves are stored in the `@hits` array. In the other case, the number of lines is stored in the `$hits` variable.

The first argument may also be a file inquiry operator that helps classify groups of files. For example, you might take a list of files and classify it according to whether the files were directories, text files, binary files, etc.

```
@text_files = grep (-T, @ARGV);      # text files
@directories = grep (-d, @ARGV);     # directories
@binary_files = grep (-B, @ARGV);    # binary files
```

There is also a block version of `grep`. In this case, the first argument is treated as a subroutine. Each element of the list is sent to the subroutine through the special variable `$_`. Whenever the subroutine returns a non-zero value, the element being processed is placed in a list. When all values have been processed, the list is returned. The example below returns a list of even numbers:

```
#   Use block-style grep to return even numbers
#
@values = (100,200,300,301,303,304);
sub test
{
    $_[0] % 2 == 0 ? 1 : 0;   # return 1 if even
}
@list = grep ( test($_), @values);
print  "@list\n";          # prints 100 200 300 304
```

4.3.8 splice

`splice` displaces a slice of a list with another list. The displacement is for a certain number of elements beginning at a specified index. The displaced list is returned. In the example below, the original list is `@members`, the list that will displace elements of `@members` is `@newbees`, and the displacement starts at position 1 for 3 positions:

```
#!/usr/bin/perl
#
#   splice.pl
#
@newbees =("Al", "Mary");
@members = ("Mike", "Bob", "Jane", "Jill"," John");
print "originals are @members\n";
print "new ones are @newbees at 1 for 3\n";
@result = splice(@members,1,3,@newbees);
print "expelled members are:  @result", "\n";
```

continued...

```
        print "now staff members are: @members", "\n";
        % splice.pl
        originals are Mike Bob Jane Jill John
        new ones are Al Mary at 1 for 3
        expelled members are:  Bob Jane Jill
        now staff members are: Mike Al Mary John
        %
```

Exercises

1. Using `splice` several times, take the following `@cities` and `@states` array and build the `@total` array:

```
@cities = (Boston, Atlanta, Chicago);
@states = (MA, GA, IL);
@total  = (Boston, MA, Atlanta, GA, Chicago, IL);
```

2. Write a Perl script that counts the total number of lines in all text files given on the command line.
3. Write a Perl program that maintains a queue. The program should contain an infinite loop. Each time through the loop, a menu of choices is printed.
   The user will select one of the following choices:

   0) exit
   1) add
   2) remove
   3) print

   If the choice is 0), the program terminates. If the choice is 1), the user is prompted for a line and this line is added to the queue. If the user selects 2), the head of the queue is removed. If the user selects 3), the queue is printed.

5

HASHES

Most programs simply cannot do without arrays. On the other hand, associative arrays, also called hashes, are never necessary, but are so efficient and so powerful that they should be mastered and applied wherever necessary. Hashes deal with paired data, and as it happens, there are a plethora of situations in software where this data structure is by far the best solution. The approach in this section is to demonstrate how any problem that can be solved with hashes may also be handled with simple arrays, albeit less efficiently. Next, we will show how hashes make your programming life easier and more efficient. Finally, we will show a variety of common problems where hashes provide the best solution.

5.1   Introduction

Most beginning Perl programmers are never taught the real power of hashes. As you will see shortly, hashes may be used to solve many different problems.

An associative array, or hash, is a collection of pairs, each of which has a key and a value. When the key is used as a subscript, the value is retrieved. Other languages refer to this type of array as a map because in mathematics, a mapping function takes one value and translates it to another. Computer scientists refer to associative arrays as hashes, so we will adopt that term for the remainder of the book.

A hash is simple to use and is supported in many languages other than Perl. C++ supports hashes through the Standard Template Library (STL), and Java supports hashes through the Collections classes.

In the final analysis, a hash is a simple yet clever technique for doing table lookups. If you've studied searching techniques, you should recall that there are three fundamental approaches: linear search, binary search, and hash search. To completely understand hashing, it helps to create your own hashes.

5.1.1 Hashes as dual arrays

If you were tasked with determining the frequency counts of words in a file, you might proceed with the following logic:

```
create a word table
create a frequency table
while(there's another word)
{
     if it's not in the word table
          add it to the word table
     add one to the count table for this word
}
foreach word you have found
{
     print the word and print the count
}
```

For each word in the input file, we place it in an array of words and then add one to a counter for that word. This requires two arrays: one for the words and one for the counts. Here's the Perl code to do this:

```
#!/usr/bin/perl
#
#    lookup.pl
#
while(<STDIN>)
{
     @words = split;
     foreach $word (@words)
     {
          for ($i = 0; $i < $count; $i++)
          {
               if ( $table[$i] eq $word )
               {
                    $howmany[$i]++;
                    last;
               }
          }
          if ( $i == $count )
          {
               $table[$count] = $word;
               $howmany[$count++] = 1;
          }
     }
}
for( $i = 0; $i < $count; $i++)
{
     print $table[$i], " ", $howmany[$i], "\n";
}
```

The program above has three nested loops: the outer loop gets a line from the input file; the middle loop delivers each word on that line; and the inner loop does all of the table work.

```
while(<STDIN>)                # get a line
{
    @words = split;
    foreach $word (@words)  # deliver each word
    {
        for ($i = 0; $i < $count; $i++)
        {                     # look up each word
        }
    }
}
```

The `if` searches the array where the strings are kept to see if the current word has been seen previously. If it has, then the count at the appropriate index is incremented and the loop is terminated.

```
if ( $table[$i] eq $word )
{
    $howmany[$i]++;
    last;
}
```

If the word is not found, then it is entered into the `table` array and the appropriate count is set to 1. The important part of this code is that the indices into the `howmany` array are always a function of the appropriate place in the `table` array. In other words, for each word in the `table` array, the count is kept at the same index in the `howmany` array.

```
if ( $i == $count )
{
    $table[$count] = $word;
    $howmany[$count++] = 1;
}
```

Finally, both arrays are printed with the `foreach` loop. In a language that does not have hashes, this solution is typical. We'll now improve on the above strategy by writing our own hashing algorithm. Keep in mind that in Perl, you do not need to write your own hashing algorithm, but you will better understand Perl's hashing techniques if you have written your own.

5.1.2   A hashing algorithm

The code above uses the linear search method to find a word and then prints the frequency of the word seen in the input. We can improve the performance by using a hash search. The next version of this program requires that we code our own hash algorithm. It is worth a look because this is exactly the step you would be saving if you had used Perl's hashing instead of your own algorithm.

A hashing algorithm takes a string and maps it to a number. There are many hashing algorithms, but all we require is a simple one. Our hashing algorithm consists of summing the numerical values for each character in the string. Then, the algorithm divides this sum by the size of the table where each string will be stored. We take the remainder of this division and use it as the index into this table. Here's the code to produce such an algorithm:

```perl
#!/usr/bin/perl
#
#    hashing.pl
#
sub hash
{
     ($string, $table_size) = @_;
     @chars = split("", $string);
     $hvalue = 0;
     foreach $character (@chars)
     {
          $hvalue += ord($character);
     }
     $hvalue % $table_size;
}
while(<STDIN>)
{
     @words = split;
     foreach $word (@words)
     {
          print "$word ",hash($word,100), "\n";
     }
}
```

The hash function is shown below. It simply takes each character of a word and gets its numerical value using the ord function. Notice the use of split to split a string into an array of single characters. The remainder of the division is returned using the modulus operator, %.

```perl
sub hash
{
     ($string, $table_size) = @_;
     @chars = split("", $string);
     $hvalue = 0;
     foreach $character (@chars)
     {
          $hvalue += ord($character);
     }
     $hvalue % $table_size;
}
```

We now show the data file and the execution of the program on a very small data file:

```
% display data
is si is life file life
%

% hashing.pl < data
is 20
si 20
is 20
life 16
file 16
life 16
%

% myhash.pl < data
is 3
life 3
%
```

Having the hashing algorithm allows us to implement a hash search. For each word, we hash it and then use the hash value as the place to store the count for the string. Here's the code:

```perl
#!/usr/bin/perl
#
#    myhash.pl
#
while(<STDIN>)
{
    @words = split;
    foreach $word (@words)
    {
        $hv = hash($word, 10);
        $count[$hv]++;
        $table[$hv++] = $word;
    }
}
for ($i = 0; $i < 10; $i++)
{
    if ( $table[$i] )
    {
        print $table[$i]," ",$count[$i],"\n";
    }
}
```

Now we have done our own hashing! There's a problem, however! More than one string could hash to the same value. This is called a *collision,* and it is evident from the program output where `is` and `si` hash to the same value, as do `life` and `file`.

In the example above, not all entries of the `@table` array will have a value. We must test each element of the array to determine which elements have a value.

```perl
if ( $table[$i] )
{
    print $table[$i]," ",$count[$i],"\n";
}
```

Of course, the counts in the above program are incorrect because of the collisions.

5.1.3   Builtin hashing

It would not be difficult to write code to handle the collisions. However, since this is a book about Perl and not data structures, we will opt instead to use Perl's support for hashing, the associative array. Whenever you code:

```perl
$table{"John"} = 21;
```

Perl stores the value `21` in the place in memory to which `John` hashes. Of course, each time `John` is hashed, it will hash to the same value. Others may also hash to that same value, but Perl handles the collisions. Here's the solution using a Perl hash:

```perl
#!/usr/bin/perl
#
#   assn.pl
#
while(<STDIN>)
{
    @words = split;
    foreach $word (@words)
    {
        $words{$word}++;
    }
}
foreach $word (keys(%words))
{
    print "$word\t$words{$word}\n";
}
```

continued...

```
% assn.pl < data
file        1
life        2
si          1
is          2
%
```

A few comments are in order relative to the code above. There are two data structures named `words`. When Perl sees a reference like the one below, the curly braces tell Perl that the reference is to a hash:

```
$words{$word}++;
```

On the other hand, the reference below is to a regular array:

```
@words
```

In this program, there was no need to subscript `@words`, but if there was a need, the reference would have been as follows:

```
$words[0]
```

That's fine for Perl. It can tell by the punctuation. For example:

```
#
#    An  array of three entries
#
@words = (Huey, Louie, Dewey};

#
#    Some hash references
#
$words{Me}  =   Moe;
$words{You} = Larry;
$words{Him} = Curly;

#
#    A scalar of three words
#
$words = "Eeny meenie miny";

print "($words[0]), ($words{Me}), ($words)\n";
#
#   prints (Huey), (Moe), (Eeny meenie miny)
#
```

Hashes are usually dynamic, but if you need to initialize a hash, you may proceed by coding in either of these styles:

```
%words = ( Me => Moe,  You => Larry, Him => Curly);
%words = ( Me,   Moe,  You,   Larry, Him,   Curly);
```

5.2   Sorting Hashes

Returning to the problem of counting word frequencies, you might wonder how we can sort the results from the hash examples above. Depending on how we change the `foreach` loop, we might sort the data either by *key* or by *value*.

5.2.1   Sorting by keys

In Perl, the native `sort` function always sorts lexicographically, and thus it is always easier to sort strings than numbers. Sorting by keys, therefore, is simple. Change the `foreach` loop to the following:

```
foreach $word (sort (keys(%words)))
{
    print "$word\t$words{$word}\n";
}
```

The keys are sorted and then presented in turn to the `foreach` loop variable.

5.2.2   Sorting by values

To sort by numerical value, in this case, the frequency, a specialized version of `sort` is required. The code to invoke `sort` would be:

```
sort numcmp keys(%words))
```

In this case, the two values sent to `sort` will be two keys. However, we want to compare the values associated with those keys and that is why the comparison expression is:

```
$words{$a} <=> $words{$b}
```

When those two frequencies are out of order, then their respective keys are swapped such that the entire array of keys ends up sorted in an order reflective of their associated values. Here's the special function:

```
sub numcmp
{
    $words{$a} <=> $words{$b}
}
```

This subroutine uses the signed comparison operator, `<=>`, which returns –1, 0, or +1, depending on the results of the comparison. Zero is returned when the two items being compared are the same, and –1 is returned when the item on the left is less than the item on the right.

```
foreach $word (sort numcmp keys(%words))
{
    print "$word\t$words{$word}\n";
}
```

It might help to see the original hash and the results:

```
sort numcmp keys(%words)
```

If the original pairs were:

```
Mike        => 5
Zeke        => 7
Alice       => 3
Mary        => 10
```

then the results of the above `sort` would be:

```
Alice   Mike   Zeke   Mary
  3      5      7     10
```

We've listed the frequencies with the keys so you can see the results of the orderings. If these keys were presented in accordance with the above `sort`, the actual output would be:

```
Alice      3
Mike       5
Zeke       7
Mary       10
```

Keep in mind that in this case, the values of the hash were frequencies, but in other cases, the values might be strings. To sort these strings, the comparison function would be as shown below. Of importance here is that you need to use the string signed comparison operator, `cmp`, rather than the numeric signed comparison operator, `<=>`.

```
sub stringcmp
{
    $words{$a} cmp $words{$b}
}
```

5.3   Hash Solutions to Common Problems

Powerful features often elicit more use than is necessary. Nevertheless, there are many common problems that are best solved through the use of hashes. We now present a few problems where a hash is the most convenient and efficient solution.

5.3.1   Finding unique words in a file

Suppose you are interested in determining the unique words that exist in a file. The solution here is not much different than the frequency count problem seen earlier. Here's a solution:

```
#!/usr/bin/perl
#
#   unique.pl
#
while(<STDIN>)
{
    @words = split;
    foreach $word (@words)
    {
        $wds{$word}= 1 if ! exists $wds{$word};
    }
}
print join("\n", keys(%wds)), "\n";
```

We use the `exists` function to determine if a particular key has already been seen. If it has not, then we enter it into the hash. The value for the hash really does not matter in this case.

5.3.2   Reverse lookups

Another common use for a hash is in performing reverse lookups. To illustrate, suppose you have a file of (*state, capital*) pairs. You might be interested in finding a state, given its capital, or you might be interested in finding a capital, given its state. In general, the technique illustrated in the program below will only work if the collection of pairs forms a 1:1 mapping. Since no two states have the same capital, the code below is fine. But the code would not work correctly if we were using state universities and nicknames. For example, Princeton and Clemson both use the name Tigers.

```perl
#!/usr/bin/perl
#
#   reverse.pl
#
open(STATECAPS, "statecaps") || die;
while(<STATECAPS>)
{
    chomp;
    ($state, $cap) = split(":");
    $states{$state} = $cap;
}
while(1)
{
    print "enter a capitol ";
    chomp($input = <STDIN>);
    last if ($input eq end);
    if  ( exists $states{$input} )
    {
        print "capital of $input is $states{$input}\n"
    }
    else
    {
        print "$input is not a capital\n";
    }
}
print "Now we'll do some reverses\n";
%caps = reverse(%states);                  # key line of code
while(1)
{
    print "enter a state ";
    chop($input = <STDIN>);
    last if ($input eq end);
    if  ( exists $caps{$input} )
    {
        print "$caps{$input} is capital of $input\n"
    }
    else
    {
        print "$input is not a state\n";
    }
}
```

The important principle above is that when you reverse a hash, the (key, value) pairs stay together, but the keys become the values and the values become the keys. The line of code that accomplishes the reverse is:

```
%caps = reverse(%states);                    # key line of code
```

It should be clear that the keys for a hash must be unique. If you execute the following code, it will be the value for the last instance of the key that will be printed:

```
$record{subject} = Perl;
$record{subject} = Java;
print $record{subject}, "\n";                # prints Java
```

If you want subject to map to both Perl and Java, you must wait for the chapter on references (Chapter 10).

It's all right to have more than one key map to a different value. For example, each of the following is fine:

```
$record {nickname} = John;
$record {fistname} = John;
```

However, if you reverse %record, it is not clear what the John key will have for its value: firstname or nickname. This was the problem to which we alluded earlier with Princeton and Clemson.

5.3.3   Selecting the top n elements from a list

Suppose you have a list and you want to determine the highest/lowest element in it. This is a simple problem. The following code will do the trick:

```
#!/usr/bin/perl
#
#   lowhigh.pl
#
@data = (Mike, Jane, Zeke, Jeb, Alan, Susan);
@array = (sort(@data))[0, -1];
print "@array\n";

% lowhigh.pl
Alan Zeke
%
```

This is straightforward. However, we can complicate the problem slightly by requesting the top or bottom n elements of the list.

```perl
#!/usr/bin/perl
#
#   lowhighn.pl
#
@d = (Mike, Jane, Zeke, Jeb, Alan, Susan);
$n = 3;
@bottom = (sort(@d))[0..($n - 1)];
print "BOTTOM: -> @bottom\n";
@top = (sort(@d))[ ($#d - ($n - 1)) .. $#d];
print "TOP -> @top\n";

% lowhighn.pl
BOTTOM: -> Alan Jane Jeb
TOP: -> Mike Susan Zeke
%
```

The code is not pretty, but it is fairly simple. Let's throw a wrinkle into the problem. Suppose you have a hash and you want to retrieve the highest or lowest keys or values. The rub here is that you need to keep the key together with its associated value. You can't simply get the keys and sort them because then you have lost the pairings. The code below gets a number from the command line, say n, and then prints from a hash the highest n values and the keys associated with them. We'll use the file named hashdata shown here:

```perl
% display hashdata
Bob        38
Sally       6
Susan      60
Mike      132
Patti       2
Kim         3
Erin       36
%

#!/usr/bin/perl
#
#   highhash.pl
#
while(<STDIN>)
{
    chomp;
    ($name, $val) = split;
    $hash{$name} = $val;
}
@keys = sort  keys(%hash);
$howmany = $ARGV[0] - 1;
```

continued...

```
@keys = @keys[0 .. $howmany ];
foreach $name (@keys)
{
    print "$name\t$hash{$name}\n";
}

% highhash.pl 3 < hashdata
Bob        38
Erin       36
Kim         3
%
```

Keep in mind that we have sorted on the names. To sort on the values, we need to supply our own comparison function, as we did earlier in this chapter. The only line in the above program that would change would be the line that sorted the data:

```
@keys=sort { $hash{$b} <=> $hash{$a} } keys(%hash);
```

The output would be:

```
% valuehash.pl 3 < hashdata
Mike       132
Susan       60
Bob         38
%
```

5.4   Builtin Associative Arrays

As you have seen, many names are built into Perl. Some of them are scalars such as $. and $_. Others are filehandles such as STDOUT and STDIN. In this section, we will examine a few builtin hashes.

5.4.1   The %ENV hash

%ENV is a builtin hash. It is through this variable that a Perl program has access to its environment. So if you wanted to access the PATH variable from within a Perl script, you might obtain its value with:

```
$path = $ENV{PATH};
```

Or, to see the value of your prompt, you could code:

```
$prompt = $ENV{PROMPT};
```

To see a listing of all your environment variables, you could do so as follows:

```
foreach $key (keys(%ENV))
{
    print "$key has value $ENV{$key}\n";
}
```

5.4.2 The %INC hash

Another builtin hash is %INC. This hash helps Perl load libraries that we'll see later.

5.5 Reading from a File into a Hash

Sometimes a hash must be built from data in a file. For example, suppose we had a file such as the one below:

```
% display datafile
Mike:1:50000:6812 Caravan Court
Susan:2:45000:9748 Basket Ring Road
Erin:3:70000:111 Main Street
Sally:4:50000:345 Flower Drum Drive
Patti:5:60000:247 Creekside Row
%
```

The following code will create a hash whose keys are names and whose values are the rest of the record. By now, you have probably realized that keys must be unique. If they are not, then the old value for a key will be replaced with the new value for the same key. Here is the code that produces the hash from the data file above. The code takes advantage of the version of split that requires a third argument.

```
#!/usr/bin/perl
#
#   database.pl
#
open(INPUT, "< database") || die "Can't open database\n";
while(<INPUT>)
{
    ($name, $data) = split(':', $_, 2);
```

continued...

```
    $names{$name} = $data;
}
while(1)
{
    print "Enter a name ";
    chomp($name = <STDIN>);
    last if ( $name eq "quit" );
    if ( exists ($names{$name} ))
    {
        print "$name: $names{$name}";
    }
    else
    {
        print "can't find $name\n";
    }
}
```

The third argument to `split` causes it to return a specific number of fields. In this case, the first field becomes the key and the rest of the line becomes the value for that key.

```
($name, $data) = split(':', $_, 2);
$names{$name} = $data;
```

After all the data has been read, the user enters a name. The `exists` function determines if this element exists in the hash:

```
if ( exists ($names{$name} ))
```

If it does, it is printed. If it does not exist, then an informative message is printed.

```
% database.pl
Enter a name Mike
Mike:1:50000:6812 Caravan Court
Enter a name Mikey
can't find Mikey
Enter a name Susan
Susan:2:45000:9748 Basket Ring Road
Enter a name quit
%
```

Exercises

1. Read a file of (number, name) pairs such as:

```
1 Mike
2 Dave
3 John
4 Mary
```

and then read a file of data such as:

```
4   6000 234567891 Austin, Texas
1 50000 246813579 Providence, R.I.
2 20000 135790124 Greenville, S.C.
3   4000 912345678 Trenton, New Jersey
```

The first field in this file is the key to the name in the first file. The program should print the name and information for each record whose balance is greater than the first argument supplied to the program. Here's a sample execution of the program:

```
% program 10000
Mike: 50000 246813579 Providence, R.I.
Dave: 20000 135790124 Greenville, S.C.
%
```

2. Write a Perl script that takes a number, say N, and a filename from the command line. The file contains lines such as the ones shown below. The program should print lines associated with the N smallest files. See the file named `filenames` among those that you downloaded.

```
129   04-17-93   9:41p 1-1.C
120   04-17-93   9:41p 1-2.C
218   04-17-93   9:41p 1-3.C
134   04-17-93   9:43p 2-3.C
304   10-22-93   8:01a 2-4.C
249   04-17-93   9:45p 5-1.C
197   04-17-93   9:45p 5-2.C
438   04-17-93   9:46p 5-3.C
451   04-17-93   9:47p 5-4.C
391   11-03-96  12:48p 6-1.C
433   07-20-93  12:32p 6-2.C


% program 2 filenames
120   04-17-93   9:41p 1-2.C
129   04-17-93   9:41p 1-1.C
%
```

REGULAR EXPRESSIONS

Many applications will have an opportunity to validate data. In Perl, this is accomplished through pattern matching with regular expressions. Although this is a common use for regular expressions, there are many other uses as well. Among all programming languages, none can match the power of regular expressions in Perl.

6.1 Introduction

A regular expression is a string of characters, some with special meaning, that describes patterns. The regular expression is compared to a target string to determine whether the target string matches the regular expression or not. The regular expression string is composed of a combination of characters, some of which represent themselves, and some of which have a special meaning.

6.2 The Match Operator

The =~ operator is used to determine whether the target string is a match or not. For example, to determine whether a string matches the string throw, you would code:

```
$input = <STDIN>;
chop($input);
if ( $input =~ m/throw/ )
{
    print "input is a match\n";
}
```

The "m" in the above expression is the match operator. The regular expression itself may be placed inside forward slashes, although other characters may also be used to enclose it. For example, each of the following is correct:

```
print "is a match\n" if ( $input =~ m#throw# );
print "is a match\n" if ( $input =~ m!throw! );
print "is a match\n" if ( $input =~ m(throw) );
```

You may also use the ! ~ operator to mean "does not match the pattern."

```
print "is a match\n" if ( $input !~ m#throw# );
print "is a match\n" if ( $input !~ m!throw! );
print "is a match\n" if ( $input !~ m(throw) );
print "is a match\n" if ( $input !~ /throw/ );
```

If you use the slashes, the m operator is not necessary.

```
print "is a match\n" if ( $input =~ /throw/ );
print "is a match\n" if ( $input =~ m#throw# );
print "is a match\n" if ( $input =~ m!throw! );
```

If the target variable is $_, then you may take some liberties in your code. Although the following are identical, the last one is the preferred coding style:

```
print "is a match\n" if ( $_ =~ m/throw/ );
print "is a match\n" if (  m/throw/ );
print "is a match\n" if (   /throw/ );
```

Be careful about spaces. A space is a character like any other. Notice the difference between the following two patterns. The first matches the five-letter pattern throw, while the second matches the seven-letter pattern throw surrounded by single blanks.

```
print "is a match\n" if (   /throw/   );
print "is a match\n" if (   / throw /  );
```

A regular expression may also be contained in a variable as in:

```
$_ = throw;
print  "matches"'  if  /$ARGV[0]/ ;
```

6.3   Regular Expression Metacharacters

In the regular expressions we have seen thus far, each character has represented itself. For example, in the expression below, the "t," "h," "r," "o," and "w" represent themselves:

```
print "is a match\n" if ( /throw/ );
```

More often, a regular expression is composed of a set of metacharacters, that is, characters that have special meanings. Regular expression metacharacters are divided into two categories: one category is concerned with single-character matches; a second category is concerned with multiple-character matches.

6.3.1   Single-character matches

Here are a few examples of single-character matches. The period character (.) matches any single character. Therefore, the pattern:

```
/h.t/
```

matches:

```
hit
hat
hot
shot
hotel
```

but does not match:

```
hunt
htdocs
```

while the pattern:

```
/h..t/
```

matches:

```
hoot
shout
haute
```

but does not match:

```
hot
```

Incidentally, all matches are case-sensitive. You can make them case-insensitive if you place the "i" character in back of the pattern. The pattern below allows the `while` loop to exit if the user types any string containing `yes`, regardless of case:

```
while(1)
{
      print "answer yes or no ";
      chomp($res = <STDIN>);
      last if $res =~ /yes/i;
}
```

The square brackets are similar to the period except that the match is limited to the characters within the brackets. Thus, the pattern:

```
/h[aeiou]t/
```

matches the three-letter patterns:

```
hat
het
hit
hot
hut
```

but does not match:

```
ht
hrt
```

6.3.2   Within square brackets

Since certain character alternatives are more popular than others, there are shortcuts you may take inside square brackets. Specifically, the dash character (-) may be used to specify certain ranges. Thus, the following pairs are equivalent:

```
[0-9]
[0123456789]
[a-z]
```

continued...

```
[abcdefghijklmnopqrstuvwxyz]

[a-fA-F]
[abcdefABCDEF]
```

The following regular expression matches a string that contains a lowercase character, followed by a digit, followed by an uppercase character:

```
/[a-z][0-9][A-Z]/
```

The dash character only has this special meaning when it is used to specify a range. In the following example, the match is against any string with a dash followed by a digit. This illustrates two distinct uses of the dash.

```
/-[0-9]/
```

The caret character (^) has a special meaning if it is the first character within square brackets. In this case, it represents all characters except those that follow. The program below prints those lines that do not contain a digit. Note the importance of chomping away the newline character. If you do not, the newline qualifies as a non-digit character.

```
while(<STDIN>)
{
    chomp;
    print "$_\n" if /[^0-9]/;
}
```

6.3.3   Multiple-character matches

You may use a set of curly braces to match multiple occurrences of characters. The numbers inside the curly braces correspond to the character indicated at the left of the curly braces. Here are several examples:

```
/x[0-9]{2}x/
```

matches exactly 2 digits surrounded by the "x" character.

```
/x[0-9]{2,5}x/
```

matches 2–5 digits surrounded by the "x" character.

```
/a[0-9]{5,}a/
```

matches at least 5 digits surrounded by the "a" character.

Several multiple-character patterns occur more commonly than others. Therefore, Perl has some special regular expression characters for these situations. ? is equivalent to zero or one of what is at its left. * is equivalent to zero or more characters of whatever appears at the left of it. + is equivalent to one or more of what is at its left. Keep in mind that these special symbols represent themselves when they are inside square brackets. Thus, the following example matches a set of optionally signed digits, that is, zero or more digits possibly preceded by either a + or a -. Note that the two +'s below have different meanings.

```
/[-+]?[0-9]+/
```

6.3.4   Other special symbols

To determine if a string contains one of a set of alternatives, use the | symbol:

```
print if /mike|michael|mickey/;
print if /10|15|19)/;              # 10, 15, or 19
print if /1(0|5|9)/;               # 10, 15, or 19
```

In the last example above, note that the parentheses were used to group a set of alternatives.

Some other special symbols that may be used as shortcuts in your regular expression code are:

- \w   Matches a word character (a-z_A-Z).
- \W   Matches a non-word character.
- \s   Matches a whitespace character (blank, tab, or newline).
- \S   Matches a non-whitespace character.
- \d   Matches a digit character.
- \D   Matches a non-digit character.

6.4   Anchoring Patterns

Earlier we saw that the expression below matches a set of optionally signed digits:

```
/[-+]?[0-9]+/
```

Keep in mind that each of the following strings matches this pattern:

```
-256hello
hello+256
1yes
the2ndone
```

If you wanted to match a string that contained only digits, then the pattern above is probably not what you intended. For example, if you asked the user for a number, you would expect responses such as the following rather than those above:

```
-256    +256     345
```

To solve this problem, we need to demonstrate how to anchor a match to certain boundaries. The caret character (^) allows you to match a pattern if it is at the beginning of a string. The $ character allows you to match a pattern if it is at the end of a string. (Note that a newline must be matched explicitly.) Finally, the \b sequence allows you to match a string at a word boundary. For example:

```
/^this/            # at beginning of string
/this$/            # at end of string
/this/             # anywhere in the string
/\bthis\b/         # if a word
/^this$/           # only if line contains 'this'
```

The code below asks the user for an integer and then checks the result with a regular expression. If the user's input is not an integer, the program asks the user to re-enter the integer. Eventually, the number of attempts for a correct match is printed.

```
#!/usr/bin/perl
#
#     integers.pl
#
print "Enter a number ";
$count = 1;
while(1)
{
     $_ = <STDIN>;
     chop;
     last if /^[-+]?[0-9]+$/;
     print "$_ is not a number, Re-enter ";
     $count++;
}
print "$count tries to enter a number\n";

% integers.pl
Enter a number a number
a number is not a number, Re-enter seven
seven is not a number, Re-enter 23.45
23.45 is not a number, Re-enter 23
4 tries to enter a number
%
```

6.5   Remembering Parts of Matches

There are occasions when you need to determine whether a string matches a pattern so that you can remember a portion of the match. For example, suppose you wish to examine a Web server log file that contains many lines, each of which contains a URL along with some other information. Your task might be to recover the XXX part from names such as www.XXX.com. When a regular expression contains a set of parentheses, the pattern does not change because of it. The following two regular expressions represent the same pattern, a set of digits:

```
/[0-9]+/
/([0-9]+)/
```

However, if a match occurs, the parenthesized portion of the match is remembered and can be recalled by using the special variable $1. In the following code, each line that contains a set of digits will have those digits printed. Only the first set will be printed in the case where there are multiple sets.

```
#!/usr/bin/perl
#
#    numbers.pl
#
while(<STDIN>)
{
    print "$1\n" if /([0-9]+)/;
}
```

Likewise, the URL problem from above may be solved as follows:

```
#!/usr/bin/perl
#
#    urls.pl
#
while(<STDIN>)
{
    push (@URLS, $1) if /\w{3}\.(.*)\.com/;
}
print join("\n",@URLS);
```

Note that in the above, a backspace character, (\), is used to escape the special meaning of the period. The backspace character is thus a metacharacter as well. Its meaning is to remove the special meaning of the character that follows. The following regular expression prints a set of digits and their surrounding square brackets if $_ contains a set of bracketed digits:

```
print "$1\n" if /(\[.\d+\])/
```

You are not limited to a single set of parentheses. For example, the following expression remembers two different parts of a match, the left and right sides of an assignment:

```
#!/usr/bin/perl
#
#    assign.pl
#
while(<STDIN>)
{
    print "LHS = $1: RHS = $2\n" if /(.+) *= *(.+)/;
}
```

In the pattern above, remember that each + and * pertains to what precedes it. Both *'s pertain to a blank and the + pertains to any character. As an illustration of the output produced by the above program, we use the following input file as the data file:

```
% display perlprog
$a = 30;
$b =$s + 10;
$c=5;
print "hello";
%

% assign.pl < perlprog
LHS = $a : RHS = 30
LHS = $b : RHS = $s + 10
LHS = $c: RHS = 5
%
```

How many remembered portions are there? As many as you want! You may also nest them. For example, the following regular expression uses four remembered parts of patterns:

```
print "$1:$2:$3:$3\n" if /(.)(.)(.)(.)/;
```

The pattern below uses six remembered parts of patterns:

```
print "$1:$2:$3:$3\n" if /((.)(.))((.)(.))/;
```

In the expression above, the bold part of the pattern:

```
((.)(.))
```

uses three sets of parentheses. Among them, the outer set can be retrieved with $1, while the two inner sets can be obtained with $2 and $3.

6.6   Greedy Regular Expressions

Examine the following program:

```
$_ = "This is an example sentence.";
print "$1\n" if / (.*) /;
```

The pattern in the above expression is "anything surrounded by single blanks." There are several matches described by the above regular expression. Here are a few of them:

```
| is |
| is an |
| is an example |
| an example |
| an |
```

In Perl, the regular expression engine takes the largest possible pattern. Sometimes, pattern matching is described as being greedy. Therefore, the following pattern is chosen:

```
| is an example |
```

If you want the smallest match to be chosen, place a ? behind the part to be matched:

```
print "$1\n" if / (.*?) /;
```

The matched pattern is now:

```
| is |
```

Note that in the above code, there may be easier ways to isolate the pattern, but the idea here is to assure that you understand the regular expression engine.

6.7   Substitutions

There are numerous examples of using a regular expression to validate a user response:

• Is the input a set of digits?

- Is the input a set of alphabetic characters?
- Is the input some form of yes, that is, yes, y, or Y?
- Is the input an email address?
- Is the input a domain name?

However, there are also many occasions when you will want to substitute one string for a matched string. In this case, you will need to use the substitute operator, s. The syntax is similar to the match operator. Here are a few examples:

```
$var =~ s/Mike/Michael/;
```

In `$var`, substitute `Michael` for `Mike`.

```
s/Mike/Michael/;
$_ =~ s/Mike/Michael/
```

In `$_`, substitute `Michael` for `Mike`.

```
s#///#/XX#;
s!///!/XX!;
```

In `$_`, substitute `XX` for `///`.

Substitutions may also have modifiers, which are single characters that slightly modify the substitution behavior.

6.7.1   The g modifier

In the above cases, the substitution only occurs on the first occurrence of the match. For example:

```
$_ = "this will illustrate the g ";
s/ll/(ll)/;
print "$_\n";
```

will produce:

```
this wi(ll) illustrate the g
```

If you wish the substitution to occur on all occurrences of the match, you must use the g modifier.

```
$_ = "this will illustrate the g";
s/ll/(ll)/g;
print "$_\n";
```

will produce:

```
this wi(ll) i(ll)ustrate the g
```

The g modifier has another use as well. Earlier we wrote the code to print a set of digits on a line. That code only printed the first set of digits. If you wanted to do something with all of the sets, you should have used the g modifier and a loop. The regular expression logic keeps track of the position in the string where the last match occurred and subsequently looks ahead for the next match.

```perl
#!/usr/bin/perl
#
#     sumnums.pl
#
while(<STDIN>)
{
    while(/(\d+)/g)
    {
        $sum += $1;
    }
}
print "$sum\n";
```

6.7.2 The i modifier

Recall that the i modifier makes the match insensitive to case.

```
s/thy/thine/ig
```

The above substitution takes all occurrences of thy, regardless of case, and replaces them with thine.

6.7.3   The e modifier

Another useful modifier is the e modifier. The replacement string is evaluated as a Perl expression and the result of the expression is substituted for the target.

```perl
#!/usr/bin/perl
#
#    square.pl
#
sub square
{
        return $_[0] * $_[0];
}
while(<STDIN>)
{
        s/(\d+)/square($1)/ge;
        print;
}



% square.pl
10 and 10 is 100
100 and 100 is 10000
%
```

In the above code, each set of digits is remembered as $1 and then used in the replacement part of the substitution. Because of the e modifier, the expression square($1) is evaluated. The result of this evaluation is then substituted for the target—the set of digits.

6.7.4   The m modifier

Another useful modifier is m (multiple). This forces Perl to treat a string as if it has several lines within it. The $ and ^ symbols are enforced at the beginning and end of each line rather than for the entire string.

```perl
$text = "This string\nhas several\nlines\n";
print $text if $text =~/^has/;       # no match
print $text if $text =~/^has/m;      # match
print $text if $text =~/ing$/;       # no match
print $text if $text =~/ing$/m;      # a match
```

6.8   Backtracking

It is useful to understand the way in which the regular expression engine works. Examine the following:

```
$_ = "this:is:the:examination:string";
/(.*):(.*):(.*)/
```

In the above expression, the match is successful if $_ has three fields separated by single colons. The regular expression is evaluated left to right, and thus the first part to be evaluated is the .* on the left side of the expression. Since .* is greedy, it consumes the entire string. Thus, $1 is set to the entire string. Now the : must be evaluated. Thus, the regular expression engine must back up to the last colon. Next, the second .* must be evaluated. This consumes the last word of the string. So now we have:

```
$1 = "this:is:the:examination"
$2 = "string"
```

Now the process must be repeated for the last :(.*) part of the expression. This yields:

```
$1 = "this:is:the"
$2 = "examination"
$3 = "string"
```

6.9   The tr Operator

Perl also has an operator named tr. It is used in situations that are similar to regular expression matching. The tr operator is modeled after the tr Unix command. In its simplest form, it transliterates a target set of characters with a replacement set. Each set of characters is delimited by forward slashes. tr performs its action on $_ if no other variable is indicated. tr also returns the number of substitutions made. The following program replaces lowercase vowels with uppercase vowels and returns the number of replacements:

```
#!/usr/bin/perl
#
#    xvowels.pl
#
while(<STDIN>)
{
    $count = tr/aeiou/AEIOU/;
    print;
```

continued...

```
        $total += $count;
}
print "$total characters replaced\n";


% xvowels.pl < xvowels.pl
#!/Usr/bIn/pErl
#
#        xvOwEls.pl
#
whIlE(<STDIN>)
{
        $cOUnt = tr/AEIOU/AEIOU/;
        prInt;
        $tOtAl += $cOUnt;
}
prInt "$tOtAl chArActErs rEplAcEd\n";
28 characters replaced
%
```

The line:

```
        $count = tr/aeiou/AEIOU/;
```

actually makes the replacements in $_ and then returns the number of replacements that were made.

You may also use some shortcuts in expressing the character sets. To replace the first 10 letters of the alphabet with their uppercase counterparts, either of the following would work:

```
tr/abcdefghij/ABCDEFGHIJ/;
tr/a-j/A-J/;
```

If the target set is larger than the replacement set, then the last character of the replacement set is used as a replacement for the excessive target characters.

The examples thus far have been with respect to $_. To apply `tr` to other variables, you may code:

```
        $howmany = $names =~tr/efgh/EFGH/;
```

Here, the transliterations are made in $names and then the total is assigned to $howmany. There are additional uses of `tr` as well. If you place any of the following characters behind the final slash, you will get a different behavior:

The d modifier causes `tr` to delete a set of characters:

```
tr/0-9//d;                 # delete digits
```

The s modifier squeezes out all but one of the repeated adjacent characters:

```
$_ = "mississippi";
tr/a-z//s;                 # yields misisipi
```

Perhaps the most useful modifier is the c option, which replaces only those characters in the complement of the target set with a single character in the replacement set. To see how this works, examine the output of the small program below, which deletes sequences of all non-alphabetic characters and replaces each of them with a single newline.

Since we have also added the s option, each set of resulting newlines is squeezed down to a single newline. This produces output of one word per line. The file displayed below is used as input to the following program:

```
% display paragraph
This produces as output one word per line.  We will use
this file as the data file.
%



#!/usr/bin/perl
#
#    words.pl
#
while(<STDIN>)
{
    tr/a-zA-Z/\n/cs;
    print;
}

% words.pl < paragraph
This
produces
as
output
one
word
per
line
We
will
use
```

continued...

```
this
file
as
the
data
file
%
```

Exercises

1. Write a Perl script that reads a file and prints those lines that contain an e-mail address and nothing else. Consider a valid e-mail address to be of the following form:

   ```
   name@something.com
   ```

   name can be composed of characters in the following set: alphabetic, digit, a period, or an underscore.
2. Write a regular expression that matches an optionally signed decimal integer.
3. Use `tr` and an associative array to count the frequency of words in a file. (Use `tr` to get rid of all punctuation.)

SUBPROGRAMS

All programming languages give developers the ability to create their own subroutines, blocks of code that allow generality and reuse. This chapter examines all of the principles having to do with subroutines in Perl.

Some languages refer to these blocks as functions, while others refer to them as subroutines; still others refer to them as procedures. In Perl, they are referred to as either subroutines or functions. There is no difference between these two terms in Perl.

7.1 Introduction

All high-level languages offer ways in which a large program may be partitioned into manageable pieces. This divide-and-conquer strategy leads to easier debugging, maintenance, and readability. Different programming languages use different names for these partitions of reusable code. Some of these names are methods, subprograms, procedures, functions, and subroutines. Perl tends to use the latter two names more than the other names.

7.1.1 Organization of subroutines

The division of labor in Perl is accomplished through the use of programmer-written subroutines, operating system calls, builtin subroutines, and library functions. To the Perl programmer, they all look the same. This section of the book concentrates on programmer-written subroutines.

A programmer-written subroutine may be defined anywhere within a Perl script. If a subroutine is defined ahead of its use, then the subroutine may be invoked in the following ways:

```
sub mysub
{
    print "reached the subroutine\n";
}
```

continued...

125

```
mysub;
&mysub;
mysub();
&mysub();
```

However, if the subroutine is defined below its use, then the first form above cannot be used unless there has been a forward reference as we will see shortly. This distinction is usually unimportant since most Perl subroutines are written, tested, and stored in libraries for use in any Perl scripts. Nonetheless, many of the examples in this section will show subroutines in the same file from which they are invoked simply so we can defer the topic of libraries for a short time.

```
#!/usr/bin/perl
#
#     subs.pl
#
sub sub2; # forward reference
sub sub3
{
    print "reached sub3\n";
}
sub3;     # ok because already defined
sub2;     # ok because of forward reference
sub1;     # not ok
sub1();   # ok
&sub1;    # ok
&sub1();  # ok
sub sub1
{
    print "reached sub1\n";
}
sub sub2
{
    print "reached sub2\n";
}
```

The comments tell most of the story in the code above. The & or ( ) operator can always be used to invoke a subroutine, even if the subroutine is defined after it is called. If you name one of your own subroutines with the name of a Perl builtin subroutine, then you must use the & operator to invoke your subroutine:

```
#!/usr/bin/perl
#
#        yourown.pl
#
sub reverse
```

continued...

```
{
    return (1,2,3);# return the list (1, 2, 3);
}
@ans = &reverse(10,20,30);
print "@ans\n";
@ans = reverse(10,20,30);
print "@ans\n";


% yourown.pl
1 2 3
30 20 10
%
```

7.2 Passing Arguments to Subroutines

Large Perl scripts should be divided into subroutines. Whenever necessary, these subroutines can be invoked from various places within the script. This is a form of code reuse. This strategy works best if each invocation of the subroutine processes specific data, called arguments to the subroutine, and the subroutines are coded using names that are known locally to the subroutine and nowhere else.

The relationship between arguments and parameters in Perl is unusual, albeit clever. In fact, there are no formal parameters as there are in other popular languages such as C++ and Java. Rather, the arguments, if there are any, are collected and passed into the subroutine, where they are available in a special array named @_ . Before we go any further, it's a good idea to drill down a little bit into the variable @_:

```
#!/usr/bin/perl
#
#   squares.pl
#
sub square
{
    $args = @_;
    print "Number of arguments: $args\n";
    print "First arg: $_[0]\n";
    print "Last arg: $_[-1]\n";
    foreach $value (@_)
    {
        push(@squares, $value * $value);
    }
    @squares;
}
@data = (5, 10, 3, 8, 12);
@results = square(@data);
print "Originals: @data\n";
print "Results: @results\n";
```

continued...

```
% squares.pl
Number of arguments: 5
First arg: 5
Last arg: 12
Originals: 5 10 3 8 12
Results: 25 100 9 64 144
%
```

The values passed to the function are stored in the array @_. Once inside the function, we use @_ in various ways for the purpose of showing you a few standard Perl idioms.

Do not confuse $_ with $_[0]. The former is the default input variable and default pattern matching variable, while the latter represents the first element of the array @_.

Although it's not apparent in this example, it is not a good idea to alter any value in the @_ array as this will alter an argument passed to the subroutine. To see how an error could result, examine the following code carefully:

```
#!/usr/bin/perl
#
#    factorial.pl
#
sub factorial
{
     $result = 1;
     while($_[0] > 1)
     {
          $result *= $_[0];
          $_[0]--;
     }
     return $result;
}
print "Enter a number ";
chop($number = <STDIN>);
$answer = &factorial($number);
print "$number factorial is $answer\n";


% factorial.pl
Enter a number 5
1 factorial is 120
%
```

The program changes $_[0], which is a reference to $number. Thus, $number is changed as well. Most programming languages have a pass by value mechanism in which a copy of each argument is saved in a parameter. But the Perl mechanism of passing arguments to functions has no parameter list, so the programmer must simulate them. It is standard practice in Perl to store arguments in local variables.

This is made possible by using my, a function that localizes a variable, or local, a Perl 4 remnant that is still useful.

7.2.1   `local` vs. `my`

`local` may be used to limit the scope of a variable to a specific subroutine and all subroutines called from it. This is known as dynamic scoping.

my defines a scope that is limited to a specific subroutine, excluding those called from within it. This is called *lexical scoping.* my is always preferred to `local`. It is always a sound practice to localize variables; otherwise, all variables referenced in a subroutine would be global variables. Here is the correct way to write the `factorial` function:

```
sub factorial
{
    my $f = $_[0];
    my $result = 1;
    while($f > 1)
    {
            $result *= $f;
            $f--;
    }
    return $result;
}


% factorial.pl
enter a number 5
1 factorial is 120
%
```

The value of `$_[0]` is saved in `$f`, a my variable. Likewise, `$result` is also localized so it will not collide with a variable of the same name potentially used in another part of the program.

7.2.2   Typeglobs

Normally, it is a big advantage to be able to pass to a subroutine an argument list whose size can vary from one invocation to another. For example, the `totals` function below may take any number of arguments and return the sum of them. Notice some of the ways in which it may be invoked:

```
#!/usr/bin/perl
#
#        totals.pl
#
sub totals
{
        my($sum) = 0;
        foreach $item (@_)
```

continued...

```
        {
                $sum += $item;
        }
        $sum;
}

@data = (1,2,3,4);
@vals = ( 10,20,30,40);
print "sum of @data is ", totals(@data), "\n";
print "sum of @vals is ", totals(@vals), "\n";
print "sum of @vals and @data is ";
print totals(@vals, @data), "\n";

% totals.pl
sum of 1 2 3 4 is 10
sum of 10 20 30 40 is 100
sum of 10 20 30 40 and 1 2 3 4 is 110
%
```

Inside the subroutine, all the arguments are collected into @_ . Even though a variable number of arguments is usually a good thing, there are some occasions when this can be a problem. One such problem occurs when the subroutine needs to differentiate between arrays.

To solve this problem, you can use a typeglob, or hard reference. We will postpone the discussion of references and concentrate on typeglobs. A typeglob creates synonyms for a family of names. Before we give a useful example of a typeglob, we will define the basics. The lines below define a set of Perl variables, all of which have the same name:

```
$friendly = "hello"
@friendly = ("hi", "aloha", "shalom");
sub friendly
{
    print "hello from sub\n"
}
```

The next line defines a few synonyms for the name friendly:

```
*amicably = *friendly;
```

The line above creates several identities. All friendly names are now amicably as well. This means that the following pairs are simply different names for the same data:

```
$friendly      @friendly      &friendly      %friendly      FRIENDLY
$amicably      @amicably      &amicably      %amicably      AMICABLY
```

Therefore, the following holds:

```
print "$friendly\n";           # hello
print "$amicably\n";           # hello
print "@friendly\n";           # hi aloha shalom
print @amicably;               # hi aloha shalom
&friendly;                     # hello from sub
&amicably;                     # hello from sub
```

Now that we have seen the basics, we will use this concept to solve the following problem. Suppose you wish to write a function that receives several arrays and returns an array consisting of the lengths of the individual arrays. The function's behavior is exhibited by the following lines:

```
@a1 = (1..10);
@a2 = (10..13);
@lengths = lengths(@a1, @a2);
print "@lengths\n";            # prints 10, 4
```

The problem is ensuring that the subroutine can distinguish between the arrays. A typeglob can solve this problem.

```
#!/usr/bin/perl
#
#   lengths.pl
#
sub lengths
{
    local(*r1, *r2) = @_;
    my($len1) = @r1;
    my($len2) = @r2;
    return($len1, $len2);
}
@a1 = (1..10);
@a2 = (10..13);
@lengths = lengths(*a1, *a2);
print "length of @a1 is $lengths[0]\n";
print "length of @a2 is $lengths[1]\n";
% lengths.pl
length of 1 2 3 4 5 6 7 8 9 10 is 10
length of 10 11 12 13 is 4
%
```

Earlier, the identities of amicably and friendly were made the same through the following assignment:

```
*amicably = *friendly;
```

In this case, the identities of a1 and r1, and likewise a2 and r2, are made the same through the argument/parameter relationship. Since the my feature was added to Perl in Perl 5, you must use local to store typeglobs. Inside the subroutine, @a1 and @a2 can be referenced using @r1 and @r2, respectively. Note that two globs must be sent to the function rather than two arrays:

```
@lengths = lengths(*a1, *a2); # correct
@lengths = lengths(@a1, @a2); # incorrect
```

Typeglobs must be used in connection with filehandles in certain cases. Filehandles are not first-class citizens; that is, there are certain operations that are disallowed on filehandles. For example, you cannot assign a filehandle or create a local one. Since filehandles don't have their own prefix (such as $, %, &, or @), Perl thinks they are constants in situations such as:

```
local(FH);
FH1 = FH2;
fun(FH);
```

If you need to parameterize a filehandle, a typeglob is necessary. Here's an example of sending a filehandle to a function:

```
#!/usr/bin/perl
#
#    handles.pl
#
sub process
{
    local (*F) = @_;
    my $ct = 0;
    $ct++ while(<F>);
    $ct;
}
print "Enter a filename ";
chomp($fn = <STDIN>);
print "processing $fn\n";
open(HANDLE1,"$fn") || die;
$lc = process(*HANDLE1);
print "$fn contains $lc lines\n";
print "Enter another filename ";
chomp($fn = <STDIN>);
print "processing $fn\n";
open(HANDLE2,"$fn") || die;
$lc = process(*HANDLE2);
print "$fn contains $lc lines\n";
```

Remember that typeglobs are synonyms. Thus, inside the function, F is just another name for whatever typeglob was passed to the function.

7.3   Returning Values from Subroutines

Although we have already seen examples of subroutines that return a value, we will give the details in this section. Without an explicit return statement, a Perl subroutine always returns the last evaluated expression. All Perl subroutines return a value. It must also be pointed out that on some occasions, the returned value is ignored.

7.3.1   Returning a scalar

Subroutines can return any type of value. The subroutine below returns a scalar which represents the larger value of the two arguments sent to it:

```
#!/usr/bin/perl
#
#   bigger.pl
#
sub bigger
{
    $_[0] >= $_[1] ? $_[0] : $_[1];
}
print "Enter two numbers ";
chomp($_ = <STDIN>);
($a, $b) = split;
print bigger($a, $b), "is larger\n";

% bigger.pl
Enter two numbers 5 10
10 is larger
%
```

Note that we have used a conditional expression. Therefore, the last expression evaluated is either $_[0] or $_[1]. In this example, it's fine to use elements of @_ directly since you are not changing them.

If you are debugging a subroutine by using print functions within the subroutine, be careful where you place your print statement. Notice what happens if we add a print statement to the subroutine above:

```
#!/usr/bin/perl
#
#   bigger2.pl
#
sub bigger
```

continued...

```
{
    $_[0] >= $_[1] ? $_[0] : $_[1];
    print "returning from bigger\n";
}
print "Enter two numbers ";
chomp($_ = <STDIN>);
($a, $b) = split;
print bigger($a, $b), "is larger\n";

% bigger2.pl
Enter two numbers 5 10
returning from bigger
1 is larger
%
```

Remember that the last expression evaluated is what is returned. In this case, it is the `print` statement that is evaluated last. Although it is rarely material, `print` returns the value 1 if successful. If you use any debugging statements inside a function, make sure the last statement inside the subroutine is not one of them.

Some subroutines can take any number of arguments, but this one requires exactly two. What happens if the wrong number of arguments is passed to a subroutine? It depends on your philosophy in writing the routine. If you desire, you can issue an error message; or, if it makes sense, you can proceed by processing the arguments received by the subroutine. We will show you how to determine if the correct number of arguments were passed, but ultimately, the decision of trapping this error or not rests with the writer of the subroutine.

In the program below, the subroutine is invoked with too many arguments. As you can see, this subroutine proceeds by processing the first two elements:

```
#!/usr/bin/perl
#
#  bigger3.pl
#
sub bigger
{
    $_[0] >= $_[1] ? $_[0] : $_[1];
}
@data = (5,10,20,30,8,50);
print bigger(@data), "is larger\n";


% bigger3.pl
10 is larger
%
```

Here is a version of the subroutine that determines if the correct number of arguments was supplied. In this case, we decided to exit, but that choice is ultimately yours.

```
sub bigger
{
    if ( @_ != 2 )
    {
        print STDERR "bigger: wrong number of args\n";
        exit;
    }
    $_[0] >= $_[1] ? $_[0] : $_[1];
}
```

It should also be pointed out that Perl is very permissive about how values are sent to subroutines. Each of the following is a correct way of sending arguments to `bigger`:

```
#
#    send the first and last elements
#    of the @data array to the subroutine
#
@data = (5,10,20,30,8,50);
$x = bigger(@data[0,-1]);
print $x;               # prints 50
#
#    split $_ on whitespace and thus
#    send the list (10 20) to the subroutine
#
$_ = "10 20";
$x = bigger(split);
print $x;               # print 20
$a = 10;
$b = 50;
#
#    send two simple expressions to the subroutine
#
$x = bigger($a + 20, $b - 25)
print $x;               # prints 30
```

7.3.2   Returning an array

You can also write subroutines that return arrays. Here's an example of a subroutine that returns a two-element array consisting of the mean and standard deviation of a set of numbers. The subroutine adds the entries and divides by the number of them to get the mean. The standard deviation is a little more complex. You need to compute the sum of the squared differences between the mean and each data item. Finally, you need to take the square root of this number divided by one less than the number of items. (It's more complicated to express this idea in English than it is to write the code in Perl.)

```
#!/usr/bin/perl
#
#    stats.pl
#
sub statistics
{
    my $mean = 0;
    my $dev = 0;
    my(@results);
    foreach $item (@_)
    {
            $mean += $item;
    }
    $mean /= @_;
    foreach $item (@_)
    {
            $dev = $dev + ($item - $mean) ** 2;
    }
    $dev = sqrt($dev/ (@_ - 1));
    push(@results, $mean, $dev);
    @results;
}
print "Enter some numbers ";
chomp($_ = <STDIN>);
@data = split;
($mean, $sd) = statistics(@data);
print "MEAN = $mean, SD = $sd\n";
% stats.pl
Enter some numbers 10 11 12 13 14 15
MEAN = 12.5, SD = 1.87082869338697
%
```

The `return` statement in the subroutine is coded as:

```
@results;
```

but it could also have been coded as:

```
return @results;
return ($mean, $dev);
($mean, $dev);
```

In the last two lines above, the parentheses are necessary. Without them, the expressions are evaluated with the comma operator in a scalar context, thus yielding the last item:

```
return $mean, $dev;          # returns $dev
$mean, $dev;                 # returns $dev
```

7.3.3   Returning other types

Perl subroutines are not limited to returning scalars or arrays. Later in the book, we will see examples of subroutines that return other types such as associative arrays or references, also known as pointers.

7.4   Perl Libraries

All of the subroutines above were written in the file where they were invoked. To make these and other programmer-written subroutines reusable, you must place them in a file and instruct Perl to include them in any script that needs them. The files where you place these subroutines are essentially Perl library files. There are a few ways of accomplishing this task.

7.4.1   The `require` function

One way of loading a file into your program is to use the Perl `require` function. To illustrate how this function works, let's take the `statistics` function and the `bigger` function from above and place them in a file by themselves. The name of the file is not significant. We will call it `mystats.pl`. This file will never be executed by itself, and therefore it is not necessary to have the `#!` line at the top of the file even if you are on Unix.

```
#
#   mystats.pl
#
sub bigger
{
    $_[0] >= $_[1] ? $_[0] : $_[1];
}
sub statistics
{   my $mean = 0;
    my $dev = 0;
    foreach $item (@_)
    {   $mean += $item;
    }
    $mean /= @_;
    foreach $item (@_)
    {   $dev = $dev + ($item - $mean) ** 2;
    }
    $dev = sqrt($dev/ (@_ - 1));
    push(@results, $mean, $dev);
    @results;
}
1;                  # see next paragraph
```

To use any of the functionality in the library file that we just constructed, we can load this file into an application that requires any of these functions. The loading is accomplished by the `require` function. `require` is written in such a way that it uses the return value from the file it is loading. Of course, the return value is the last expression evaluated in the file that is loaded. All Perl libraries must have their last expression evaluate to true, or non-zero. By convention, Perl programmers use the value 1, as we saw above in `mystats.pl`. Here is a program that uses this library:

```perl
#!/usr/bin/perl
#
#    usemystats.pl
#
require "mystats.pl";
print "Enter some numbers ";
chomp($_ = <STDIN>);
@dat = split;
($mean, $sd) = statistics(@dat);
print "MEAN = $mean, SD = $sd\n";
print "LARGEST of (@dat[0,1]):", bigger(@dat[0,1]);

% usemylib.pl
Enter some numbers 10 11 12 13 14 15
MEAN = 12.5, SD = 1.87082869338697
LARGEST of 10,11: 11
%
```

7.4.1.1 The @INC array. There's another issue that needs to be addressed. The library file above needs to be placed in a directory in the filesystem where Perl can find it. This is where Perl uses the builtin array `@INC`.

The `@INC` array contains a colon-separated set of directories where Perl looks to find required files. You can place a library file in any directory as long as you add this directory to the `@INC` array. When you install Perl, the `@INC` variable will already have some directories in it. One of them is called `site`. This is a good place for your libraries.

One way of adding a directory to the `@INC` array is to either `push` or `unshift` it there. Of course, you would have to do this in every program that needed to use the library.

```perl
push(@INC, "c:/perl/site");
```

Another way to do this is to use the `-I` flag on the command line:

```perl
% perl -I/perl/site usemystats.pl
```

Perhaps the best way is to use the `PERL5LIB` environment variable. This variable should contain the set of directories where your libraries exist. If this variable exists, Perl will check it to determine where to look for libraries. How you set the environment variable depends on your operating system. If you are using Unix, it depends on which shell you are using.

```
C:> set PERL5LIB=C:\libs            # Windows
$ PERL5LIB=/$HOME/libs              # Unix Korn Shell
```

One final note about the @INC array. It's not absolutely required. Instead, you could use long pathnames. However, the more you type, the more errors you will make. Here's how your code would look if you used long pathnames:

```
require "c:/perl/site/mylib.pl";
```

7.5   The Perl Standard Library

As we have seen, programmers can always build their own libraries. There is, however, a standard Perl library that is delivered with the Perl distribution and located in the lib sub-directory of your Perl installation. This library contains many useful functions for Perl programs. We will illustrate the use of this library with the ctime function, which delivers the date and time as a string. You do not need to worry about @INC here because it has been pre-set to include the standard library directory.

```
#!/usr/bin/perl
#
#   usestdlib.pl
#
require "ctime.pl";
$time = time;              # builtin time function
print "$time";             # as an integer
$x=&ctime($time);          # standard library function
print $x;                  # date format
% usestdlib.pl
999800151
Thu Sep 6 14:15:51 2001
%
```

7.6   Packages

The scope of a variable refers to that section of the program where the variable can be accessed. In a Perl program without any subroutines, all variables are global to the program. We've seen how scope can be limited to a subroutine either dynamically with local, or lexically through the use of my variables. Now we will look at the Perl package capability that allows for a further division of scope.

By default, a program has one package, the main package. You can create other packages by using the package statement. Packages provide a separate namespace so that you can avoid naming collisions. These collisions may happen if you are using libraries from two different sources and each source happens to choose the same name for a function or for a variable. Below is a simple package contained in Banking.pl:

```
#   Banking.pl
#
package Banking;
$name="Inside the Banking package";
sub deposit
{
    print "depositing $_[0]\n";
}
sub withdraw
{
    print "withdrawing $_[0]\n";
}
1;
```

In Perl, there is the notion of a default package. When a Perl program begins, the default package is the main package. To use symbols from another package, you must use the : : operator to make qualified references. First, however, you must use require to load the new package. In one sense, packages are nothing more than named libraries. Here's an application that uses the Banking.pl library:

```
#!/usr/bin/perl
#
#   Bankapp.pl
#
$name = "Inside the main package";
print "$name\n";          # default package is main
require "Banking.pl";
Banking::deposit(50);     # need qualified reference
Banking::withdraw(50);
print "$Banking::name\n";
package Banking;          # change default package to Banking
deposit(50);
withdraw(50);
print "$name\n";
print "$main::name";      # now need to qualify name
package main;             # change default package to main
print "$name\n";

% Bankapp.pl
Inside the main package
depositing 50
withdrawing 50
Inside the Banking package
depositing 50
withdrawing 50
Inside the Banking package
Inside the main package
Inside the main package
%
```

When the program begins, all references are assumed to be for the default package, which is `main`. To make references to another package, you must qualify the reference with the `::` operator:

```
Banking::deposit(50);
Banking::withdraw(50);
print "$Banking::name\n";
```

You can always change the default package name with a `package` statement:

```
package Banking;
```

Now, `Banking` is the default package. To reference symbols from the `main` package, you need the `::` operator:

```
print "$main::name";
```

Note that Perl builtin variables such as `$!` and `$_` always belong to the `main` package and thus never have to be referred to using the `::` operator. `my` variables, on the other hand, are never part of a package; thus, they can never be referenced using the `::` operator.

7.6.1 Modules and use

If a file contains a package, the package is usually fully contained in that file, but this is not a requirement. A file could consist of more than one package. Likewise, a package could be spread out over more than one file. However, neither of these arrangements are common occurrences. The name of the file in which a package is defined is irrelevant in Perl 4. Most files that define packages in Perl 4 were conventionally named `something.pl`.

In Perl 5, a more systematic approach is used. There is a tight connection between the filename and the package name. For example, if a package is named `Math`, then the file must be named `Math.pm`. In this approach, only one package must be defined per file. Files that follow the Perl 5 approach are called Perl modules. Modules are included in a program with the `use` statement.

The `use` statement only loads files whose names end in `.pm`, that is, a Perl module as described above. When you use `use`, you need to omit the `.pm` portion of the file you are loading:

```
use Math;
use English;
use Cwd;
```

There is also a technical difference between use and require. The former is executed during the first pass of the Perl interpreter, whereas the latter is executed during execution of the Perl program. Thus, the following will not work properly:

```
$name = "Math";
use $name;
```

There are many Perl modules (.pm files) that now ship with the Perl distribution. We will take a closer look at these modules in Chapter 11. Until then, here is a simple example using the Cwd module. This module allows you to keep track of which directory you are in, regardless of which system you are using, Windows or Unix.

```
#!/usr/bin/perl
#
#    pwd.pl
#
use Cwd;
package Cwd;                  # make Cwd the current package
$current = getcwd();         # get current directory name
print "Current directory is $current\n";
print "changing to $ARGV[0]\n";
chdir ($ARGV[0]);            # change to directory $ARGV[0]
$pwd = getcwd();
print "Current directory is now $pwd\n";
print "Changing to $current\n";
chdir ($current);
print "Current directory is $current\n";
% pwd.pl ..
Current directory is C:/perlbook/examples/7
changing to ..
Current directory is now C:/perlbook/examples
Changing to C:/perlbook/examples/7
Current directory is C:/perlbook/examples/7
%
```

The program above uses a system call, chdir, to change to the directory given as the first argument on the command line, and then changes back to the previous current directory.

7.7 Predefined Subroutines

You can code a subroutine named BEGIN anywhere in your Perl script. This subroutine will execute when your script is being translated, that is, before your program really begins execution. Awk programmers will recognize this subroutine.

```
sub BEGIN
{
    print "From the BEGIN block\n";
    push(@INC, "newdir");
}
```

Likewise, there is an END subroutine that can be coded anywhere in your script. This code gets executed after your Perl script has terminated. Note the way the following script executes:

```
#!/usr/bin/perl
#
#     specsubs.pl
#
print "Real program: line 1\n";
BEGIN
{
    print "starting\n";
}
END
{
    print "ending\n";
}
print "Real program: line 2\n";
% perl specsubs.pl
starting
Real program: line 1
Real program: line 2
ending
%
```

Occasionally, you will call a Perl subroutine that does not exist. This usually happens as a result of a typing error. When this occurs, you will see an error message on your display. Your Perl script typically halts when this happens.

```
#!/usr/bin/perl
#
#        bug.pl
#
sub process
{
        print "text is @_\n";
}
printtext("hello");
printext("hello");
print "last line of program\n";
```

It's probably obvious to you that there is an error in the code above. Nevertheless, here is what happens when you execute this program:

```
% bug.pl
text is hello
Undefined subroutine &main::printext called at bug.pl line 10
%
```

Perl provides the AUTOLOAD subroutine, which will be called when a function cannot be found as above. All arguments are also passed to this subroutine in addition to the function name. A trivial use of this function is to find all misspelled function names during a single execution of the program:

```
#!/usr/bin/perl
#
#   autoload.pl
#
sub AUTOLOAD
{
    print "MISSING FUNCTION IS $AUTOLOAD\n";
    print "ARGS are @_\n\n";

}
fun1(1, 2, 3);
fun2(a, b, c);
fun3(10,20,30);

% autoload.pl
MISSING FUNCTION IS main::fun1
ARGS are 1 2 3

MISSING FUNCTION IS main::fun2
ARGS are a b c

MISSING FUNCTION IS main::fun3
ARGS are 10 20 30
%
```

Exercises

1. Write different Perl subroutines that return:
   a. The *largest* value from a list of numbers
   b. The *smallest* value from a list of numbers
   c. Both the smallest and the largest values from a list of numbers
   d. Both the largest value and its index
2. Remove the subroutines in Exercise 1 and place them in a separate file named `subs` in the same directory as the code. Add the necessary `require` statement in your driver program and test the driver program.
3. Take the solution to Exercise 2 and place the file containing all the subroutines in a separate directory. Now, try to make your program work. Add this directory to your `@INC` variable to see if this makes a difference.
4. Write a calculator, that is, a Perl program that reads parentheses-free notation such as:

```
10    20   -   4   8 +   *   =
```

that represents the expression:

```
(10 - 20 )  *   ( 4 + 8 )  =
```

and displays the result: `-120`.

5. Add to the `Banking` package presented earlier so that the following code works correctly:

```
&deposit(50, "Mike");          # deposit into account
&deposit(80, "Jane");          # deposit into account
&withdraw(40,"Mike");          # withdraw from account
print &balance("Mike");        # get account balance
print &total();                # get total funds in bank
```

8

GENERATING REPORTS
IN PERL

Perl has the ability to generate reports. These reports are typically written by system administrators to summarize user and file activity. Perl can automatically generate headers and format a report body. This chapter gives the details of the rudimentary report writing capabilities of Perl.

8.1 Introduction

In addition to the Perl functionality that we have seen, Perl also has report writing capabilities. Output from Perl applications can be formatted for human readability using `format` statements and the `write` function. A `format` statement has the form shown below:

```
format NAME =
    picture line
    argument line
    picture line
    argument line
    etc.
.
```

NAME is a filehandle, which is STDOUT by default. A *picture line* consists of one or more formats from certain `format` specifiers and possibly some text. An *argument line* is one or more expressions separated by commas. There should be as many `format` specifiers as there are expressions. There can be as many (picture line, argument line) pairs as required. Any picture line containing text without a `format` is printed literally. The entire structure ends with a left-adjusted period alone on a line. Each pair is treated together. When a Perl program executes a `write` command, the data items in the argument line are written according to the `format` items in the associated picture line. If a picture line has no accompanying argument line, the picture line is written as pure text.

8.2   `format`

Each `format` in a picture line starts with either the @ or ˄ character. The length of the field is supplied by padding out the field with zero or more characters from the following set:

```
<                           left-adjust
>                           right-adjust
|                           center
##.###                      numerical data, possible non-integer
@                           normal value
˄                           multi-line text block fill
```

The following is an illustration of writing a report in Perl, including:

- The data file from which the report was built
- The running of the program producing the report
- The program that produced the report

```
% display data
EVAL1     PL          92  02-07-01  4:53p  eval1.pl
CALC      PL         242  02-08-01  9:28a  calc.pl
HTML      PL         394  02-08-01  8:45a  html.pl
OOPS      PL         203  02-08-01  9:29a  oops.pl
TR        PL         134  02-08-01  7:09a  tr.pl
QUOTES    PL         234  02-07-01  8:03p  quotes.pl
HASHSORT  PL         299  02-08-01  8:15a  hashsort.pl
SORTS     PL         250  02-08-01  9:33a  sorts.pl
WORDS     PL          68  02-08-01  8:08a  words.pl
HEREHTML  PL         340  02-08-01  9:20a  herehtml.pl
DEBUG     PL         316  02-07-01  9:08p  debug.pl
REMEMBER  PL         115  02-08-01  3:34p  remember.pl
HERE~1    HTM        126  02-08-01  9:21a  here.html
PACK      PL         339  02-08-01  1:37p  pack.pl
MAKEHTML  PL         398  02-08-01  8:49a  makehtml.pl
FILE~1    HTM        126  02-08-01  8:52a  file.html
BIN       PL         126  02-08-01  2:13p  bin.pl
%
```

The output from the program will list files with a suffix given on the command line whose file size is greater than a specific size, which is also given on the command line. In other words, to list all files whose size is greater than 200 and whose name ends in "PL," we would execute the program as follows:

```
% report1.pl PL 200
CALC            242
HTML            394
OOPS            203
QUOTES          234
HASHSORT        299
SORTS           250
HEREHTML        340
DEBUG           316
PACK            339
MAKEHTML        398
%
```

Next, we will show the Perl program producing the report:

```
#!/usr/bin/perl
#
#    report1.pl
#
die "$0: extension size\n" unless $#ARGV == 1;
format STDOUT =
@<<<<<<<<<<<    @>>>>>>>
$info[0],       $info[2]
.
open(FILES, "< data") || die "error: 'files'\n";
while(<FILES>)
{
    @info = split;
    write if ($info[1] eq $ARGV[0] && $info[2] > $ARGV[1]);
}
```

The program reads lines from the data file and splits them into fields. Each line is sent to the report if it matches the file extension, which is given as $ARGV[0], and if the file size is greater than the number given, which is $ARGV[1]. The write command causes the data to be written in accordance with the default format, STDOUT.

The report format has one picture line and one argument line. The picture line has one format to left-adjust in a field of 12 and another format to right-adjust in a field of 8. The formats pertain to $info[0] and $info[2], respectively. The comma is necessary on the argument line, but the argument placement on that line is irrelevant. They happen to be placed under their associated format for clarity, as you can see below:

```
format STDOUT =
@<<<<<<<<<<<    @>>>>>>>
$pieces[0],     $pieces[2]
.
```

8.2.1   A different view

Suppose you wanted two lines of output information for each line in a file. For example, say you wanted your layout to appear as follows, rather than the way it appears above:

```
CALC              242
02-08-01        9:28a
=====================
HTML              394
02-08-01        8:45a
=====================
```

To achieve this particular layout, you could use the following `format` (see `report2.pl`):

```
format STDOUT =
@<<<<<<<<<<    @>>>>>>>
$info[0],    $info[2]
@<<<<<<<<<<    @>>>>>>>
$info[3],    $info[4]
========================
.
```

In this `format`, each time the `write` command is executed, then:

```
$info[0] and $info[2]
```

are displayed using:

```
  @<<<<<<<<<<    @>>>>>>>
```

Likewise, the items:

```
$info[3] and $info[4]
```

are displayed using:

```
  @<<<<<<<<<<    @>>>>>>>
```

And finally, the last line:

```
========================
```

is written out as pure text since there are no `formats` on the next line.

8.2.2 Multi-line formatting

There will be times when you want to have several data items in a column, another longer data item in a block paragraph, and show the two side-by-side.

```
item1                                    this is all
item2                                    part of the
item3                                    same item4
```

You can achieve the above formatting by using `^` rather than `@` as the `format` specifier. For the blocked text, the line break is on a space, a newline, or a hyphen. The value of the variable is truncated as it is printed. Be sure to allow enough picture and argument lines for the blocked item.

```perl
#!/usr/perl/bin
#
#   blocked.pl
#
format STDOUT =
NAME: @>>>>>>>>>>>    ^<<<<<<<<<<<<<<<<<<<<<<<
$name                        $sum1
AGE:  @>>>>>>>>>>>    ^<<<<<<<<<<<<<<<<<<<<<<<
$age                         $sum1
CITY: @>>>>>>>>>>>    ^<<<<<<<<<<<<<<<<<<<<<<<
$city                        $sum1
~~                   ^<<<<<<<<<<<<<<<<<<<<<<<
                             $sum1
-------------------------------------------------
.
$name = "Smith";
$age = 25;
$city = "Raleigh";
$sum1= "Smith is an excellent worker, but he ";
$sum1 .= "is sometimes prone to inactivity.";
write;
$name = "Jones";
$age = 31;
$city = "Baltimore";
$sum1= "Jones is not right for this job, but he ";
$sum1 .= "would be right for many others.";
write;
```

When you run out of items in the left "column," use the ~~ characters. Perl uses this convention to replicate the format for as many lines as it needs. Here's the output from the above code:

```
% blocked.pl
NAME:          Smith    Smith is an excellent
AGE:              25    worker, but he is
CITY:         Raleigh   sometimes prone to
                        inactivity.
-----------------------------------------------------
NAME:          Jones    Jones is not right for
AGE:              31    this job, but he would
CITY:        Baltimore  be right for many others.
-----------------------------------------------------
```

8.3   Top-of-page formatting

Perl reports also have builtin page-sensing capabilities. You can arrange to print page headings, page numbers, etc. with a top-of-page format. This format is similar to any other format except for the filehandle portion. The suffix _TOP must be added to the name of the format:

```
format STDOUT_TOP =
#
#   format body
#   goes here
#   just as before
.
```

Perl triggers the writing of this format automatically at the top of every page. The following special variables are used in connection with top-of-page output:

```
$=      maximum number of lines per page
$-      number of lines remaining on this page
$%      current page number
```

Most reports will typically print $% at the top of each page. $- yields the number of lines left on the page. If you set this variable to zero, the top-of-page format will be executed automatically when you execute the write. $= reports the page size. To demonstrate these, we will add a top-of-page format to the file report. Note that we have also printed the date at the top of each page and added several columns. The new report looks like this:

```
% report3.pl PL 200
1            Fri Feb  9  8:55:04 2001            1
FILE          SIZE         DATE         TIME
==============================================
CALC          242          02-08-01     9:28a
HTML          394          02-08-01     8:45a
OOPS          203          02-08-01     9:29a
QUOTES        234          02-07-01     8:03p
HASHSORT      299          02-08-01     8:15a
SORTS         250          02-08-01     9:33a
HEREHTML      340          02-08-01     9:20a
DEBUG         316          02-07-01     9:08p
PACK          339          02-08-01     1:37p
MAKEHTML      398          02-08-01     8:49a
%
```

Here is the code producing the report:

```
#!/usr/bin/perl
#
#   report3.pl
#
require "ctime.pl";
die "$0: extension size\n" unless $#ARGV == 1;
$date = ctime(time);
chomp($date);

format STDOUT_TOP =
@|||           @>>>>>>>>>>>>>>>>>>>>>>>            @|||
$%,            $date,                              $%
FILE                SIZE          DATE       TIME
==================================================


.

format STDOUT =
@<<<<<<<<      @>>>>>>>       @>>>>>>>       @>>>>>>>
$pieces[0],    $pieces[2],    $pieces[3],  $pieces[4]
.

open(FILES, "< data") || die "open failed\n";
while(<FILES>)
{
    @pieces = split;
    write if ($pieces[1] eq $ARGV[0] &&$pieces[2]>$ARGV[1]);
}
```

8.4   The `select` Function

In Perl, there is the notion of the "currently selected filehandle." By default, it is STDOUT. The output from all prints, printfs, and writes will be sent to the display. The default for the currently selected filehandle can be changed using the select function. select takes a filehandle or scalar containing the filename and makes this argument the new currently selected filehandle. select returns the old filehandle so it may be restored later if this is desired. Here is a small illustration:

```
#!/usr/bin/perl
#
#   select.pl
#
open(NEWFILE, "> output");
print "This goes to STDOUT by default\n";
$oldhandle = select(NEWFILE);
print "This goes to NEWFILE so you won't see it\n";
select($oldhandle);
print "STDOUT has been restored now\n";
```

You'll sometimes see a different file being selected in a subroutine and the original file being reselected before the subroutine returns.

8.4.1   Special formatting variables: `$~` and `$^`

`$~` is the name of the report format for the currently selected output filehandle. You can use this variable to change the format of the currently selected filehandle. By default, its value is STDOUT.

Likewise, `$^` is the name of the top-of-page format for the currently selected output filehandle. You can use this variable similarly to `$~`. Its default is STDOUT_TOP.

```
#!/usr/bin/perl
#
#   formats.pl
#
format ONE =
This is format # 1
.

format TWO =
This is format # 2
.

format ONE_TOP =
This is format # 1 top of page
.

format TWO_TOP =
```

continued...

```
This is format # 2 top of page
.
$^ = ONE_TOP;
$~ = ONE;
write;
$- = 0;          # force top of page
$~ = TWO;
$^ = TWO_TOP;
write;
```

Note that you can always force a top-of-page `format` to be printed by making `$-` have the value 0. Remember that this variable represents the number of lines remaining on the printed page. If you set it to 0, Perl thinks you now want a top-of-page `format`.

```
% formats.pl
This is format # 1 top of page
This is format # 1
This is format # 2 top of page
This is format # 2
%
```

8.5 Bottom-of-Page Formatting

There is no automatic bottom-of-page `format` generation, but you could create one yourself by using `$-` or your own counter to detect when you are near the bottom of a page. Once you've done that, you could install the new `format` for the bottom of the page, execute the `write`, and then reinstall the old `format` for the body of the next page. Here is the output from running the program `bottom.pl`. The source code is shown after the output.

```
% bottom.pl PL 200
1            Sat Sep  8 10:24:21 2001            1
FILE         SIZE         DATE              TIME
==============================================
CALC          242         02-08-01          9:28a
HTML          394         02-08-01          8:45a
OOPS          203         02-08-01          9:29a
QUOTES        234         02-07-01          8:03p
HASHSORT      299         02-08-01          8:15a
SORTS         250         02-08-01          9:33a
HEREHTML      340         02-08-01          9:20a

======================================
THIS IS THE BOTTOM OF THE PAGE FORMAT
Sat Sep  8 10:24:21 2001     PAGE   1
```

continued...

```
==========================================
   2              Sat Sep  8 10:24:21 2001            2
FILE            SIZE             DATE             TIME
==========================================================
DEBUG             316           02-07-01             9:08p
PACK              339           02-08-01             1:37p
MAKEHTML          398           02-08-01             8:49a
%
```

And here is the code producing the above output:

```perl
#!/usr/bin/perl
#
#   bottom.pl
#
require "ctime.pl";
die "$0: extension size\n" unless $#ARGV == 1;
$date = ctime(time);
chomp($date);
format BOTTOM =
=====================================
THIS IS THE BOTTOM OF THE PAGE FORMAT
@<<<<<<<<<<<<<<<<<<<<<<<<     PAGE @||||
$date,       $%
=====================================
.
format STDOUT_TOP =
@|||           @>>>>>>>>>>>>>>>>>>>>>>>           @|||
$%,            $date,                             $%
FILE            SIZE           DATE        TIME
=============================================================
.
format STDOUT =
@<<<<<<<<<    @>>>>>>       @>>>>>>>>       @>>>>>>>>
$pieces[0],   $pieces[2],    $pieces[3], $pieces[4]
.
open(FILES, "< data") || die "open failed\n";
while(<FILES>)
{
    @pieces = split;
    if ( $-  == 50 )
    {
        $~ = BOTTOM;
        write;
        $~ = STDOUT;
        $- = 0;
    }
    write if ($pieces[1] eq $ARGV[0] &&$pieces[2]>$ARGV[1]);
}
```

Exercises

1. Produce a table of powers where the base (2) in the example and the end range (10) in the example are given as command-line arguments:

```
% 8-1 2 10
-----------------------------------
POWERS TABLE Page num:  1
BASE        POWER RESULT
-----------------------------------
     2        1        2
     2        2        4
     2        3        8
     2        4       16
     2        5       32
     2        6       64
     2        7      128
     2        8      256
     2        9      512
     2       10     1024
%
```

2. Write a stock report based on the `stocks` file in the `solution` directory for Chapter 9. That file looks like this:

NAME	SHARES	PURCHASE	CURRENT	SYMBOL
MICROSOFT	100	50	100	MSFT
SUN	200	75	100	SUNW
SYBASE	300	15	10	SYBS

Your program should produce the following report:

```
% 8-2
STOCK REPORT: PAGE       1
TODAYS DATE IS:    Sat Sep  8 10:42:16 2001
===========================================
STOCK            SYMBOL          GAIN
=====            ======          ====
MICROSOFT        MSFT            5000
SUN              SUNW            5000
SYBASE           SYBS           -1500
%
```

3. Try printing a summary for Exercise 2. The output for this problem will be as shown here:

```
% 8-3
STOCK REPORT: PAGE        1
TODAYS DATE IS:      Sat Sep  8 10:44:44 2001
================================================
STOCK               SYMBOL           GAIN
=====               ======           ====
MICROSOFT           MSFT             5000
SUN                 SUNW             5000
SYBASE              SYBS             -1500
================================================
TOTAL FOR 3 ITEMS IS                 8500
%
```

4. Write a report that is based on the non-directory files in any directory given on the command line. Your output should look as follows:

```
% 8-4 .
PAGE    1       REPORT Sat Sep  8 200
COUNT           FILENAME   SIZE         LAST_MOD_DATE
  1             9-1         554     Sat Sep  8 10:33:12 2001
  2             9-2         730     Sat Sep  8 10:33:27 2001
  3             9-3         735     Sat Sep  8 10:33:43 2001
  4             9-4        1178     Sat Sep  8 10:49:57 2001
  5             STOCKS       80     Sat Feb 20 12:03:10 1999
================================================
TOTAL NUMBER OF FILES =            5
AVERAVE SIZE OF FILES =         655.40
LARGEST FILE IS                1178
```

9

ACCESSING SYSTEM RESOURCES

This section examines the functions that are built into the operating system. Since Perl comes from Unix, there is a strong Unix flavor to these functions. Many of them have been implemented on Windows so that they have a consistent behavior regardless of the operating system. However, this is not possible with all of the functions. When there is a difference, it will be pointed out.

9.1   Introduction

From the beginning of this book, we have been using builtin subroutines. These are subroutines that are built into the Perl executable. Examples of these are `open`, `print`, `split`, `join`, etc. In the previous chapter, we saw how to write our own subroutines. We also saw subroutines from the Perl standard library. In this section, we will look at another class of functions: those that are built into the operating system. These are referred to as system calls because they give you access to operating system resources such as the filesystem.

Since there will always be a strong tie between Perl and Unix, some of these calls may work only on Unix, or they may work on both Unix and Windows, but deliver slightly different information. Where that is the case, we will point it out. If the reader has programmed in C, many of these calls will be familiar.

9.2   File and Directory System Calls

There are a number of important system calls involving directories and files that can be useful in a wide variety of Perl scripts. These functions will be demonstrated with a series of programs.

9.2.1 `mkdir`

You can create a directory in Perl using the `mkdir` system call. `mkdir` takes a directory and a set of permissions for the directory. The permissions may only be meaningful on Unix-derived systems. `mkdir` returns a 1 on success and a 0 on failure. Here are a few examples of using this system call:

```
mkdir ($ARGV[0],0755) || die "$!\n";
mkdir ("mydirectory",0700) || die  "$!\n";
```

If the `mkdir` fails, then the value 0 is returned and the `die` function executes. It's your choice as to whether you wish the program to terminate or not. You could also write the code as follows:

```
#!/usr/bin/perl
#
#       mkdir.pl
#
print "Enter directory name ";
chomp($dirname = <STDIN>);
while(($result = mkdir($dirname)) == 0)
{
        print "$!\n";                   # error message
        print "Enter directory name ";
        chomp($dirname = <STDIN>);
}
print "Created $dirname\n";
```

9.2.2 `chdir`

The `chdir` command requires one argument, the directory to which you wish to change. This call also returns the value 1 on success and the value 0 on failure. Often in a program, you need to toggle between two directories. The small program below is a variation of one that we have seen previously:

```
#!/usr/bin/perl
#
#   whereto.pl
#
use Cwd;
$cwd = getcwd();
print "Current dir is $cwd\n";
print "Change to which directory? ";
chomp($newdir = <STDIN>);
chdir($newdir);
```

continued...

```
print "Current directory is now ", getcwd(), "\n";
print "Changing back to $cwd\n";
chdir($cwd);
print getcwd(), " is current directory again\n";

% whereto.pl
Current dir is D:/newones/8
Change to which directory? c:\windows
Current directory is now c:/windows
Changing back to D:/newones/8
D:/newones/8 is current directory again
%
```

Keep in mind that when a Perl script executes, it does so in its own environment. When the script finishes, the current directory will be the same as it was when the script was started, even if there was a change to a new directory within the script. There is no notion of a Perl script executing in the same environment as its starting environment the way there is with a Unix shell script.

9.2.3   `opendir, readdir,` **and** `closedir`

`opendir` is similar to the `open` function in that it requires a filehandle and a name. The name should be the name of a directory. The filehandle is used with `readdir`, which returns a list of files from the directory associated with the filehandle. `opendir` returns a 0 on failure and a 1 on success. `closedir` closes the handle created with `opendir`. To illustrate these system calls, the program below displays the files and the number of lines in all files in the directory named on the command line:

```
#!/usr/bin/perl
#
#   lines.pl
#
die "usage: lines.pl directory\n" unless $#ARGV == 0;
die "usage: arg must be a directory\n" unless -d $ARGV[0];
die "can't open $ARGV[0]\n" unless opendir(DIR, $ARGV[0]);
@files = readdir(DIR);
close(DIR);
chdir($ARGV[0]);
print "FILENAME\tLINES\n";
foreach $file (@files)
{
        next if ( -d $file);
        open(THISFILE, $file);
        while(<THISFILE>) { }
        print "$file\t$.\n";
        close(THISFILE);
}
```

This program, more than any other we have seen thus far, illustrates the beauty of Perl. The program is succinct and yet there is quite a bit going on within it. Before we explain it, here is a run of the program with (.), the current directory given as the command-line argument:

```
% lines.pl .
FILENAME    LINES
mkdir.pl    13
whereto.pl  14
lines.pl    21
%
```

The user feeds the program a command-line argument. The first few lines in the program check for errors. There are several different problems that could occur in this script. The first check is to assure that an argument was provided. The next check assures that the argument was a directory. The final check assures that the directory could be opened.

```
die "usage: lines.pl directory\n" unless $#ARGV == 0;
die "usage: arg must be a directory\n" unless -d $ARGV[0];
die "can't open $ARGV[0]\n" unless opendir(DIR, $ARGV[0]);
```

Next, the files are read into the `@files` array. Then, each file is tested to assure that it is not a directory. Finally, each file is opened and read to the end. The line count and filename are printed and the process is repeated for each file in the directory.

There are a few subtleties in this program. First, each file must be closed after it is read or `$.` will not be reset to zero. Second, the filenames may have been generated in a particular directory, but the program itself is started in its own directory. Thus, the `chdir` assures that the names of the files are relative to the directory from which they came.

9.2.4 `unlink` **and** `rename`

In the Unix operating system, a file can have more than one name. This is not true for all operating systems. The Perl `unlink` system call removes a name from the filesystem. If this is the only name for the file, the file is removed. In any case, `unlink` has several interfaces.

```
@files = (datafile, textfile, books);
unlink ("onefile");            # remove this name
unlink (@files);               # remove a list of names
unlink <chap*>                 # remove names starting with
                               # chap
```

The `rename` system call gives an existing file a new name as follows:

```
rename("original", "newname");
```

9.3   **Process Creation**

A process is a program in execution. A process includes the executing program and some operating system information related to it. This information may differ from system to system, but it would typically include items such as the current directory, the owner of the file, the size of the executable, environment variables, etc.

9.3.1   exec

The `exec` system call replaces the program running in a process. For example, the program below prints the time of day and then calls the `DIR` command. The argument to the `exec` command must be a command that can be executed on your operating system's command line.

```
#!/usr/bin/perl
#
#   exec.pl
#
require "ctime.pl";
$date = ctime(time);
print "$date";
print "Starting the DIR command \n";
print "---------------------------\n";
exec("DIR /B");
print "finishing the DIR command\n";
% exec.pl
Fri Sep  7 23:20:29 2001
Starting the DIR command
---------------------------
exec.pl
mkdir.pl
whereto.pl
lines.pl
%
```

If you examine the program closely, you will see that everything proceeds as expected until the `exec` is executed. It is at that point that the `DIR /B` command is executed. If you are using Unix, use `ls -l` instead of `DIR`. It's the manner in which it is executed that is important. It actually replaces the Perl program in memory. Technically, the Perl program running in the process is replaced by the `DIR` executable. Thus, the Perl program is erased from memory. That is why the last `print` in the program is never executed. The program performing the `exec` never returns.

9.3.2 `fork` and `wait`

The Perl program above was offered to explain how `exec` works. In reality, it would be rare if a program performed the `exec` as it was done above. You do not simply dismiss a program in the middle of its execution.

`exec` usually works in connection with the `fork` system call. `fork` creates a child process, which is a clone of its parent. One would use a `fork` and then `exec` a process in the child.

The `exec`ed process and the parent process run at the control of the operating system scheduler. The parent process can wait for the child to terminate by executing the `wait` system call. Not all operating systems allow `fork`. Some versions of Windows allow `fork`, while other versions do not.

The difficult part to understand about `fork` is that at the instant at which it is executed, there is a second process that is created. The value returned by `fork` may be used to see which is the parent and which is the child. The operating system arranges to return zero to the child process, while in the parent, the returned value from `fork` is some value greater than zero. On Unix, the value is the child process identification number. This may not make sense for all operating systems.

Here's a program that uses `fork`, `exec`, and `wait`:

```perl
#!/usr/bin/perl
#
#    fork.pl
#
require "ctime.pl";
if ($x = fork)
{
    $date = ctime(time);
    print "Parent Waits at $date";
    wait;
    $date = ctime(time);
    print "Parent returns at $date";
}
else
{
    print "Child executes dir in 2 seconds\n";
    $date = ctime(time);
    print "child sleeps at $date";
    sleep 2;
    $date = ctime(time);
    print "child starts dir at $date";
    exec "dir /B";
}
print "parent continues at ", ctime(time);
```

continued...

```
% fork.pl
Parent Waits at Fri Sep  7 23:35:39 2001
Child executes dir in 2 seconds
child sleeps at Fri Sep  7 23:35:39 2001
child starts dir at Fri Sep  7 23:35:41 2001
exec.pl
mkdir.pl
whereto.pl
lines.pl
fork.pl
Parent returns at Fri Sep  7 23:35:41 2001
parent continues at Fri Sep  7 23:35:41 2001
%
```

The `wait` call in the parent assures that the parent does not progress until the child finishes. `sleep` causes a suspension in the program for a specified number of seconds.

9.3.3   system

The `system` call may be used to execute any command-line command from your Perl script. `system` is similar to the combination of `fork` and `exec`, except you do not have to handle any of the details. `system` can be invoked in any of the following ways:

```
#
#  A string
#
system("dir");                      # on Windows, for example
#
#  A list whose first argument is a command
#
@command = ("ls", "-l", "/");    # on Unix, for example
system(@command);
```

`system` returns the value 0 on success and some non-zero value on failure. To determine whether it has succeeded or not, just code as below:

```
system(@list) || die "your own message here\n";
```

9.3.4   Back quotes

When you use `system`, it is not possible to retrieve the standard output from the command you are executing. It is sent to the display. To execute a command-line command and have the output sent to your program, you may use the same technique that Unix shell programmers use.

You may place your command-line command within a set of back quotes. Perl will execute the command and return the standard output from the command. In the following example, the date command is executed:

```
$date = `date`;
```

Remember that the text inside the back quotes must be a meaningful command-line command on your operating system. The following two commands work fine on Unix systems:

```
$date = `date`;
$current_directory = `pwd`;
```

However, Windows does not have a pwd command. Also be aware that on Windows, the date command behaves differently than it does on Unix. The portable way to handle each of these is as follows:

```
require "ctime.pl";
$date = ctime(time);

use Cwd;
$current_directory = cwd();
```

In the examples thus far, all of the output from the command is being captured in a scalar. It may be more convenient to capture the output in an array:

```
@files = `dir`;
```

In this case, each line of output generated by the back quoted command becomes an element in the @files array.

The content inside the back quotes may be arbitrarily complex and may involve Perl variables. The only restriction is that it must resolve to a command-line command.

```
$pattern = EOF;
@filenames = (text1, text2, text3);
@files = `grep -l $pattern @filenames`;
```

In the above sequence, we are using the Unix grep command to give us the names of the files that contain the string "EOF."

Be careful not to code the former when you mean the latter of the two constructions below. They give you very different results. The first gives you the exit status of the execution of the system command, while the latter gives you the output from the date command.

```
$date = system("date");
$date = "date";
```

9.4 Updating Files

Earlier in this book, we spoke of opening files for either reading or writing. Although we also mentioned how to open files for both reading and writing, we did not show how that was accomplished. In this section, we will show an example of updating a file. We must first mention a few system-like calls that allow the user to gain information about processing a disk file.

9.4.1 tell

As you read data from a file, the operating system maintains a pointer into that file so it can fetch data from the correct place for future reads. Likewise, when you are writing data into a file, the operating system maintains a pointer into that file so future writes to the file will be placed just beyond the previous write. The tell function tells you where, as a byte offset from the beginning of a file, you are in a file. The function takes one argument, a filehandle. If the filehandle is omitted, tell works on the last file that was read. Here is an example of how the tell function works:

```
#!/usr/bin/perl
#
#          tellme.pl
#
open(DISK, "> diskfile") || die "can't open diskfile\n";
print "Before first write: pos ", tell(DISK), "\n";
while(1)
{
        print "Enter some data: ";
        chomp($data = <STDIN>);
        last if ( $data eq quit );
        print DISK "$data\n";
        print "Next write at pos ", tell(DISK), "\n";
}
print "Diskfile is ", tell(DISK), " bytes in length\n";


% tellme.pl
Before first write: pos 0
Enter some data: the first line of data
Next write will be at pos 25
Enter some data: now the next
Next write will be at pos 41
Enter some data: quit
Diskfile is 41 bytes in length
%
```

There are several things to notice. Before you write any data to the file, you are positioned at the beginning of the file. `tell` tells you that you are at position 0. When you are at the end of the file, `tell` returns the file size. If you attempt to use `tell` on a closed filehandle, `-1` is returned.

9.4.2 seek

There are many applications where you must perform both reads and writes on the same file. The classic example is when you are updating a file; that is, perhaps you are changing a date or a name for certain records. In these situations, you must first read a record, test to see if it needs to be changed, make the change on the in-memory copy of the record, and then write the changes to the disk. We will assume that the records are actually lines.

In problems such as these, once you have read a record, you are positioned at the end of the record. You must move the file pointer back to the beginning of the record before you do the writing of the in-memory modified record.

Perl provides the `seek` function to move the file pointer. This function takes three arguments: a filehandle, an offset, and an origin. The pointer for the filehandle is moved offset number of bytes from the origin. The origin is given as an integer: 0, 1, or 2, representing the beginning position, the current position, or the end position of the file. Here are a few examples:

```
open(DISK, "+<") || die;        # open for both read and write

seek(DISK, 0, 0);               # seek 0 bytes from origin
                                # i.e., rewind

seek(DISK, 0, 2);               # seek 0 bytes from end
                                # i.e., move to end of file

seek(DISK, -30, 1);             # seek 30 bytes toward the
                                # the beginning of the file
                                # from current position
```

In some problems, you may need to read a data file more than once. You may always close the file and reopen it, but it is more efficient to seek back to the beginning of the file. In the following example, `search.pl`, the user types words on the command line. The program displays lines from a file that contains those words. Every time a search is made for the next word, the input file needs to be "rewound."

```
#!/usr/bin/perl
#
#       search.pl
#
die "usage: inputfile patterns....\n" unless $#ARGV >= 1;
open(DISK, "< $ARGV[0]") || die "can't open datafile\n";
```

continued...

```
#
#    shift the filename away
#    leaving just the words
#
shift;
foreach $argument (@ARGV)
{
        $. = 0;
        while(<DISK>)
        {
                print "$. $_" if /$argument/;
        }
        seek(DISK, 0, 0);
}

% search.pl
usage: inputfile patterns....
%
% search.pl search.pl if while foreach
8 # shift the filename away
11 shift;
17                     print "$. $_" if /$argument/;
15          while(<DISKFILE>)
12 foreach $argument (@ARGV)
%
```

Don't be misled by the output. The word "shift" contains the word "if," and thus, it is printed.

9.4.3 Modifying records

There are many applications that need to modify disk files. For example, you might write an application that updates an employee's record on receiving a promotion. Or, an application might change an address when an employee moves.

Some files have records of varying lengths. Making a change in these files is difficult because a change to one field may overwrite another field. Other files have fixed-length fields. These files are easier to modify.

Here is an example of a fixed-length file. Each record contains a first name, a last name, a city, and a state. The first two fields are 10 positions in length, and the last two fields are 15 characters in length. The name of the file is info.

```
% display info
Michael    Saltzman   Columbia       Maryland
Susan      Saltzman   Charleston     South Carolina
Maria      Gonzalez   Pikesville     Maryland
Erin       Flanagan   Annapolis      Maryland
AlexandriaMacPhersonJefferson City Missouri
Michael    Jones      Palm Beach     Florida
%
```

If we attempt to read a record above in the conventional way, we quickly get into trouble. That is, if you read in a line at a time and try to use `split`, you have forgotten that these fields have no delimiters. They are of fixed length. The proper way to deal with this kind of file is to use the `unpack` function. The details of this function will be shown later. The file should be read in the following way:

```
while($_ = <DATABASE>)
{
    chop;
    ($fname,$ln, $ct, $st) = unpack("A10 A10 A15 A15", $_);
}
```

`unpack` takes a series of formats and the variable to be unpacked and returns a list of values. The `Ax` format specifies that x characters are to be extracted and any trailing blanks are to be thrown away.

The example program below is used to change all records having a name given on the command line as the first argument to the replacement name given as the second argument. Once the data has been read into the program, it's easy to see if the name for a particular record matches `$ARGV[0]`. If it does, it is also easy to replace it with the replacement name given as `$ARGV[1]`. However, there are still a few wrinkles to smooth out.

In particular, when you find a record that must be changed, you have already read to the end of that record. You now need to "back up" an amount equal to the size of the record. Then you can write the record "over itself."

Before you write the record, you must format it correctly. Use `pack` to accomplish this. Here is the code:

```
if ( $fname eq $ARGV[0] )
{
    $fname = $ARGV[1];
    $newrec = pack("A10 A10 A15 A15",$fname,$lname,$city,$state);
    seek(DATABASE, -52, 1);
    print DATABASE "$newrec\n";
}
```

In the above code, the amount to back up might depend on the system you are using. I first ran the above code on Windows. Files there map the newline character into the two characters carriage return and line feed. Therefore, the amount to back up is `10 + 10 + 15 + 15 + 2`, or `52`. When I ran this code on a Unix system, I used the value `51` as the amount to back up. You can always use the special Perl variable $^O to determine the operating system.

One final item must be considered. There is a lot of operating system input and output in the program that performs the update. To be sure that the buffering of all these reads and writes is correct, we turn it off. This is done by first opening the input file, then selecting it, and then setting $|$ to the value 1. Finally, we select STDOUT so that if the program issues any prints, they will find their way to the display.

```
open(DATABASE, "+< info") || die;
select(DATABASE);
$| = 1;
select(STDOUT);
```

Here is the entire program, update.pl:

```
#!/usr/bin/perl
#
#   update.pl
#
die "usage: update.pl target newvaln" unless $#ARGV == 1;
open(DATABASE, "+< info") || die;
select(DATABASE);
$| = 1;
select(STDOUT);
while($_ = <DATABASE>)
{
    chop;
    ($fn, $lnm, $ct, $st) = unpack("A10 A10 A15 A15", $_);
        if ( $fn eq $ARGV[0] )
            {
            print "Changing $ARGV[0] to $ARGV[1]\n";
            $fn = $ARGV[1];
            $newrec=pack("A10 A10 A15 A15",$fn,$lnm,$ct,$st);
            seek(DATABASE, -52, 1);
            print DATABASE "$newrec\n";
            }
}

% update.pl Michael Mike
changing Michael to Mike
changing Michael to Mike
% display info
Mike        Saltzman    Columbia        Maryland
Susan       Saltzman    Charleston      South Carolina
Maria       Gonzalez    Pikesville      Maryland
Erin        Flanagan    Annapolis       Maryland
AlexandriaMacPhersonJefferson City Missouri
Mike        Jones       Palm Beach      Florida
%
```

Exercises

1. Write a Perl script that determines the total number of times a word occurs over all text files in a directory.

   ```
   $ howmany word directory
   ```

2. Write a Perl program that takes a directory as input and lists the sizes of all files in the first-level subdirectories of that directory.

   ```
   $ sizes directory
   ```

10

PERL REFERENCES

This is the first chapter where the concepts are slightly advanced. We will concentrate on a thorough treatment of references, Perl's version of pointers. References are used for almost all advanced Perl topics.

10.1 Introduction

When Perl transitioned from Perl 4 to Perl 5, one of the most significant changes to the language was the introduction of references. If you are a C programmer, you will find references very similar to pointers. Of course, the syntax for Perl references is different than the syntax for C pointers. References have many uses in Perl. We will see a myriad of them in this and future chapters.

10.1.1 What is a reference?

You can think of a Perl reference as a scalar whose value is the address in memory where a piece of data is stored. Of course, the piece of data may be a simple value such as a string:

```
[mike]
```

or it might be more complex such as a record consisting of a name, an occupation, and a series of elements relating to the occupation:

```
[mike]        [instructor]      [C, C++, Perl, Java]
```

In Perl, a reference is a scalar variable that contains the address of some arbitrarily complex piece of data.

10.1.2   Scalar references

One way to create a reference is by using the \ symbol. You can think of this symbol as the "address of" symbol because that is what it returns. Here's an example of creating a reference:

```
$data = 20;              # scalar: integer value of 20
$rdata = \$data;         # reference: address of $data
```

The scalar $rdata is a reference to $data, which is itself a scalar. Once a reference to a variable is created, you may use it to access the variable that is being referenced. To access a variable through a reference, you will need to use $, the scalar dereferencing operator. Assembly language programmers will recognize this as indirect addressing. All of the ideas above are collected into the following example:

```
#!/usr/bin/perl
#
#   scalarref.pl
#
$data = 20;
$rdata = \$data;         # create the reference
print "$data\n";         # print the data directly
print "$rdata\n";        # print the reference
print "$$rdata\n";       # print the data indirectly
$$rdata = 50;            # change the data indirectly
print "$data\n";         # prove it

% scalarref.pl
20SCALAR(0xbe7420)20
50
%
```

If you print a reference, you'll get an address. Normally, this is not what you want, so don't forget to put the extra $ in front of the reference to get the value to which it is pointing.

10.1.3   Array references

References to any of Perl's data types can be created. To create a reference to an array, you would proceed as follows:

```
@values = (10, 20 , 30);
$rvalues = \@values;
```

As before, if you access $rvalues, you get the following:

```
ARRAY (0xbe742c)
```

To get the actual array through the reference, you need to use the array dereferencing operator, @:

```
print "@$rvalues";          # prints 10 20 30
```

Or, if you wanted any element of the array, that is, one of the scalars inside the array, then you would use the scalar dereferencing operator, $:

```
print "$$rvalues[0]";       # prints  10
print "$$rvalues[1]";       # prints  20
print "$$rvalues[2]";       # prints  30
print "$$rvalues[-1]";      # prints  30
```

Here's a program that puts these ideas together:

```
#!/usr/bin/perl
#
#    arrayref.pl
#
@values = ( 10, 20, 30);
$rvalues = \@values;                 # create the reference
for ( $i = 0; $i < @$rvalues; $i++)
{
    print "$$rvalues[$i]\n";         # access an element
                                     # via the reference
}
@$rvalues = (120,130,140);           # change the array
                                     # through the reference

print "@values\n";

% arrayref.pl
10
20
30
120 130 140
%
```

References to arrays have great utility in Perl. For example, the subroutine `lengths` receives array references and returns an array consisting of the lengths of the arrays being referenced. We wrote a similar program previously using typeglobs. The function below can receive any number of arrays:

```
#!/usr/bin/perl
#
#   lengths.pl
#
sub lengths
{
    my(@ans);
    foreach $array (@_)
    {
        push(@ans, scalar(@$array));
    }
    @ans;
}
@v1 = (10, 20, 30, 40, 50, 60);
@v2 = (10, 20, 30, 40, 50);
@v3 = (10, 20, 30, 40);
@results = lengths(\@v1, \@v2, \@v3);
print "@results\n";
% lengths.pl
6 5 4
%
```

In the program above, the subroutine receives three references and loops through them in the `foreach` loop. In each case, a scalar context is forced through the use of the builtin `scalar` function. Thus, the length of each array referred to is pushed on to the `@ans` array, which is ultimately returned to the caller.

Keep in mind that if you do not pass references in this case, and instead pass arrays, they will be flattened into one long list and received in `@_`.

10.1.3.1 Prototypes.   The program above works fine, but there is a slight burden to the user of the `lengths` subroutine. The user must remember to pass references rather than arrays. It would be nice if the user could pass the actual array and have the subroutine behave as if references were sent. This is where a Perl prototype is useful.

A prototype is a set of symbols that inform Perl about incoming parameter types. These symbols are placed within a set of parentheses in back of the function name. Some of the symbols that may be used are:

$ Force scalar context on incoming arguments

\@   Force array reference context

;   Rest of arguments are optional

In our example, we would like to have at least one argument and arbitrarily up to five arguments in total. Thus, we would code:

```
sub lengths(\@;\@\@\@\@)
{
    my(@ans);
    foreach $array (@_)
    {
        push(@ans, scalar(@$array));
    }
    @ans;
}
```

The calling program would now be:

```
@v1 = (10, 20, 30, 40, 50, 60);
@v2 = (10, 20, 30, 40, 50);
@v3 = (10, 20, 30, 40);
@results = lengths(@v1, @v2, @v3);
print "@results\n";
```

The only restriction is that the caller must not use the & symbol to invoke the subroutine.

10.1.4   Hash references

You may also create a reference to a hash. As usual, the reference operator is \, but this time, % is the dereferencing operator:

```
#!/usr/bin/perl
#
#   hashref.pl
#
%names = (    "The Kid"        =>     "Ted Williams",
              "The Babe"       =>     "Babe Ruth",
              "The Iron Horse" =>     "Lou Gehrig"
          );
$rnames = \%names;
#
#   print all the keys - a likely event
#
print join("\n",keys(%$rnames)), "\n\n";
#
#   print a value from a key - the most likely event
#
print $$rnames{"The Kid"}, "\n";$ hashes
```

In the above code, you should notice that `%$rnames` is the entire associative array and `$$rnames{"The Kid"}` is the scalar resulting from the "The Kid" key.

```
% hashref.pl
The Kid
The Iron Horse
The Babe

Ted Williams
%
```

10.1.4.1 A relaxed notation.   It should also be noted that Perl allows other notations that are more pointer-friendly for the dereferencing of both arrays and hash references. Suppose we have the following:

```
@data = (10,20,30,40);
$rdata = \@data;
```

We have seen above that to retrieve an element of the array `@data` through the reference `$rdata`, you can code:

```
$$rdata[0];
```

However, there is another notation that is more pointer-friendly:

```
$rdata->[0]
```

Just be careful; when you use this notation, you should refrain from using quotes in expressions such as:

```
print "$rdata->[0]\n";
```

because the `->` will not be meaningful within single or double quotes.

There is also an alternative notation for hash references so that if you have a hash such as:

```
%states = (     MD => Annapolis,
                CA => Sacremento,
                NY => "New York City"
          );
```

and a reference to a hash such as:

```
$rhash = \%states;
```

you can retrieve values from the hash in either of the following ways:

```
print "$$rhash{NY}\n";          # New York City
print $rhash -> {NY}, "\n";     # New York City
```

10.1.5   References to subroutines

Any Perl data type can have a reference. Thus far, we've seen references to arrays, hashes, and scalars. We will now examine references to subroutines. The code below shows how to create a reference to a subroutine and how to invoke the subroutine through the subroutine dereference operator, &:

```
sub square
{
   $_[0] * $_[0];
}
$sref = \&square;               # create reference
$ans = &$sref(10);              # dereference
print "$ans";                   # prints 100
```

Now that we know the mechanics of referencing subroutines, we can show an example of sending both an array and a subroutine as arguments to a subroutine:

```
#!/usr/bin/perl
#
#    compute.pl
#
sub square
{
    $_[0] * $_[0];
}
sub cube
{
    $_[0] * $_[0] * $_[0];
}
```

continued...

```
sub compute
{
    my($array,$function) = @_;
    foreach $item (@$array)
        $item = &$function($item);
    }
}
@values = (10,20,30);
compute(\@values,\&square);
print "@values\n";
@data = (5,6,7);
compute(\@data,\&cube);
print "@data\n";
```

In the above code, there are two calls to the `compute` function:

```
compute(\@values,\&square);
compute(\@data,\&cube);
```

In each case, the arguments are an array reference and a subroutine reference. Therefore, inside the subroutine, we can access each of the arguments through the my variables defined in the following statement:

```
my($array,$function) = @_;
```

`$array` is a reference to a real array, and `$function` is a reference to a real function. The `foreach` loop calls the function on each element of the array and changes that element. It will either be changed to its square or its cube, depending on which function is sent during the call to `compute`.

```
foreach $item (@$array)
{
    $item = &$function($item);
}
```

Remember that within a `foreach` loop, the iterating variable is a synonym for the actual array element to which it is bound. Thus, the following statement actually changes an array element:

```
$item = &$function($item);
```

10.2 Anonymous References

The examples that we have seen thus far have included only named arrays and hashes. In some cases, you will want to take another approach. It's possible to create an array that has no name. When you do this in Perl, the address of where the array is located is generated for you. This is called an anonymous array.

10.2.1 Anonymous arrays

The syntax for creating an anonymous array is shown in the following example. Keep in mind that the address returned by this array will be stored in a scalar, so you must code as shown below:

```
$refa = [10, 20, 30];
print "The entire array -> @$refa\n";
print "A single element -> $$refa[0]\n";
print "Alternative notation", $refa->[0], "\n";
```

It would be a logical error to code:

```
@refa = [10, 20, 30];
```

This would simply create an array of one element whose value was the address of wherever data 10, 20, and 30 were stored. The important notion here is that the expression:

```
[10, 20, 30]
```

is a reference in the same sense that $ref is a reference in the line below:

```
@data = (200, 300, 400);
$refa = \@data;
```

10.2.2 Anonymous hashes

You may also have anonymous hashes. In the code below:

```
$states = { MD => Annapolis,
            CA => Sacramento,
            NY => "New York City"
          };
print "$$states{NY}\n";
print  $states->{NY}, "\n";
```

$states is an anonymous hash, that is, it points to a hash that has no name. Notice the curly braces are used here as opposed to a set of parentheses, which usually encloses a set of hash initializers.

10.2.3 Anonymous scalars

It is also possible to define a reference to an anonymous single value, a scalar. In this way, you can define constants in Perl.

```
$PI = \3.14159;
$$PI++;                         # illegal
```

10.3 Complex Data Structures

We'll now explore some complex data structures such as higher dimensional arrays, hashes whose values are complex, and several others.

10.3.1 Two-dimensional arrays

Suppose you wanted to build an array with two dimensions. Conceptually, you might think of this as rows and columns, but Perl thinks of this as an array of arrays. A first attempt may result in something like:

```
@a1 = (10,20,30);
@a2 = (100,200,300);
@matrix = (@a1, @a2);
print "@matrix"; # prints 10,20,30,100,200,300
```

but this simply creates one flat array with six elements. Instead, you could populate an array with references. The easiest way to do this is to use a set of anonymous references:

```
#!/usr/bin/perl
#
#   twodim.pl
#
@twodim = (      [10, 20, 30],
                 [40, 50, 60],
                 [70, 80, 90]
           );
print "@twodim\n";
print "$twodim[0]";
print "$twodim[1]";
print "$twodim[2]";
```

continued...

```
% twodim.pl
ARRAY(0x176f09c) ARRAY(0x17650f4) ARRAY(0x176516c)
ARRAY(0x176f09c)
ARRAY(0x17650f4)
ARRAY(0x176516c)
%
```

The first `print` above simply prints all the elements of the array, which of course are simply references to anonymous arrays. From this, it follows that the last three `prints` print single references. To get at the actual data in these anonymous arrays, you must dereference them.

How you actually perform the dereferencing depends on which chunk of data you wish to access. To print each row, you can simply dereference each anonymous array reference:

```
foreach $row (@twodim)
{
    print "@$row\n";
}
```

The simplest way to get at a particular element is to use two subscripts:

```
print $twodim[0][0]          # prints the 10
print $twodim[0][1]          # prints the 20
print $twodim[1][0]          # prints the 40
```

Two-dimensional arrays may also be built on-the-fly. For example, if the first access to an array in your program is:

```
data[5][6] = 0;
```

then you have an array of 42 elements. Remember, array subscripts start at 0, not 1.

Finally, you may have a jagged array, one where there is a different number of elements in each row.

```
#!/usr/bin/perl
#
#    disparate.pl
#
@values = (        [1, 2, 3, 4, 5 ],
                   [Mike, Judy, Joel],
                   [Prov, Boston]
             );
for ( $i = 0; $i < @values; $i++)
```

continued...

```
{
    for ($j = 0; $j < @{$values[$i]}; $j++)
    {
        print $values[$i][$j], " ";
    }
    print "\n";
}
```

The outer loop performs three iterations, one for each reference in the array. In a scalar context, @values yields 3. Since the array is not rectangular, the number of inner loop iterations will depend on how many elements are contained within each reference.

The following expression used in a scalar context will yield the correct number of elements in each row:

```
@{$values[$i]}

% disparate.pl
1 2 3 4 5
Mike Judy Joel
Prov Boston
%
```

There is yet another approach we could take. We could have a reference to a bunch of references. If you are a C programmer, you may know this idiom as a pointer to a bunch of pointers—similar to argv.

```
$t =     [      [1, 2, 3, 4, 5 ],
                [Mike, Judy, Joel],
                [Prov, Boston]
         ];
```

$t is a reference to three anonymous references. To get at any of the elements, there needs to be an additional indirection with respect to previous array examples:

```
print "$t \n";                 # ARRAY ref
print "$$t[0]\n";              # ARRAY ref
print "$$t[1]\n";              # ARRAY ref
print "$$t[2]\n";              # ARRAY ref
print "$$t[0][0]\n";          # 1
print "$$t[1][0]\n";          # Mike
print "@{$$t[2]}\n";          # Prov Boston
```

10.3.2   **Complex hashes**

We have concentrated mostly on arrays thus far. We now turn to hashes. A hash maps a key to a value. The value can be arbitrarily complex, that is, it could be a scalar, an array, another hash, a subroutine, or any other complex data that you need. The following hash contains a few (name, value) pairs. Each name is mapped to an anonymous array.

```
%courses = (    Mike  => [Cpp, Java, Perl],
                Alan  => [OOAD, Java, UML],
                Roger => [UNIX, C, Cpp]
           );
```

To display the courses that `Mike` teaches, we could simply dereference the expression `$courses{Mike}`. The code would be:

```
print @{$courses{Mike}};
```

If we wanted a particular course, we could just supply the appropriate subscript on the previous expression. For example, the following expression would display `Java`:

```
print @{$courses{Mike}}[1];
```

Thus, we could use the following to print all the courses:

```
foreach $key (keys(%courses))
{
    print @{$courses{$key}}, "\n";
}
```

Each `$courses{key}` reference above returns a reference to an array which then must be dereferenced with @. To build an array of all the courses, we could code:

```
foreach $key (keys(%courses))
{
    foreach $course (@{$courses{$key}})
    {
        push(@courses, $course);
    }
}
```

Rather than having an actual hash, we could have a reference to one. This would change the notation a bit.

```
$fac = {    Mike  =>    [Cpp, Java, Perl],
            Alan  =>    [OOAD, Java, UML],
            Roger =>    [UNIX, C, Cpp]
       };
print @{$$fac{Mike}}, "\n";
foreach $key (keys(%$fac))
{
    print @{$$fac{$key}}, "\n";
}
```

Note that a reference to an anonymous array uses the [ ] notation:

```
$anonarray = [ 10, 20, 30 ];
```

whereas a reference to an anonymous hash uses the { } notation:

```
$hash = {  a => b, c=> d };
```

10.3.3   Two-dimensional hashes

Hashes are not limited to a single dimension. A key may map to another hash. For example, suppose your organization employs several salespeople, each of whom can sell different products, say personal computers (pc) and desktop computers (dt). We could define a hash as follows: Each key represents a salesperson. Each key maps to a hash that represents sets of product and revenue pairs.

The easiest way to represent this data structure is with a reference to an anonymous hash whose elements are keys, each of which maps to an anonymous hash of (product, revenue) pairs. Here is such a reference. Assume that the numbers represent total revenues for a particular product.

```
$revenues = { Mike  =>    { pc =>  10, dt => 20 },
              Jane  =>    { pc => 100, dt => 200 },
              Susan =>    { pc => 200, dt => 300 },
            };
```

Of course, the question now becomes: "How do we get at the data?" To simplify such a complex data structure, note that at the outer level, we simply have a set of (key, value) pairs and retrieving them is not difficult. Each key is a person's name. However, the value for that key is an anonymous hash.

```
while(($key, $value) = each(%$revenue))
{
    print "$key $value\n";
}
```

What is printed, therefore, is the anonymous hash for each key.

```
Jane HASH(0x176f218)    # address of {pc =>  10, dt =>  20}
Susan HASH(0x17651d4)   # address of {pc => 100, dt => 200}
Mike HASH(0x176f134)    # address of {pc => 200, dt => 300}
```

Now we must take the $value variable from above and treat it as a hash reference.

```
while(($k, $v ) = each(%$value))
{
    print "$k, $v\n";
}
```

Here's a program that packages all of these ideas:

```
#!/usr/bin/perl
#
#   hashhash.pl
#
$revenue = { Mike  =>    { pc =>  10, dt => 20 },
             Jane  =>    { pc => 100, dt => 200 },
             Susan =>    { pc => 200, dt => 300 },
           };
while(($key, $value) = each(%$revenue))
{
    print "$key:\n";
    while(($k, $v ) = each(%$value))
    {
        print "$k, $v\n";
    }
}
```

continued...

```
% hashhash.pl
Jane:
pc, 100
dt, 200
Susan:
pc, 200
dt, 300
Mike:
pc, 10
dt, 20
%
```

A problem such as this could be defined in a slightly different way. We might suppose that each line in a file contained a transaction that detailed a salesperson, a product, and a revenue. Then, we could write a program to print summaries, that is, how much revenue did each salesperson create by selling a particular product. Here is such a file, `hashdata`:

```
% display hashdata
Tom PC 500
Sue PC 400
Tom DT 300
Sue DT 400
Tom PC 100
Sue PC 200
Mike PC 400
%
```

At issue here is the creation of the hash dynamically rather than building it into the program through initialization. Here is a program that processes the previous file:

```perl
#!/usr/bin/perl
#
#    revenue.pl
#
while ( <STDIN> )
{
    ($name, $product, $amt) = split;
    $revenues{$name}{$product} += $amt;
}
while (($name, $hash) = each(%revenues))
```

continued...

```
{
    print "$name:\n";
    $tot = 0;
    while(($prod, $amt) = each(%$hash))
    {
            print "$prod $amt\n";
            $tot += $amt;
    }
    print "Total for $name: $tot\n\n";
}
```

The top `while` reads the data from the file and dynamically builds the complex hash.

```
($name, $product, $amt) = split;
$revenues{$name}{$product} += $amt;
```

The last line above builds entries with the same structure you saw when the hash was initialized—well, almost the same structure. This hash is real and the previous one was pointed to by a reference.

The first of the nested `while`s loops through the outer hash and `each(%revenues)` returns a key, which is a name, and the value for that key, which is itself a hash reference. The inner loop takes that hash reference and returns a product and the total amount associated with it. Here is the output of the program when it is run on the real `hashdata` file which comes with your download:

```
% revenue.pl < hashdata
Tom:
DT 600
PC 600
Total for Tom: 1200

Sue:
DT 800
PC 1600
Total for Sue: 2400

Erin:
DT 600
PC 800
Total for Erin: 1400

Mike:
DT 200
PC 1600
Total for Mike: 1800

%
```

10.4 Collections of Records

A record is a set of related data fields. For example, name, address, phone number, etc. is a set of fields which, when taken together, forms a payroll record. Keep in mind that Perl does not have any formal treatment of records; thus, the programmer must be creative. Most programmers keep track of records by using anonymous hashes. If you are a C programmer, you will appreciate the similarity between record creation in C and Perl. The C approach might be:

```c
struct record {
    char name[100];
    int age;
};
typedef struct record RECORD;
RECORD create(char *name, int age)
{
    RECORD r;
    strcpy(r.name, name);
    r.age = age;
    return r;
}
main()
{
    struct record a,b;
    a = create("Mike",54);
    printf("%s %d\n", a.name, a.age);
}
```

In Perl, the record would be constructed as:

```perl
sub create
{
    my($name,$age) = @_;
    my $rec =    {    name => $name,
                      age => $age
                 };
    $rec;
}
$a = create("Mike",54);
print $a -> {name}, "\n";
print $a -> {age}, "\n";
```

create is a function that takes its input and inserts it into a hash keyed by two meaningful field names: name and age. The important issue is that the hash is anonymous, and thus, the result is stored in a reference. When the subroutine returns this reference, the "record" is created.

Collections of these records can be built and references to them can be stored in lists, then they can be manipulated using Perl's powerful list manipulation functions such as push, pop, shift, and unshift.

The following program, getrecs.pl, reads a file of records and builds a list of references. We will assume that the file contains lines of space-separated triplets such as [name age city].

```
% display recdata
Susan 37 Columbia
Bob 57 Boston
Erin 25 Odenton
Mike 54 Columbia
%

#!/usr/bin/perl
#
#   getrecs.pl
#
sub create
{
    my($name, $age, $city) = @_;
    my $emp  = {   name => $name,
                   age => $age,
                   city => $city
               };
    return $emp;
}
while(<STDIN>)
{     @info = split;
      $record = create(@info);
      push(@list, $record);
}
while(@list)
{     $x = pop(@list);
      print "RECORD #: ", ++$ct, "\n";
      print "NAME: $x->{name}\n";
      print "AGE:  $x->{age}\n";
      print "CITY: $x->{city}\n";
      print "--------------\n";
}
```

The main part of the program reads lines from the input file and splits them on whitespace. These values are sent to the create method, where a hash reference is created and filled with this data. Each reference is added to the @list array.

The rest of the program is simply a loop that pops off one reference at a time from the @list array until it is empty. Each record is then printed one field at a time.

Here is the execution of the program:

```
% getrecs.pl < recdata
RECORD #: 1
NAME: Bob
AGE:  57
CITY: Boston
--------------
RECORD #: 2
NAME: Erin
AGE:  25
CITY: Odenton
--------------
RECORD #: 3
NAME: Susan
AGE:  37
CITY: Columbia
--------------
RECORD #: 4
NAME: Mike
AGE:  54
CITY: Columbia
--------------
%
```

10.4.1   Sorting based on a key field

Now, suppose we want to sort a record based on a particular field. We know from previous experience with sorting that we will have to write some custom subroutines.

```
@keys = sort custom_sub (@list);
```

In the above line, the sort routine will repeatedly pass two references to its comparison algorithm. The trick is to have the reference point to the field that we want sorted. Based on how the fields compare, the references must be placed in an order that reflects the comparison. Here's a program that sorts on the name field:

```
#!/usr/bin/perl
#
#    namesort.pl
#
sub create
{
    my($name, $age, $city) = @_;
    my $emp =    {    name => $name,
                      age  => $age,
                      city => $city
                 };
    return $emp;
```

continued...

```
}
while(<STDIN>)
{
    @info = split;
    $record = create(@info);
    push(@list, $record);
}
sub byname        { $a->{name} cmp $b->{name};  }
@sorted = sort byname(@list);
print "SORTED BY NAME\n";
foreach $item (@sorted)
{
    print "$$item{name} $$item{age} $$item{city}\n";
}

% namesort.pl
SORTED BY NAME
Bob 57 Boston
Erin 25 Odenton
Mike 54 Columbia
Susan 37 Columbia
%
```

To sort by age, we simply change the special comparison function to:

```
sub byage
{
    $a->{age}  <=> $b->{age};
}
@sorted = sort byage(@list);

% agesort.pl
SORTED BY AGE
Erin 25 Odenton
Mike 54 Columbia
Susan 37 Columbia
Mike 54 Columbia
Bob 57 Boston
%
```

10.4.2 References to references

Data structures can be arbitrarily complex. In most of the previous examples, the references that we used were pointing to data. However, there is no reason why they cannot point to other references that point to data.

Here's an example involving passengers and flights. Each flight has a flight number, a destination city, and a departure city as well as several passengers. Each passenger has a name, a hometown, and a meal. A passenger can be built with an anonymous hash reference. Each flight will contain several passengers.

First, we will create a few passengers:

```perl
sub booking
{
    my $pass;
    my($name, $seat, $meal) = @_;
    $pass = {   name => $name,
                seat => $seat,
                meal => $meal
            };
    $pass;
}
$p1 = booking(Mike, "21B", eggs);
$p2 = booking(Susan, "37C", toast);
$p3 = booking(Erin, "21C", eggs);
$p4 = booking(Bob, "37B", toast);
```

Each item above is a reference to a passenger. Now, we can build a flight that contains these passengers. Each flight will contain a flight number, a destination city, a departure city, and an array of passengers.

```perl
sub makeflight
{
    my $flight;
    my($number, $from , $to, @passes) = @_;
    $flight =    {          number => $number,
                            from => $from,
                            to => $to,
                            log => [@passes]
                };
    $flight;
}

$f1 = makeflight("257", Boston, Miami, $p1, $p2);
$f2 = makeflight("389", Raleigh, Boston, $p3, $p4);
```

Flight logs may be printed with:

```perl
sub printlog
{
    my($f) = @_;
    my($log) = $f->{log};
    print "PASSENGER LIST: FLIGHT: ", $f->{number};
    print " FROM: ",$f->{from},"->",$f->{to}, "\n";
```

continued...

```
       foreach $p (@$log)
       {
           print $p->{name}, " ",
                 $p->{seat},  " ",
                 $p->{meal}, "\n";
       }
}
```

The `printlog` subroutine is passed a reference to a hash, and thus, the initial `prints` simply fetch the flight number and cities. Then the fun starts. The `$log` variable contains a reference to the anonymous hash containing the passenger references. Since `@$log` is the array of passenger references, each of them in turn is fed to `$p`. Then, the passenger information is fetched through `$p`.

Here is the complete code for this application followed by a run of the program:

```
#!/usr/bin/perl
#
#   flights.pl
#
sub makeflight
{
    my $flight;
    my($number, $from , $to, @passes) = @_;
    $flight =    {    number => $number,
                      from => $from,
                      to => $to,
                      log => [@passes]
                 };
    $flight;
}
sub booking
{
    my $pass;
    my($name, $seat, $meal) = @_;
    $pass =      {    name => $name,
                      seat => $seat,
                      meal => $meal
                 };
    $pass;
}
sub printlog
{
    my($f) = @_;
    my($log) = $f->{log};
    my($num) = 1;
    print "PASSENGER LIST: FLIGHT: ", $f->{number};
    print " FROM: ", $f->{from}, "->", $f->{to}, "\n";
```

continued...

```
        foreach $p (@$log)
   {
        print $num++, " ", $p->{name}, " ",  $p->{seat},
                      " ",  $p->{meal}, "\n";
   }
}
$p1 = booking(Mike, "21B", pizza);
$p2 = booking(Susan, "37C", vegan);
$p3 = booking(Erin, "21B", lemon);
$p4 = booking(Bob, "37B", gourmet);
$p5 = booking(Maria, "21C", tamales);
$p6 = booking(Patti, "42C", chocolate);
$p7 = booking(Dave, "17C", "Dr. Pepper");

$f1 = makeflight("257", "Boston", "Miami",$p1,$p2,$p3,$p4);
$f2 = makeflight("389", "Baltimore", "Boston",$p5,$p6,$p7);
printlog($f1);
printlog($f2);
% flights.pl
PASSENGER LIST: FLIGHT: 257 FROM: Boston->Miami
1 Mike 21B pizza
2 Susan 37C vegan
3 Erin 21B lemon
4 Bob 37B gourmet
PASSENGER LIST: FLIGHT: 389 FROM: Baltimore->Boston
1 Maria 21C tamales
2 Patti 42C chocolate
3 Dave 17C Dr. Pepper
%
```

Exercises

1. Write a program that reads a file such as the one below, creates a two-dimensional array, and then prints it:

```
10 20 30 40
20 30 40
40 50 60 70
```

2. Create a hash that consists of pairs where the first element of the pair is a state and the second element is a set of cities. Write a subroutine that takes the hash as an argument and returns a list of all of the cities.
3. Write a subroutine that takes any number of arrays as input and returns a list consisting of the sum of each individual array.

OBJECT-ORIENTED PROGRAMMING

With the success of graphical user interfaces, or GUIs, the software world has gone object-crazy! Object-oriented (OO) software offers developers rich rewards down the road. Programs are easier to maintain and understand. This chapter gives the details of object-oriented programming (OOP) in Perl.

11.1 Introduction

When Perl transitioned from Perl 4 to Perl 5, one of the major enhancements to the language was the introduction of OOP. If you are familiar with this style of programming in languages such as Smalltalk, C++, and Java, you may be a little surprised with Perl's implementation when you see it later in this chapter. Many Perl modules are written using this style of programming, and thus it will serve you well to master the OO paradigm in Perl.

The approach in this section is to build a new data type, a class, and then demonstrate how to use this class in an application by creating an object or two, each of which uses some of the behavior defined in the class. We will demonstrate all of the OO terms with a series of examples that increase in complexity.

11.2 The Vocabulary of Object Orientation

Before we actually learn how to write OO programs in Perl, we must develop an OO vocabulary. In the real world, we commonly think of anything physical as an object. In software, we extend this notion to things that are conceptual. Thus, you can think of anything that is physical or conceptual as an object. Some examples of objects are a bank account, a file, a person, a stack, and a circle.

Typically, a particular application is built to solve problems in a domain-specific area. Any such application would likely have many objects in it. For example, banking software would have many account objects in it; an operating system would have many file and job objects in it.

Every object has a set of attributes collectively referred to as the state of the object. For example, a mortgage object would have among other things, a name, a loan amount, a payment amount, and so on. Thus, the state of a mortgage is the collection of its data items such as name, loan amount, and payment. Note that attributes tend to be nouns.

Each object functions in various ways. The collection of these functions can be thought of as the behavior of the object. For example, a mortgage has behaviors such as create, make payment, get balance, etc. Behaviors tend to be verbs.

Thus, every object has state and behavior.

In the OO software world, different languages tend to use different words to describe the same phenomena. For example, some synonyms for attributes are fields, traits, characteristics, object data, and instance data. The last two are used most often.

Behavior refers to the collection of actions that an object can perform. Behavior is sometimes referred to as actions, functions, operations, procedures, and methods. The term "method" is the most often used term. To ensure that these points are clearly understood, a few simple examples follow.

Suppose we have a car object—call it `MyCar`. Instance data for `MyCar` would include `length`, `height`, `color`, `model`, etc. The collection of this data is called the state of the object.

Methods for `MyCar` would include `start`, `stop`, `drive`, `turn_left`, etc. The collection of these functions is called the behavior of the object.

Every object contains data and behaves in a particular way based on the class to which it belongs. A class is like a blueprint or template from which objects are created. An object is composed of many pieces of data. The level of complexity of an object is completely determined by the class from which it was instantiated.

The behavior of an object is implemented by a Perl method that is defined in the file where the class definition is kept. The class definition is always kept in a `.pm` file, the contents of which are organized in a particular way. We will describe this organization as we move through this chapter.

For example, a class named `Mortgage` would be defined in a file named `Mortgage.pm`. Each method that can be executed on a particular `Mortgage` object would also be defined in this file.

Unlike traditional OO languages such as C++ and Java, in Perl there is no keyword named `class`. Rather, a class is just a Perl module, a `.pm` file, with certain other prerequisites.

11.3 Defining and Using Objects

A class usually provides a method for creating an object as well as methods for defining the behavior of an object. Although you may name the creation method whatever you wish, it is usually named `new` in honor of both C++ and Java, where it is mandatory.

The data contained in an object is composed of many pieces. A `Student` object, for example, might contain the attributes NAME, MAJOR, and COURSES. One way to model this in Perl code is to create an anonymous hash as follows:

```
#!/usr/bin/perl
#
#  object.pl
#
$student = {
    NAME => Mike,
    MAJOR => Math,
    COURSES => [Calc, Trig, DiffE ]
};
print $student->{NAME},"\n";
print $student->{MAJOR},"\n";
print "@{$student->{COURSES}}", "\n";
print "@{$student->{COURSES}}[1]", "\n";

% object.pl
Mike
Math
Calc Trig DiffE
Trig
%
```

The above code demonstrates a way to create a set of related data. But an object should be constructed more formally, and in such a way that it knows to which class it belongs. In particular, there should be a way to create as many new `Student` objects as an application requires. What is needed is correct packaging. To do this, we create a `Student.pm` file whose first line is:

```
package Student;
```

Ultimately, we are creating a new data type named `Student`. In this file, we place a method for the creation of a `Student` object. Any code in this method would look similar to the code above. The application could use this method as many times as it wished to create as many `Student` objects as it needed. Methods to implement behaviors for `Student` objects are required as well. We will see them shortly. Here's how the file would appear with this new packaging:

```
#  Student.pm
#
package Student;
sub new
{
    my($pkg, $name, $major, @courses) = @_;
```

continued...

```
    my $s = {    NAME => $name,
                 MAJOR => $major,
                 COURSES => [ @courses ]
              };
    bless $s, $pkg;
    return $s;
}
1;
```

The first method that we will illustrate is called `new`. Its purpose is to construct a new
`Student` object. Note that the name of this method is irrelevant, but in deference to both
C++ and Java, most Perl coders choose the name `new`. Further, this method is typically
referred to as the constructor for the `Student` class because it is used to construct new
`Student` objects.

The intent is to invoke the constructor and pass to it the arguments it needs to build a
`Student` object. The Perl syntax for invoking the constructor is shown below. For reasons
that will become clear shortly, we also pass the package name as the first argument.

```
@courses = (Calc, Trig, DiffE);
$s1 = Student::new(Student, Mike, Math, @courses);
```

There is an alternative and equivalent way in which to invoke the `Student::new`
method:

```
$s1 = new Student(Mike, Math, @courses);
```

The alternative method is closer to the C++ and Java syntax. When you use this form,
Perl translates it to the original form. The following two statements are equivalent:

```
$s1 = new Student(Mike, Math, @courses);
$s1 = Student::new(Student, Mike, Math, @courses);
```

There is a third notation that is equivalent to the first two:

```
$s1 = Student->new(Mike, Math, @courses);
```

The `new` method creates a reference to an anonymous hash, and then fills the hash with
parameters. Before this method returns the reference, it adds to the reference an additional
property, the package name, that is, `Student`. This is accomplished with the `bless` function. Now the reference is a blessed hash reference and not simply a hash reference. This
additional property will be useful when we discuss inheritance. Inheritance is the cornerstone of object orientation. It allows you to derive one class from another. For example, a
`GradStudent` class could be derived from a `Student` class.

```
bless $s, $pkg;
```

An application using a `Student` object might look like this:

```
#!/usr/bin/perl
#
#    Student1.pl
#
use Student;
@courses = qw(Calc Trig DiffE);
$s1 = new Student(Mike, Math, @courses);
print $$s1{NAME}, "\n";
print $s1->{MAJOR}, "\n";
print "@{$$s1{COURSES}}", "\n";
print @{$s1->{COURSES}}[0], "\n";
```

```
% Student1.pl
Mike
Math
Calc Trig DiffE
Trig
%
```

11.3.1   Information hiding

Although the above code works fine, there are a few problems with it. First, it is cumbersome to use all of the punctuation symbols to satisfy the syntax requirements of Perl. Second, it places a burden on the writer because the writer must be familiar with the field names. For example, see if you can determine why the code below would produce incorrect results:

```
use Student;
@courses = (Calc, Trig, DiffE);
$s1 = new Student(Mike, Math, @courses);
print $$s1{name}, "\n";
print $s1->{name}, "\n";
print "@{$$s1{COURCES}}", "\n";
print @{$s1->{COURCES}}[0], "\n";
```

The developer misspelled the last two indices. They should be COURSES, not COURCES. Users of the `Student.pm` file, that is, users of the `Student` class, should not have to worry about any information inside the `Student.pm` file, let alone the spelling of the keys.

These problems may be overcome by writing methods that deliver object data rather than allowing direct access to the data. The disallowance of direct access to object data is called information hiding. Most OO languages will generate a compiler error when direct access to hidden data is attempted. Perl just expects you to "play by the rules," as it has no such feature.

11.3.2   Accessor and mutator methods

A good class is expected to provide methods to retrieve data from an object. These methods are called accessor methods. Likewise, a good class is expected to provide methods to alter the state of an object. These methods are called mutator methods.

Other methods might simulate other behavior. For example, in the Student class, there could be a method that determines how many courses a student is taking.

The Student class should have methods that allow the setting and getting of object data. Functionality like setname and getname should be supported.

```
use Student;
$s1 = new Student(Mike, Math, Trig, Calc);
$s2 = new Student(Susan, Dynamics, Statics, Art);
$s1 -> setname(Michael);
$name1 = $s1->getname();
```

When a method is called on a blessed reference, such as the last two lines above, Perl knows to look in the appropriate .pm file to find the correct function. In reality, Perl turns the last two above calls into:

```
Student::setname($s1, Michael);
Student::getname($s1);
```

so the reference is always passed as the first argument to the method in question. Here is a revised Student.pm file:

```
#   Revised Student.pm
#
package Student;
sub new
{   my($pkg, $name, $major, @courses) = @_;
    my $s = {         NAME => $name,
                      MAJOR => $major,
                      COURSES => [ @courses ]
             };
    bless $s, $pkg;
    return $s;
}
```

continued...

```
sub getname
{   my ($ref) = shift;
    $ref->{NAME};
}
sub setname
{   my ($ref, $name) = @_;
    $ref -> {NAME} = $name;
}
1;
```

11.3.3   Other instance methods

A real class would have some other methods as well. Here are some suggestions:

```
@courses = $s1 -> getcourses();
$s1 -> addcourses(Geometry, Algebra);
$numcourses = $s1 -> numcourses();
$s1 -> getcourse(1);
```

We'll show how to write the `addcourses` method. Check the `Student.pm` file for the others.

```
sub addcourses
{
        my($ref, @newones) = @_;
        push(@{$ref ->{COURSES}}, @newones);
}
```

11.3.4   Writing an accessor and a mutator as one method

Remember that an accessor method retrieves the value of some object data.

```
$s1 = new Student(Susan, Dynamics, Statics, Art);
$name1 = $s1->getname();
```

Also, recall that a mutator method sets the value for some object data.

```
$s1 = new Student(Susan, Dynamics, Statics, Art);
$s1->setname("Soozie");
```

Some Perl programmers use the same function to perform both the getting and setting of object data. To do this, the programmer takes advantage of the fact that in the setting of object data, there is one real argument passed to the method, while in the getting of object data, there are zero real arguments sent to the method. If we call this method `name`, then the code for both uses would be as follows:

```
$s1 = new Student(Susan, Dynamics, Statics, Art);
$s1->name("Soozie");              # set the name
$thename = $s1->name();           # get the name
```

You can see above that in the setting of name, there is no need to capture the returned value from this method, although if you wanted, you could write the function so that it returned the old value of name. Here's the code for the dual-purpose name method:

```
sub name
{
    my $ref = shift;
    if ( @_ )          # if another argument
    {                  # then must be setting the name
        my($oldname) = $ref->{NAME};
        $ref->{NAME} = shift;
        $oldname;
    }
    else               # if no other args
    {                  # then must be getting the name
        $ref->{NAME};
    }
}
```

As usual, the first argument is the reference and it is shifted into $ref. Then, @_ is tested to see if any arguments remain. If there is one, the old name is tucked away in $oldname, the new name is shifted into the hash, and $oldname is returned. If there are no remaining arguments, the current name is returned.

If name is invoked with an argument, it could be used in two ways:

```
#
#   simply set name and ignore the returned value
#
$s1->name("Michael");
#
#   set the name, but remember the previous name
#
$oldname = $s1->name("Michael");
```

11.3.5 Destructors

Some classes use resources such as files and sockets. It's essential that these resources be given back to the system when the object that is using them is no longer in use. Toward this end, Perl will execute the special subroutine DESTROY if you provide it in your class. OO languages refer to such a method as a destructor. It must be named DESTROY and it will be called automatically whenever the space for an object is garbage-collected.

In the previous `Student` example, a destructor is not needed because no resources are used. If we provided one, it would still be executed each time a blessed reference was no longer in use.

Here's an example of the `DESTROY` method. Keep in mind that most of the work in this particular `DESTROY` method is for illustrative purposes:

```perl
sub DESTROY
{
    my ($ref) = shift;
    print "destroying ";
    print $ref -> {NAME}, "\n";
}

#!/usr/bin/perl
#
#   destroy.pl
#
use Student;
$s1 = new Student(Mike, Math, Trig, Calc);
{
    my($s2) = new Student(Jane, Math, Trig);
}
$s3 = new Student(Peter, Math, Trig, Calc);

% destroy.pl
destroying Jane
destroying Peter
destroying Mike
%
```

Notice that the objects are destroyed when zero references are pointing to them or when the program terminates.

11.3.6   Class methods

Thus far, the data that we have seen is contained within each object. Likewise, the methods that we have seen are executed on objects. However, some programs may require that there be data "of a class" rather than "of an object." This can be accomplished by using `my` variables at file scope. For example, suppose we wanted to track the number of objects that were currently allocated at any given time in a program. We would add the following `my` variable to the `Student.pm` file:

```perl
my $count = 0;
```

add the following line to the constructor:

```
$count++;
```

add the following line to the destructor:

```
$count--;
```

and add the function howmany to return $count:

```
sub howmany
{
    return $count;
}
```

The interesting thing about the howmany method is that it does not operate on an object, but rather it operates on the class.

Here is a program that uses the method named howmany. Notice how it is invoked vs. how object methods are invoked:

```
Student::howmany()
print $s3->getname();


#!/usr/bin/perl
#
#   count.pl
#
use Student;
$s1 = new Student(Mike, Math, Trig, Calc);
print Student::howmany(), " objects\n";
{
    my $s2 = new Student(Jane, Math, Trig);
    print Student::howmany(), " objects\n";
}
$s3 = new Student(Peter, Math, Trig, Calc);
print Student->howmany(), " objects\n";
print $s3->getname();

% count.pl
1 objects
2 objects
destroying Jane
2 objects
peter
destroying Peter
destroying Mike
%
```

11.4 Inheritance

The `bless` function gives more information to a reference. It forces the reference to be of a type, `Student` in this case. This has several uses in Perl as we shall see. Using "public" methods to access "private" data is not the only benefit of the OO approach. Another important principle, inheritance, is the cornerstone of object orientation.

Inheritance is one of the principle ways of implementing code reuse. Like all powerful features, it should only be used when necessary. Inheritance implements the "is-a" relationship. The following are examples of inheritance relationships:

- A `Directory` is a type of `File`.

- A `Manager` is a type of `Employee`.

- A `Car` is a type of `MovingVehicle`.

- A `Circle` is a `Shape`.

In the `File`/`Directory` relationship, we say that `File` is the superclass and `Directory` is a subclass. Likewise, `Shape` is the superclass and `Circle` is a subclass. C++ programmers tend to use the words base class and derived class for superclass and subclass, respectively.

If we already have a `File` class, we should not have to build the `Directory` class from scratch. Since a `Directory` is a `File`, any `Directory` object should be able to reuse (without rewriting) all of the `File` methods.

To illustrate inheritance, suppose that we have a special kind of student, a `GradStudent`. For simplicity, let's say a `GradStudent` is a `Student` with a salary. The `GradStudent` class needs to specify that it is a derived class of `Student`. This is done by using the special `@ISA` array, as you will see below. Any `GradStudent` object can reuse all methods defined in the `Student` package.

`GradStudent` must implement a constructor and possibly a destructor, and any incremental behavior that specializes a `GradStudent`, such as `getsalary`, and `setsalary`.

11.4.1 SUPER

The constructor for a derived class can call its parent class constructor by using the keyword `SUPER`. Here is the constructor for a `GradStudent`. Notice how `SUPER` is used in the new method in the file `GradStudent.pm`:

```
#
#    GradStudent.pm
#
package GradStudent;
use Student;
#
#    The next line tells Perl that
#    GradStudent is derived from Student
#
ISA=qw(Student);
#
#    GradStudent's new
#
sub new
{
    my $pkg = shift;
    my ($name, $major, $salary, @subjs) = @_;
#
#    Call new in the SUPER (Student) class
#    In the call, $pkg == GradStudent
#
    my $obj=$pkg->SUPER::new($name, $major, @subjs);
    $obj ->{'SALARY'} = $salary;
    $obj;
};
sub salary
{
    my($pkg) = shift;
    @_ ? $pkg ->{SALARY} = shift : $pkg ->{SALARY};
}
1;
```

When a new GradStudent is created, the data for it is passed to the new constructor in the same way that a Student's new constructor is called. Then, there is a call to the Student constructor. It is necessary for the GradStudent constructor to call the Student constructor to construct the Student portion of the GradStudent.

```
    my $obj=$pkg->SUPER::new($name, $major, @subjs);
```

The line above calls the new method in the Student class in such a way that the first argument in the call is GradStudent. This is because GradStudent is the value of $pkg. When Student::new returns, the returned reference has been blessed as a GradStudent, not as a Student. Finally, the salary field is added to the reference and the reference is returned.

The line:

```
@ISA=qw(Student);
```

tells Perl that the `GradStudent` class is a subclass of `Student`, and thus any `GradStudent` object can freely reuse all `Student` methods. Here's a program that demonstrates the use of the `GradStudent` class:

```
#!/usr/bin/perl
#
#   grad.pl
#
use Student;
use GradStudent;
$stu1 = new Student(Mike, Math, Alg, Calc, Trig);
print $stu1->getname(), "\n";
print $stu1->getmajor(), "\n";
$gs=new GradStudent(Dave, Math, 25000, Calc, Trig);
#
#   reuse Student functionality
#
print $gs->getname(), "\n";
print $gs->getmajor(), "\n";
#
#   a new method
#
print $gs->salary(), "\n";
```

11.4.2   Polymorphism

Consider a set of classes related through inheritance. The classic example is a set of classes derived from a geometric `Shape` class. Each class, say `Circle`, `Square`, `Triangle`, etc. would have its own `draw`, `area`, and `perimeter` methods. Each of these methods would have a class-specific implementation. The skeleton code for an application for such a scenario would be:

```
$circle1 = new Circle(5);        # create a circle
$square1 = new Square(10);       # create a square
print $circle1->area(),"\n";     # area of circle
print $square1->area(),"\n";     # area of square
```

The capability of a language to differentiate among several methods, all of which have the same name in the same inheritance hierarchy, is called polymorphism. Polymorphism is implemented in Perl through the `bless` function. When an object is blessed, it is bound to a class. When a method is called on the object, the chosen method comes from the class bound to the object.

Here's an example to illustrate polymorphism with respect to `Student` and `GradStudent`. To add credibility to the example, we added a method named `type` to each class. This function reveals the type of the reference; that is, it simply returns either the string `Student` or `GradStudent`.

```perl
#!/usr/bin/perl
#
#  poly.pl
#
use Student;
use GradStudent;
$s1 = new Student(Mike, Math, Calc,  Trig);
$s2= new Student(Susan, Dynamics, Statics, Art);
$gs1 = new GradStudent(Alan, Math, 25000, Calc);
$gs2 = new GradStudent(Roger, Math, 25000, Trig);
@people = ($s1, $s2, $gs1, $gs2);
foreach $person (@people)
{
    print $person -> getname();
    print ": ",  $person -> type(), "\n";
}


% poly.pl
Mike Student
Susan Student
Alan GradStudent
Roger GradStudent
destroying Roger
destroying Susan
destroying Alan
destroying Mike
%
```

Of importance is the fact that @people contains references to both `Student` and `GradStudent` objects. Nevertheless, when the `type` method is invoked, the correct class-specific `type` method is chosen based on the class into which the reference was blessed. `type` represents a method whose behavior varies over derived classes. The situation is different for the `getname` method, where the behavior is invariant over specialized classes; thus, it is simply reused by all derived classes.

Exercises

1. Create a class named `Vehicle`. Any `Vehicle` object should have the following attributes: `fuel` and `mpg`. Write methods so that the following code will execute:

```
$car = new Vehicle("20gallons", "30mpg");
print $car->fuel(), "\n";        #    20
print $car->mpg(), "\n";         #    30
print $car->range(), "\n";       #   600
$car ->fuel(40);
print $car->range(), "\n";       #  1200
```

2. Now, derive the `Airplane` class from `Vehicle`. `Airplane` objects should have an additional attribute, `airspeed`. `Airplane` should also add the method `getspeed`.

3. Create a class named `Shape` that stores an important value for a few `Shape` objects (such as `radius` for `Circle` and `side` for `Square`). `Shape` should also define a method called `parameter` that returns the key value. Next, define a few shapes such as `Circle` and `Square`. For each of these, define particular `area` and `perimeter` methods. Create a few objects of each type, place them in an array, and loop through the array calling all three methods on each object in the array.

12

CLIENT/SERVER APPLICATIONS

This chapter explores some of the possibilities of writing client/server applications with sockets. After reviewing some networking fundamentals, we'll give some examples of writing clients that connect to real servers. Then we will write a few servers.

12.1 Introduction

A server is a program in execution that provides some service. One server may offer a file transfer service, while another server may offer the time of day. A client is a program that needs some service, such as a file transfer or the time of day. In this chapter, we will show how to write clients and servers, and how to connect them to each other.

12.1.1 TCP networks

Two programs communicate over a network using a set of rules called protocols. Several well-known protocols are in wide use today. Among them, the Transmission Control Protocol, TCP, and the Internet Protocol, IP, are two standard protocols for communicating over the Internet.

TCP/IP provides two types of data delivery mechanisms: TCP and the User Datagram Protocol, or UDP. TCP is a reliable data delivery service. This service guarantees data delivery by using error detection mechanisms and acknowledgments. Before any data transmission, both communicating programs need to establish a TCP connection.

UDP is a best-effort data delivery service that is connectionless and does not guarantee reliable data delivery. For instance, an application delivering sound or images might use UDP service.

Typically, a server starts execution first and continues to accept requests without terminating. A client starts execution only when a service is required and usually terminates after its request has been satisfied; or, after the service is provided, the client may make another request of the server. For example, the client may request another file.

12.1.2 Internet addresses

A client/server application is an example of two communicating programs on a network. The server program provides a service to the client program. Typical server applications include echo service, daytime service, telnet service, and File Transfer Protocol (FTP) service.

Each computer on the Internet has a name and a 32-bit address. The name is referred to as the domain name and the address is referred to as the IP address. The IP address is typically expressed as four dot-separated integers.

```
www.sun.com              192.18.97.241
www.ford.com             164.109.71.245
www.microsoft.com        207.46.230.220
```

The Domain Name System (DNS) translates a domain name into an IP address whenever this is necessary.

12.1.3 Ports

Since there may be more than one service running on the same machine, each service is assigned a port. A client wishing to communicate with a server needs to know the address of the server and the port assigned to it. Well-known services, such as `ftp` (21) and `http` (80), are assigned reserved ports. On Unix, port numbers under 1000 cannot be used unless you are the root user. Initially, a server establishes the port number on which the communication will occur. When a client connects to a server, the server obtains the address of the client and can therefore send information back to the client if necessary.

The two communicating programs may reside on different machines, provided the two machines are connected by a similar network, or the two communicating programs may reside on the same machine.

12.1.4 Sockets

A socket is a software abstraction that behaves as an endpoint for communicating processes. Sockets were originally developed for Berkeley Unix systems in the 1970s, but a version of this abstraction currently exists on all operating systems.

The socket programming interface takes various arguments that specify which protocols should be used in the underlying data exchange. We will describe only those parameters that are used to do TCP/IP programming in the Internet domain, although other domains exist.

In older Perl programs, the `socket` subroutine required several parameters as shown below:

```
$AF_INET = 2;                     # AF = address family
$SOCK_STREAM = 1;                 # Stream Socket
$proto_numb = (getprotobyname('tcp'))[3];
socket(S, $AF_INET ,$SOCK_STREAM, $proto_numb) || die "$!";
```

The constants specify the type of stream. There are different stream types for different delivery services. For example, TCP requires one type of stream, while UDP requires another. There are also different domains, or families, such as the Internet domain or the Unix domain. Consult a networking text to get all the details of these parameters. The last argument to the socket call is the protocol number of the protocol being used.

Once you have a socket, you need to bind the client address to the socket. However, the bind function must have this information in the correct format. It is this kind of detail that makes this style of programming difficult.

```
$sockaddr = 'S n a4 x8';          # correct format
$hostname = 'localhost';          # hostname
($client_addr) = (gethostbyname($host_name))[4];
$client = pack($sockaddr, $AF_INET,0, $client_addr);
bind(S, $client) || die "bind: $!";
```

Now the client must execute the connect function to connect to the server. Of course, the server must already have been started or the client will fail at this step. The second parameter to the connect function must be a packed address of the remote server. The packing and connecting code is as follows:

```
$port_number = 1500;              # for example
$server_name = 'localhost';       # hostname of server
($server_addr) = (gethostbyname($server_name))[4];
$server = pack($sockaddr, $AF_INET, $port_number, $server_addr);
connect(S, $server) || die "connect: $!";
```

Once the connect function has been executed, the client can send data over socket S. In other words:

```
print "send to display\n";
print S "sent to server\n";
```

If you put all of this together, you have:

```
$AF_INET = 2;                          # AF = address family
$SOCK_STREAM = 1;                      # stream socket
$proto_numb = (getprotobyname('tcp'))[3];
socket(S, $AF_INET ,$SOCK_STREAM, $proto_numb) || die "$!";
$sockaddr = 'S n a4 x8';               # correct format
$hostname = 'localhost';
($client_addr) = (gethostbyname($host_name))[4];
$client = pack($sockaddr, $AF_INET,0, $client_addr);
bind(S, $client) || die "bind: $!";
$port_number = 1500;                   # for example
$server_name = 'localhost';
($server_addr) = (gethostbyname($server_name))[4];
$server = pack($sockaddr, $AF_INET, $port_number, $server_addr);
connect(S, $server) || die "connect: $!";
```

12.1.5 `Socket.pm`

Beginning with the Perl 5.04 distribution, there is an easier way to create a socket for a client. Included with this distribution is the file `Socket.pm`. This module encapsulates many of the details from above, which are correct for the host operating system. By using this module, the Perl programmer is freed from the burden of knowing all the details.

Using `Socket.pm`, here is the equivalent code for the more lengthy code shown above:

```
use IO::Socket;
$site = 'localhost';
$sock = IO::Socket::INET->new(    PeerAddr => $site,
                                  PeerPort => 1500,
                                  Proto => 'tcp',
                                  Type => SOCK_STREAM
                     ) or die "can't create socket\n";
```

The variable `$sock` is the same as socket `S` in the previous code.

12.2 Writing Clients

Eventually, we will write our own clients and connect them to our own servers. In this section, we will demonstrate how to write a few clients, each of which connects to some real, existing service.

12.2.1 A daytime client

The U.S. government has a site at which a daytime server is running. Similar to other servers, this server waits for a connection from clients. When a client connects, the time of day is passed back to the client. The exact format of the time may be different for different daytime servers. Here is the daytime client using `Socket.pm`:

```perl
#!/usr/bin/perl
#
#  daytime.pl
#
use IO::Socket;
$site = "time-A.timefreq.bldrdoc.gov";
$sock = IO::Socket::INET->new(     PeerAddr => $site,
                                   PeerPort => 13,
                                   Proto => 'tcp',
                                   Type => SOCK_STREAM
                          ) or die "can't create socket\n";

$bytes = read($sock, $time, 100);
$time = substr($time, 1);
chop($time);
print "It is $time at $site";
```

And here are the results of running this program:

```
% daytime
It is 52167 01-09-15 15:49:42 50 0 0 793.0 UTC(NIST) * at
time-A.timefreq.bldrdoc.gov
%
```

The `read` function requests to have a specific number of bytes from any handle. In this case, the data comes from the socket `$sock`, that is, from the daytime server. The actual number of bytes transferred is returned from `read`. Various daytime servers send the time of day in various formats. You can see above that the actual time of day is the string listed below:

```
01-09-15 15:49:42
```

12.2.2   An echo client

In the above example, the client did not send any data to the server. Rather, the server sent the time of day and the client read the response with:

```
$bytes = read($sock, $time, 100);
```

In some cases, the client will send some data to the server and then the server will send a response back to the client. As an example, there are some servers that offer an echo service on Port 7. This may be useful if you wish to test your server. The echo client below connects to the echo server running on my local machine:

```perl
#!/usr/bin/perl
#
#       echoclient.pl
#
use IO::Socket;
$sock = IO::Socket::INET->new(     PeerAddr => 'localhost',
                                   PeerPort => 7,
                                   Proto => 'tcp',
                                   Type => SOCK_STREAM
                      ) or die "can't create socket\n";
print "ENTER DATA\n";
while(<STDIN>)
{
        chop;
        print "Just got $_ from user\n";
        print $sock "$_\n";
        $response = <$sock>;
        print "FROM SERVER: $response";
}
```

There is nothing special here. The client requests the user to enter some data. It is sent to the server that is waiting on Port 7 and then the server responds with the same string. The two lines below do the sending and receiving, respectively:

```perl
print $sock "$_\n";          # send to server
$response =  <$sock>;        # get from server
```

12.2.3   An FTP client

Most computers already have a client that handles file transfers to and from some foreign host. The program is typically called ftp. However, you might want to write your own client to automate certain parts of the process. To do this in Perl, you will need the Net::FTP module, which you can download from the Comprehensive Perl Archive Network (CPAN). Start your search at www.perl.com and look for the CPAN link. Once you have that module, you can code as follows:

```perl
#!/usr/bin/perl
#
#       ftpclient.pl
#
BEGIN {
   push(@INC, "libnet-1.0704");    # library dir
```

continued...

```
}
use Net::FTP;
$ftp = Net::FTP->new("172.16.1.53") || die;
$username = "user8";
$password = "password";
$ftp->login($username, $password) || die;
print "ftp'ed to 172.16.1.53\n";
foreach $file (@ARGV)
{
    $ftp -> put($file);
}
```

You can connect to the foreign host using either an IP address or a domain name:

```
$ftp = Net::FTP->new("172.16.1.53") || die;
```

Once connected, you'll have to go through the login and password phase of `ftp`:

```
$username = "user8";
$password = "password";
$ftp->login($username, $password) || die;
```

In the example above, we decided to transfer files whose names were given on the command line.

```
foreach $file (@ARGV)
{
    $ftp -> put($file);
    print "$file\n";
}
```

We also could have received a file using the following:

```
$ftp -> get($file);
```

There are more methods in the `FTP.pm` module than we have shown, but we wanted to demonstrate the main points here. The program would be executed as follows:

```
% ftpclient.pl file1 file2 file3
print "ftp'ed to 172.16.1.53\n";
sent file1
sent file2
sent file3
%
```

12.3 Writing Servers

A server is a program that exists to provide a service to as many clients that wish to connect to it. A server is usually started when a system is booted. After it has started, it usually runs forever. On Unix systems, these programs are called daemons.

12.3.1   A daytime server

Previously, we saw a daytime client connecting to a real daytime server. We could also have written the daytime server ourselves. The next example shows such a server. If you choose the pre-Perl 5 method of writing a server, the code gets a bit detailed and lengthy. However, in the interest of completeness, we will show how to write such a server.

The first part is getting the port number. We'll allow the user to enter the number on the command line. If the user does not enter a port number, then we will assume it's Port 2345. We'll also ensure that the port is composed of digits only.

```perl
($port_number) = @ARGV;
$port_number = 2345 unless $port_number;
if ($port_number !~ /^\d+$/) {
    print "$port_number is not an integer\n";
    die "Usage: $0 [port_number]\n";
}
```

The next part is getting a socket handle to communicate with the client. Once again, the socket call needs a few parameters:

```perl
($name,$aliases,$protocol_number) = getprotobyname('tcp');
$AF_INET = 2;              # DOMAIN
$SOCK_STREAM = 1;         # TYPE
socket(CS,$AF_INET, $SOCK_STREAM, $protocol_number)
                          || die "socket: $!";
```

Once a socket has been created, it must be attached to an address. This is the purpose of the bind function.

```perl
$sockaddr = 'S n a4 x8';
$server = pack($sockaddr, $AF_INET, $port_number,
                          "\0\0\0\0");
bind(CS, $server) || die "bind: $!";
print "Socket is bound...\n";
```

Next, the server listens for a connection with listen. listen alerts the operating system that this process will wait for no more than a certain number of requests on the socket. This is not a limit on the number of connections, but on the number of processes that can be waiting at a particular instant. The function returns a 1 if it succeeds or 0 if there is a problem.

```perl
listen(CS, 5) || die "listen: $!";
print "listening ...\n";
```

The server will now wait for a connection at the `accept` call. `accept` waits until a connection is made to this process and returns either the IP address of the connecting process or `FALSE` if there is a problem. `accept` also creates a second handle, `DS`, though which data is transmitted to and from the client.

```perl
($client_addr = accept(DS, CS)) || die $!;
```

As you can see once again, when you use the Perl 4 style of obtaining a socket, there is a wealth of possibilities for errors. The corresponding Perl 5 code, including the actual data transfer, would be:

```perl
#!/usr/bin/perl
#
#   newdaytimeserver.pl
#
require "ctime.pl";
use IO::Socket;
$server = IO::Socket::INET->new (LocalPort => 2345,
                        Type => SOCK_STREAM,
                        Reuse => 1,
                        Listen => 10
                        ) or die "can't create socket\n";
$connect = 1;
print "waiting for connection #$connect\n";
while($cli = $server->accept())
{       $date = ctime(time);
        print $cli "$date\n";
        $connect++;
        print "waiting for connection #$connect\n";
}
```

The slightly modified client is shown below. The client reads data in a slightly different way.

```perl
#!/usr/bin/perl
#
#   newdaytimeclient.pl
#
use IO::Socket;
```

continued...

```
$socket = IO::Socket::INET->new (  PeerAddr => 'localhost',
                                   PeerPort => 2345,
                                   Proto => "tcp",
                                   Type => SOCK_STREAM)

                          or die "can't create socket\n";
print "got a socket\n";
$date = <$socket>;
print "it is $date";
```

12.3.2   An expression server

In the next example, we will show a server that evaluates expressions sent by a client. The client receives the expressions from a user. This kind of processing introduces a little more complexity since both the client and server are sending data to one another. In this example, the client asks the user for a Perl expression and then sends it to the server for evaluation. The client ends when the user enters Q rather than an expression. The server is handed an expression and uses eval to evaluate it. It then returns the evaluated expression. Here is the client followed by the server:

```
#!/usr/bin/perl
#
#        evalclient.pl
#
use IO::Socket;
$socket = IO::Socket::INET->new (PeerAddr => 'localhost',
                    PeerPort => 2345,
                    Proto => "tcp",
                    Type => SOCK_STREAM)
                    or die "can't create socket\n";
while(1)
{
        print "Enter an expression or 'Q' to quit ";
        $expr = <STDIN>;                   # get user input
        chop;                              # nix the newline
        last if ( $expr =~ /^Q/i );        # should we quit?
        print $socket "$expr";             # send to server
        $ret = <$socket>;                  # receive results
        print "Received $ret\n";           # print results
}
close ($socket);
#!/usr/bin/perl
#
#        evalserver.pl
#
require "ctime.pl";
use IO::Socket;
$server = IO::Socket::INET->new (LocalPort => 2345,
                    Type => SOCK_STREAM,
```

continued...

```
                        Reuse => 1,
                        Listen => 10
                        )
                        or die "can't create socket\n";

$connect = 1;
print "waiting for connection #$connect\n";
while($cli = $server->accept())          # connection
{
       while(<$cli>)
       {
               print "Received $_";      # for debugging
               $result = eval ($_);      # eval expression
               print "Result is $result\n";
               print $cli "$result\n"; # return to client
       }
       $connect++;                       # count connections
       print "waiting for connection #$connect\n";
}
```

What follows is a session demonstrating the client's interaction with the user and the server. We must assume that the server has already been started.

```
% evalclient.pl
Enter an expression or 'Q' to quit 2 + 4
Received 6

Enter an expression or 'Q' to quit $b = 10
Received 10

Enter an expression or 'Q' to quit $b * 3
Received 1000

Enter an expression or 'Q' to quit Q
%
```

12.4 Iterative Servers

The previous example demonstrated how data can be exchanged in both directions over a socket. However, when a client connects to a server, the server should not only process that client's request, but it should also be capable of accepting other client requests. Here is an example of a server that exhibits this behavior:

```perl
#!/usr/bin/perl
#
#    iterative.pl
#
require "ctime.pl";
use IO::Socket;
$server = IO::Socket::INET->new
               (
                       LocalPort => 2345,
                       Type => SOCK_STREAM,
                       Reuse => 1,
                       Listen => 10
               )
               or die "can't create socket\n";
$connect = 1;
print "waiting for connection #$connect\n";
while($cli = $server->accept())
{
        if ( fork() == 0 )
        {
                print "received connection #$connect\n";
                while(<$cli>)
                {
                        print "received $_";
                        $result = eval ($_);
                        print "result is $result\n";
                        print $cli "$result\n";
                }
                print "terminating connection #$connect\n";
                exit 0;
        }
        $connect++;
        print "waiting for connection #$connect\n";
}
```

In the code above, when a connection from a client occurs, the server forks a copy of itself. If the fork returns zero, then the newly created Perl child process will handle this request while the Perl parent process will announce that it is waiting for another connection. When the child process finishes processing lines from the client, it must exit.

Not all operating systems are able to perform a fork. Originally, fork was implemented on Unix systems. As recently as 2000, fork was implemented on Windows NT systems. You'll have to check your system to see if it is able to perform the fork function.

Exercises

1. Create a client/server application where the client receives a filename from a user and then passes the name to the server. When the server returns the file to the client, the client then displays the file.

13

CGI PROGRAMMING
WITH PERL

When the Internet became commercialized, a lot of new ideas began to mushroom. With the advent of the World Wide Web and browser software, a new style of programming was born. Web pages now abound with HTML fill-in forms that are processed by back-end programs, most of which are Perl scripts. This style of programming, usually called Common Gateway Interface (CGI) scripting, is the subject of this chapter.

13.1 Introduction

The CGI is a standard by which applications external to Web servers can communicate with form documents rendered by browsers. CGI makes static Web pages come alive with dynamic content.

13.1.1 CGI languages

CGI programs are commonly referred to as scripts. However, not all CGI programs are written in a scripting language. For the most part, you choose whichever language you wish to implement a CGI. If you choose a compiled language, then your CGI program will exist as an executable file on your server. Some common programming languages used to implement the CGI standard include C, C++, Visual Basic, the Unix shells, and Perl. Among these, Perl is typically the language of choice because of its power in handling regular expressions and hashes. It should also be noted that a Java servlet provides functionality that is similar to a CGI script.

To develop Web applications using CGI, you must have at least a modest familiarity with HTML and knowledge of a programming language such as Perl. There are other bodies of knowledge that are integrated into the mix as well, including the Hypertext Transfer Protocol (HTTP), the client/server relationship, and the use of your browser.

13.1.2   HTML forms

CGI is typically used in conjunction with an HTML form to build database applications. The CGI standard specifies how your Web server interfaces with programs to extend the functionality of the Web server. Information on the CGI specification may be found at the World Wide Web Consortium site: `www.w3.org/hypertext/WWW/CGI`

CGI allows Web servers to execute programs and incorporate their output into text, graphics, etc., which are sent to Web browsers. Without CGI, the Web consists only of static documents and links to other pages or servers.

HTML forms on the Web are typically used for writing interactive quizzes, guestbook registrations, games, and a host of other e-commerce applications. Shown in Figure 13.1 is a typical form for a mortgage.

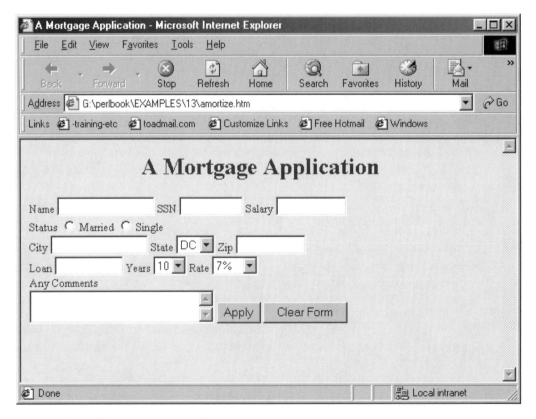

Figure 13.1   A mortgage application.

13.1.3 Web servers

A Web server is a piece of software whose task is to locate resources on the Web, as instructed by a user's request through a browser, and to respond with the requested resource. The resource is usually a file. There are many Web servers in use today. Probably the two most popular servers are the Apache Web Server for Unix machines and the Internet Information Server (IIS) for Windows machines.

13.1.4 Web browsers

The two most commonly used browsers are the Internet Explorer from Microsoft and various Navigator versions from Netscape. A browser is usually referred to as a client because it uses services provided by a Web server. When a browser talks to a server, it does so by sending the server a Uniform Resource Locator (URL). A URL is composed of several distinct parts with punctuation in between. The URL contains a protocol, a domain name, and perhaps some other information.

- Protocol   HTTP, telnet, FTP
- Domain name   `www.trainingetc.com`
- Rest of URL   other information

13.1.5 Starting a CGI program

A typical CGI application involves the following: A human fills out a form displayed by the browser. The browser collects this form data, determines the first part of the URL from the HTML, contacts the server, and supplies the remainder of the URL to the server. The server translates the remaining part of the URL into a path and filename. If this part of the URL points to a program instead of a static file, the server prepares the environment for the CGI program and launches it.

The CGI program executes and then reads the environment variables set up by the server, STDIN, or both. The CGI program sends the proper MIME (Multi-purpose Internet Mail Extention) headers to STDOUT. The CGI program sends the remaining output to STDOUT and terminates. The server sees when the CGI script terminates and breaks the connection with the browser. The browser displays the CGI output.

13.2 HTML and Forms

The hypertext markup language (HTML) is a language that is used to construct files to be displayed by a browser. HTML documents, that is, disk files, contain two types of information: keywords in the HTML language, called tags, and text to be displayed by a browser as a function of the tags. The tags themselves are enclosed in angled brackets (< >). A browser will display files differently depending on the type of file it is sent. Possible types include text files, directories, HTML files, image files, sound files, etc.

HTML documents contain two parts: a head part and a body part. Each part is delimited by tags. Ending tags are the same as beginning tags except that an ending tag also has the

/ character. Header information is placed within the HEAD tags, while the body of an HTML document is enclosed within BODY tags. All tags are enclosed within angled brackets. Here is a small HTML file and its rendering. Note that the <HTML> tag identifies the file as an HTML file. Comments may be placed in the file if you include them within a beginning tag, <!--, and an ending tag, -->.

```
<!--small.htm -->
<HTML>
<HEAD>
<TITLE>
This is the title
</TITLE>
</HEAD>
<BODY>
<H1>The body</H1><H2>of the document</H2>
<H3>is placed here</H3>
</BODY>
</HTML>
```

The text between the TITLE tags will appear as the title of the document when it is rendered. Various H tags control the relative height of the text. Consult a good HTML text for the entire set of tags, their meanings, and their attributes. Figure 13.2 is the rendering of the above file, small.htm.

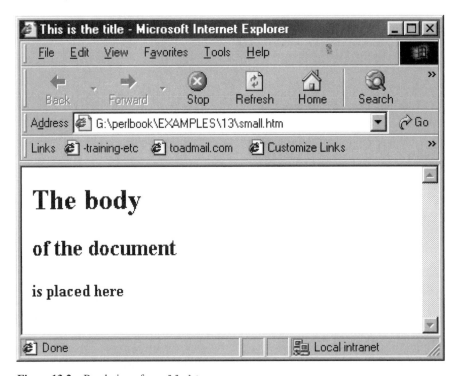

Figure 13.2   Rendering of small.htm.

Now we present a more complicated HTML file, the one that rendered the mortgage application earlier in this chapter. You will want to match these tags with their rendering, which is also displayed earlier in this chapter.

```
<!- amortize.htm -->
<HTML>
<HEAD><TITLE>A Mortgage Application</TITLE>
</HEAD>
<BODY BGCOLOR=Yellow Text=Blue>
<CENTER><H1>A Mortgage Application</H1></CENTER>
<FORM METHOD=GET ACTION="http://localhost/cgi-bin/mortgage.pl">
Name    <INPUT TYPE=text SIZE=15 NAME=name>
SSN     <INPUT TYPE=text SIZE=9 NAME=ssn>
Salary  <INPUT TYPE=text SIZE=10 NAME=salary>
<BR>
Status  <INPUT TYPE=radio NAME=status VALUE="Yes">
Married <INPUT TYPE=radio NAME=status VALUE="No"> Single
<BR>
City    <INPUT TYPE=text SIZE=15 NAME=city>
State   <SELECT NAME=state>
        <OPTION>DC<OPTION>MD<OPTION>VA
        </SELECT>
Zip     <INPUT TYPE=text SIZE=10 NAME=zip>
<BR>
Loan Amt<INPUT TYPE=text SIZE=10 name=loan>
Years   <SELECT name=years>
        <OPTION>10<OPTION>20<OPTION>30
        </SELECT>
Rate    <SELECT name=rate>
        <OPTION>7%<OPTION> 7.5%<OPTION> 8%
        <OPTION>8.5%<OPTION> 9%<OPTION> 9.5%
        <OPTION> 10%
        </SELECT>
<BR>Any Comments<BR>
<TEXTAREA ROWS=2 COLS=25 name=comments> </TEXTAREA>
<INPUT TYPE=submit VALUE="Apply">
<INPUT TYPE=reset VALUE="Clear Form">
</FORM>
</BODY>
</HTML>
```

13.2.1   Form tags

The HTML seen above is responsible for the previous mortgage form, although we have altered the text somewhat so it would fit on this printed page. A form can be placed anywhere in an HTML document. The form is created by the <FORM> and </FORM> tags. When the user clicks the Apply button, the browser sends the form data to the server. When the user clicks the Clear Form button, the form data is erased.

Note that the FORM tag has an ACTION attribute whose value is a URL, the CGI script to be executed when this form is submitted. In this case, the script is on the local machine and its name is amortize.pl in the server's cgi-bin directory. Where the scripts are actually kept on a server is a server configuration issue.

FORM tags have many INPUT tags. Each INPUT tag places a form element on the form. The TYPE attribute determines the kind of element that is placed on the form, that is, a text field, a button, a checkbox, or some other type. There are also a few special types, SUBMIT and CLEAR, which yield buttons. In the HTML code, there are several text fields, a few mutually exclusive radio buttons, a few list boxes, a text area, an Apply button, and a Clear Form button.

It's very important to notice that all of the INPUT types must have a NAME attribute associated with them. When the CGI script processes the form data, these names and the values entered into these elements become associated and ultimately parsed by the CGI script.

13.2.2   GET method vs. POST method

Another important aspect of the CGI is the method used to send form data to the server and ultimately to the Perl script. There are several methods, but the most common ones are GET and POST, either of which is specified by the ACTION attribute of the FORM tag. When the GET method is used, the data is sent to the script through environment variables. When the POST method is used, the data is sent to the script via STDIN. Your script determines which request method is used via the %ENV associative array constructed by the server and used by all CGI scripts. The exact reference is $ENV{REQUEST_METHOD}.

GET is the default method. It sends request information as a set of parameters appended to the URL. These parameters are also available through the %ENV array. GET limits the amount of data that can be sent to the script, whereas POST has no limit. If your HTML form specifies the POST method, then the form data filled in by the user is ultimately sent to the script via STDIN. The script must be prepared to read the data regardless of how it is sent.

To illustrate what the URL string looks like when the GET method has been chosen, let's look at a simple form. First the HTML will be shown, and then we will show the rendering of the page by the browser (see Figure 13.3).

```
<!-- calc.htm -->
<HTML>
<HEAD>
<TITLE>CALCULATOR</TITLE>
</HEAD>
<BODY BGCOLOR=Red Text=White>
<H1><CENTER>A CALCULATOR</CENTER></H1>
<FORM METHOD=GET ACTION="http://localhost/cgi-bin/eval.pl">
<CENTER>Enter Expression</CENTER>
<CENTER><INPUT TYPE=text NAME=expression></CENTER>
<PRE>            <!-- PRE preserves the spacing -->
<CENTER><H2>
```

continued...

```
decimal <INPUT TYPE=radio NAME=base VALUE=decimal CHECKED>
octal   <INPUT TYPE=radio NAME=base VALUE=octal>
binary  <INPUT TYPE=radio NAME=base VALUE=binary>
hex     <INPUT TYPE=radio NAME=base VALUE=hex></H2> </CENTER>
</PRE>
<HR>
<CENTER><INPUT TYPE=submit VALUE="Evaluate Expression">
</CENTER>
<BR>
<CENTER><INPUT TYPE=reset VALUE="Clear Expression"></CENTER>
<HR></FORM></BODY></HTML>
```

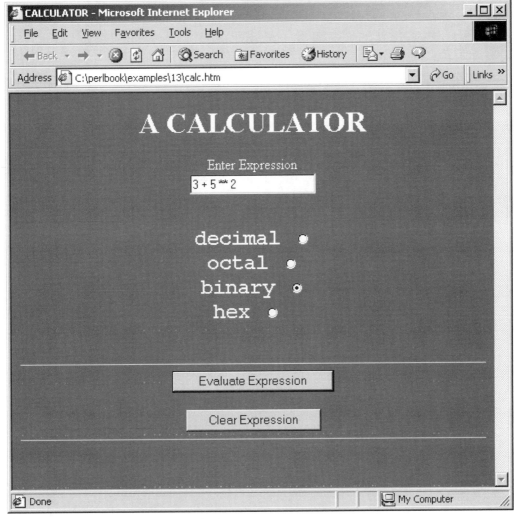

Figure 13.3 An Expression calculator.

When the user selects the `Evaluate Expression` button, the browser constructs the data string that will be appended to the URL string in the `ACTION` attribute of the `FORM` tag. For example, in the form above the user has entered the expression 3 + 5 ** 2 and has checked `binary`.

13.2.3 HTML form element names

This is where the names of the elements enter the picture. From the HTML form, you can see that the text field has the name `expression`, while the radio buttons have the name `base`. The browser constructs pairs of information. There is one pair for each input element. The pair consists of the name of the element taken from the HTML file and the value of the element as entered by the user. For a text field, the value is what the user types; for a set of radio buttons, the value is whatever appears in the `VALUE` attribute of the checked item. In this example, we have:

```
expression=3 + 5 ** 2
base=binary
```

13.2.4 URL encoding

There is another issue. When the browser sends punctuation or blanks to the server, the browser encodes them using a simple scheme known as URL encoding. In this scheme, each blank becomes a plus sign (+) and most punctuation characters become %xx, where each x represents a hexadecimal digit. Thus, the actual data sent to the server is:

```
expression=3+%2B+5+**+2
base=binary
```

The browser takes each of the pairs above and joins them with a & between the pairs so that the encoding now becomes:

```
expression=3+%2B+5+**+2&base=binary
```

Finally, the browser takes the value of the `ACTION` attribute of the `FORM` tag, joins a ? to it, and then joins the above pairs. The final URL constructed by the browser is:

```
http://localhost/cgi-bin/eval.pl?
expression=3+%2B+5+**+2&base=binary
```

Eventually, the server will send all information following the ? to the CGI program via the environment variable $ENV{QUERY_STRING}.

The server is also responsible for setting the environment for the script. The CGI script needs to determine how the data is sent. It simply checks the environment array, $ENV{REQUEST_METHOD}. If the value there is GET, the script reads the data from $ENV{QUERY_STRING}; if the value is POST, the script must check $ENV{CONTENT_LENGTH} and then use the read function to read the data from STDIN. In either case, the script needs to parse data of the form:

```
var1=value1&var2=value2&var3=value3...etc.
```

13.3   Relationship between Server and CGI Script

Keep in mind that servers extend their functionality by using CGI scripts. The server starts these scripts, and the two processes together constitute a parent and child relationship. When the CGI script wants to send output back to the server, it does so by using the print command.

HTTP demands that the server response contain header information before any data is sent. One of these headers is the content-type header, which must precede any data that the script sends and must be followed immediately by a blank line. Thus, all scripts will have the following line, which specifies the type of document being returned as the first print function. There are other headers, but we are not concerned with them here.

```
print "content-type: text/html\n\n";
```

Beyond that, the script contains the "business logic" for which it was invoked.

Below we will show the script, eval.pl, that does the expression calculation. To test this script or any other script, you will not only need an HTTP server, but you will also need to know where in the server directories to install your Web pages and scripts. Since this is a server-dependent activity, you will need to consult your server documentation.

13.3.1   A Perl CGI script

Now we will look at an actual Perl script, the one that processes the expression form from above. In general, the Perl script needs to parse the data from the query string, implement any business logic it deems necessary, and formulate some HTML to send back to the browser through the server. Often, there are some database inquiries that are part of the business logic.

```perl
#!/usr/bin/perl
#
#   eval.pl
#
require "ctime.pl";
$date = ctime(time);
print "content-type: text/html\n\n";
print "<H1><CENTER>EVALUATOR<CENTER></H1>";
print "<H1><CENTER>ON $date<CENTER></H1>";
if ( $ENV{REQUEST_METHOD} eq "GET" )
{
    $data = $ENV{QUERY_STRING};
}
else
{
    read(STDIN, $data, $ENV{CONTENT_LENGTH});
}
@pairs = split('&', $data);
foreach $item (@pairs)
{
    ($name, $value) = split("=", $item);
    $value =~ s/\+/ /g;
    $value =~ s/%([0-9A-Za-z][0-9a-zA-Z])/
                      pack("c",hex($1))/ge;
    $input{$name} = $value;
}
print "<H1><CENTER>YOU HAVE CHOSEN<CENTER></H1>";
print "<H1><CENTER>$input{base}<CENTER></H1>";
$result = eval $input{expression};
if ( $input{base} eq "octal")
{
    $val = sprintf "%o", $result;
}
elsif ( $input{base} eq "hex")
{
    $val = sprintf "%x", $result;
}
elsif ( $input{base} eq "binary")
{
    $val = unpack("B32",pack("N", $result));
    $val =~ s/^0*//;
}
else
{
    $val = $result;
}
print "<TABLE BORDER=2 ALIGN=CENTER>";
print "<TH>EXPRESSION</TH><TH>VALUE</TH>";
print "<H1><TR><TD ALIGN=CENTER>$input{expression}</TD>";
print "<TD ALIGN=CENTER>$val</TD></TR>";
print "</TABLE>";
```

The HTML shown in the `eval.pl` script is a little complex if you do not understand tables.

The HTML code prepares an HTML table. These tables contain table header tags, `<TH>`, table row tags, `<TR>`, and table data tags, `<TD>`. After returning the content type and date, the script determines the method by which it was invoked and reads the form data accordingly:

```
if ( $ENV{REQUEST_METHOD} eq "GET" )
{
    $data = $ENV{QUERY_STRING};
}
else
{
    read(STDIN, $data, $ENV{CONTENT_LENGTH});
}
```

The next step is to take the query string and split it into (name, value) pairs:

```
@pairs = split('&', $data);
```

The script then splits each pair into its corresponding name and value. Each `$value` must now be decoded:

```
$value =~ s/\+/ /g;
$value =~ s/%([0-9A-Za-z][0-9a-zA-Z])/
            pack("c",hex($1))/ge;
```

Blanks are restored from their encoded plus signs. With vintage Perl, the `%xx` encodings are decoded into their original character. And finally, an associative array named `%input` is built from each of the (name, value) pairs:

```
$input{$name} = $value;          # add element to %input
```

Recall that a set of parentheses in a regular expression causes Perl to remember the parenthesized portion of a match. In this case, we are looking for `%xx`, but only remembering the xx portion of the match. If we find a match, it is replaced with a single character produced by the `pack` function. `hex` is a function that takes hexadecimal digits, `$1` in this case, and returns their decimal value.

Next, the script takes each name and value and builds an associative array. The expression typed by the user may be easily recalled by fetching the value:

```
$input{expression}
```

Recall that the expression typed by the user was entered into an HTML text item whose name was `expression`.

The `eval` function does the work of evaluating any Perl expression, and thus we use it to evaluate the expression input by the user.

To fetch the user's response to the radio buttons, we fetch the value of:

```
$input{base}
```

The formatting is easy using `sprintf`, except there is no binary format, so we have to resort to the `pack` function and then get rid of the beginning zeroes:

```
elsif ( $input{base} eq "binary")
{
    $val = unpack("B32",pack("N", $result));
    $val =~s/^0*//;
}
```

13.3.2 Here strings

You can see that the above script sends a lot of information to the server. This is accomplished through many uses of the `print` function. There's too much room for error, so a better approach is to use a `here` string. The syntax for this construction is borrowed from the Unix shell's `here document` syntax. The following series of `prints`:

```
print "<TABLE BORDER=2 ALIGH=CENTER>";
print "<TH>EXPRESSION</TH><TH>VALUE</TH>";
print "<H1><TR><TD ALIGN=CENTER>$input{expression}</TD>";
print "<H1><TD ALIGN=CENTER>$val</TD></TR>";
print "</TABLE>";
```

can be more easily encoded as:

```
print <<EOF;
<TABLE BORDER=2 ALIGH=CENTER>
<TH>EXPRESSION</TH><TH>VALUE</TH>
<H1><TR><TD ALIGN=CENTER>$input{expression}</TD>
<H1><TD ALIGN=CENTER>$val</TD></TR>
</TABLE>
EOF
```

In this series of `prints`, the programmer has to worry too much about double quotes and semicolons. It's easier to use the `here` string syntax. This construction surrounds whatever is to be printed with a delimiter string of your own choosing. We've chosen the string "EOF." Don't forget the semicolon at the end of the first use of the delimiter! The last use of the delimiter must be on a line by itself, flush left. Notice also how variables in the middle of `here` strings are replaced with their values.

13.3.3 Environment variables

We have already seen some CGI-related environment variables and the way in which they are accessed.

```
$ENV{REQUEST_METHOD}
$ENV{QUERY_STRING}
$ENV{CONTENT_LENGTH}
```

To see a complete list of these variables, you could load the following page into your browser. Make sure your server is running and that `showenv.pl` is in the correct server-dependent place on your disk.

```
<!-- showenv.htm -->
</HTML>
<HEAD>
<TITLE>
ENVIRONMENT
</TITLE>
</HEAD>
<BODY>
<H2> Click below to see the Environment Variables</H2>
<A HREF="http://localhost/cgi-bin/showenv.pl">SHOW ENV HASH<A>
</BODY>
</HTML>
```

When you click the `SHOW ENV` link, the `showenv.pl` script will be executed. It simply prints all of the environment variables in an HTML table. Here's that Perl script:

```
#!/usr/bin/perl
#
#   showenv.pl
#
print "content-type: text/html\n\n";
print "<TABLE BORDER=2 ALIGH=CENTER>";
print "<TR><TH>ENV VARIABLE</TH><TH>VALUE</TH></TR>";
foreach $key (keys(%ENV))
{
        print "<H1><TR><TD ALIGN=CENTER>$key</TD>";
        print "<H1><TD ALIGN=CENTER>$ENV{$key}</TD></TR>";
}
print "</TABLE>";
```

Here's a list of some of the variables that are displayed:

SERVER_ADMIN:	E-mail address of server administrator
SERVER_SOFTWARE:	Specific server software that launched the CGI
REMOTE_HOST:	Machine domain name of client
REMOTE_ADDR:	Machine IP address of client
REMOTE_USER:	Full name of user issuing request
REMOTE_IDENT:	Login name of user
CONTENT_TYPE:	MIME type
HTTP_USER_AGENT:	Browser software
HTTP_REFERER:	URL of the document containing the link to this script

13.4 `cgi-lib.pl` and `cgi.pm`

In the Perl script that evaluated expressions, we decoded the form values ourselves. Since this is such a common piece of code, a few libraries have been written to perform this task. In older Perl 4 scripts, the library is called `cgi-lib.pl`. That library contains a `ReadParse` subroutine that builds an associative array for you using typeglobs.

```
require "CGI-LIB.pl";
&ReadParse(*input);
```

Note the use of a typeglob as the input to `ReadParse`. In Perl 5, there is a module named `CGI.pm` that contains a `ReadParse` routine. You simply code as below and the data will be prepared in an associative array named `%in`:

```
use CGI;
CGI::ReadParse();
```

13.5 CGI Scripts and Databases

In the evaluation script, there was very little work to do besides using `eval` and testing to see which base the user required. Most CGI scripts need to access a database to add, modify, or retrieve records. For example, if you use the Web to make airline or hotel reservations, much of the data that is displayed for you comes from a real database such as Oracle or Sybase. The next CGI application is one in which we present the user with a registration form and then ask the user to either log their information or view a history of what has been logged to date. In the interest of simplicity, we use a simple text file rather than an actual database.

Figure 13.4 is the rendering of the HTML file, followed by the HTML code and CGI script itself:

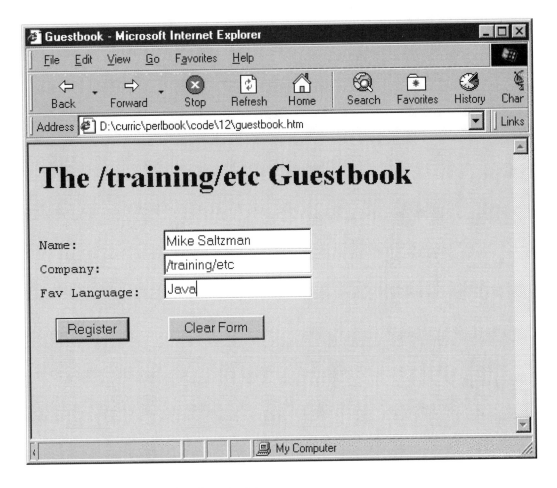

Figure 13.4 Rendering of guestbook.htm.

And here is the HTML file:

```
<!-- guestbook.htm -->
<HTML>
<HEAD>
<TITLE>Guestbook</TITLE>
</HEAD>
<BODY BGCOLOR=Yellow>
<H1>The /training/etc Guestbook</H1>
<PRE>
<FORM
    METHOD=GET
    ACTION=http://localhost/cgi-bin /guestbook.pl>
Name:            <INPUT TYPE=text NAME=name>
```

continued...

```
Company:           <INPUT TYPE=text NAME=company>
Fav Language:      <INPUT TYPE=text NAME=language>
<INPUT TYPE=submit VALUE=Register>
<INPUT TYPE=reset VALUE="Clear Form">
</PRE>
</FORM>
</BODY
</HTML>
```

When the user clicks the `Register` button, the following Perl script is executed:

```perl
#!/usr/bin/perl
#
#    guestbook.pl
#
require "ctime.pl";
$date = ctime(time);
substr($date, 20, 3) = "";
use CGI;
CGI::ReadParse();
$name = $in{name};
$company = $in{company};
$language = $in{language};
print "content-type: text/html\n\n";
print <<EOF;
<HTML>
<HEAD><TITLE>LOG IT</TITLE>
<HEAD>
<BODY BGCOLOR=Yellow>
<H1><CENTER>Hi $name</H1></CENTER>
<H1><CENTER>Today is $date</H1></CENTER>
<H1><CENTER>How's business at $company?</CENTER></H1>
<H1 ><CENTER>I love $language also</CENTER></H1>
<FONT SIZE=4 FACE=ARIAL>Now you have some choices:</FONT>
<OL>
<LI><A HREF="http://localhost/cgi-bin/mylog.pl?
        $ENV{QUERY_STRING}">Log This Entry!</A>
<LI><A HREF="http://localhost/cgi-bin/ myhistory.pl"> See History of
    Registrations</A>
</OL></FORM></BODY></HTML>
EOF
```

The program uses the `ReadParse` subroutine from the `CGI.pm` module to parse the input. Then the program uses a `here` document to respond with a virtual HTML document whose rendering we will see in Figure 13.5.

The HTML returned by the Perl program includes a few links. If any of these are selected, then another CGI script is executed. One of the problems here is in getting data from one script to another. Notice the way it is done in this script:

```
<A HREF="http://localhost/cgi-bin/mylog.pl?
        $ENV{QUERY_STRING}">Log This Entry</A>
```

We simple pass the query string into the `myhistory.pl` script. (You can also use hidden variables to accomplish the same task!) Here's the rendering from the Perl script `guestbook.pl`:

Now the user has a choice of what to do. If he or she clicks the history link, then the script `myhistory.pl` gets executed; if he or she clicks the log link, then `mylog.pl` gets executed.

```
<LI><A HREF="http://localhost/cgi-bin/mylog.pl?
        $ENV{QUERY_STRING}">Log This Entry!</A>
<LI><A HREF="http://localhost/cgi-bin/ myhistory.pl"> See history of
    Registrations?</A>
```

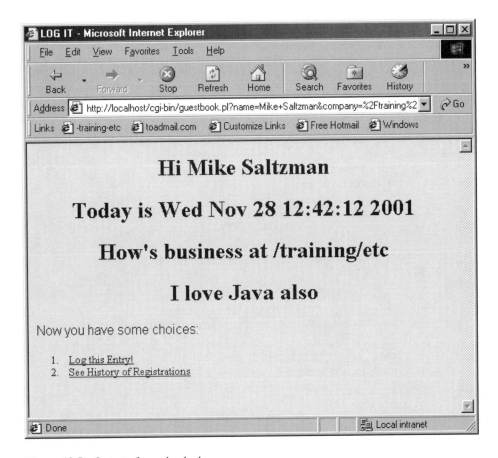

Figure 13.5   Output of guestbook.pl.

Now we will look at the script `mylog.pl`, the one that logs the data to a file. We'll use flat files here rather than an actual database such as Oracle, Sybase, or Access. However, all major databases do have an interface from Perl, the `DBI.pm` module, and later in this book, we will take a look at reading from these databases.

```perl
#!/usr/bin/perl
#
#    mylog.pl
#
require "ctime.pl";
$date = ctime(time);
substr($date, 20,3) = "";
chomp($date);
use CGI;
CGI::ReadParse();
print "content-type: text/html\n\n";
$name = $in{name};
$company = $in{company};
$language= $in{language};

if ( ! open(MYLOG, ">> logfile" ))
{
    print "OPEN FAILED";
}
else
{
    print <<EOF;
    LOGGING THE FOLLOWING ENTRY
    <OL>
    <LI>DATE: $date</LI>
    <LI>NAME: $name</LI>
    <LI>COMPANY: $company</LI>
    <LI>LANGUAGE:$language</LI>
    </OL>
EOF
    print MYLOG "$date;$name;$company;$language\n";
    close(MYLOG);
}
```

The script above gets the date and then parses the arguments with `ReadParse`.

Next, the LOGFILE is opened for appending. If the open fails, we will send a message back to the browser; if the open succeeds, we will write the "record" to the disk file. Below is the script that reads the log file:

```
#!/usr/bin/perl
#
#   myhistory.pl
#
require "ctime.pl";
$date = ctime(time);
substr($date, 20, 3) = "";
chomp($date);
use CGI;
CGI::ReadParse();
print "content-type: text/html\n\n";
if ( ! open(MYLOG, "logfile") )
{
    print "OPEN FAILED";
}
else
{
    print <<EOF;
    <TABLE BORDER=2 ALIGN=CENTER>
    <BR><PRE><TH>DATE</TH><TH>NAME</TH>
<TH>COMPANY</TH><TH>LANGUAGE</TH><BR>
EOF
    while(<MYLOG>)
    {
        ($d, $n, $c, $la) = split(';');
        print <<EOF;
        <TR ALIGN=CENTER>
        <TD>$d</TD><TD>$n</TD><TD>$c</TD><TD>$la</TD>
        </TR>
EOF
    }
    print <<EOF;
    </TABLE><HR>
<FORM><CENTER><INPUT TYPE=button VALUE='ANY OTHERS?'
    onClick='window.history.go(-2)'>
</CENTER>
</FORM>
EOF
}
```

There is nothing complicated about the previous script except that we threw in some JavaScript. Your browser tracks the pages you have visited with a history mechanism. Browsers also define events, or user interactions with Web pages. When you click the ANY OTHERS? button, an OnClick event is generated. As the writer of the HTML page, you can register an action when this event occurs. In our case, we have instructed the browser to go back two pages in the history mechanism. This will bring up the original form:

```
<FORM><CENTER><INPUT TYPE=button VALUE='ANY OTHERS?'
    onClick='window.history.go(-2)'>
```

Beyond that, the script simply reads lines from the log file and formats them nicely into a table. Figure 13.6 shows what the output from `myhistory.pl` looks like.

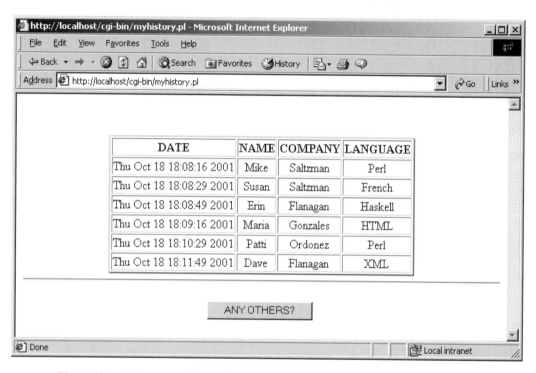

Figure 13.6   Output of myhistory.pl.

Exercises

1. Write an HTML file producing a form with two text fields (see Figure 13.7): one for NAME and one for YEAR OF BIRTH. Now, write a CGI script that displays the age of a person based on his/her entry.

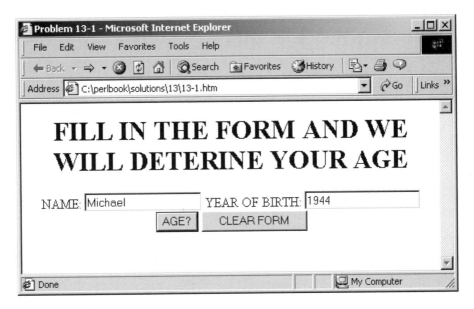

2. Write an HTML file that displays a quiz (see Figure 13.8). Then write a CGI script to grade the quiz. The rendering of the quiz might look something like what is shown on the next page:

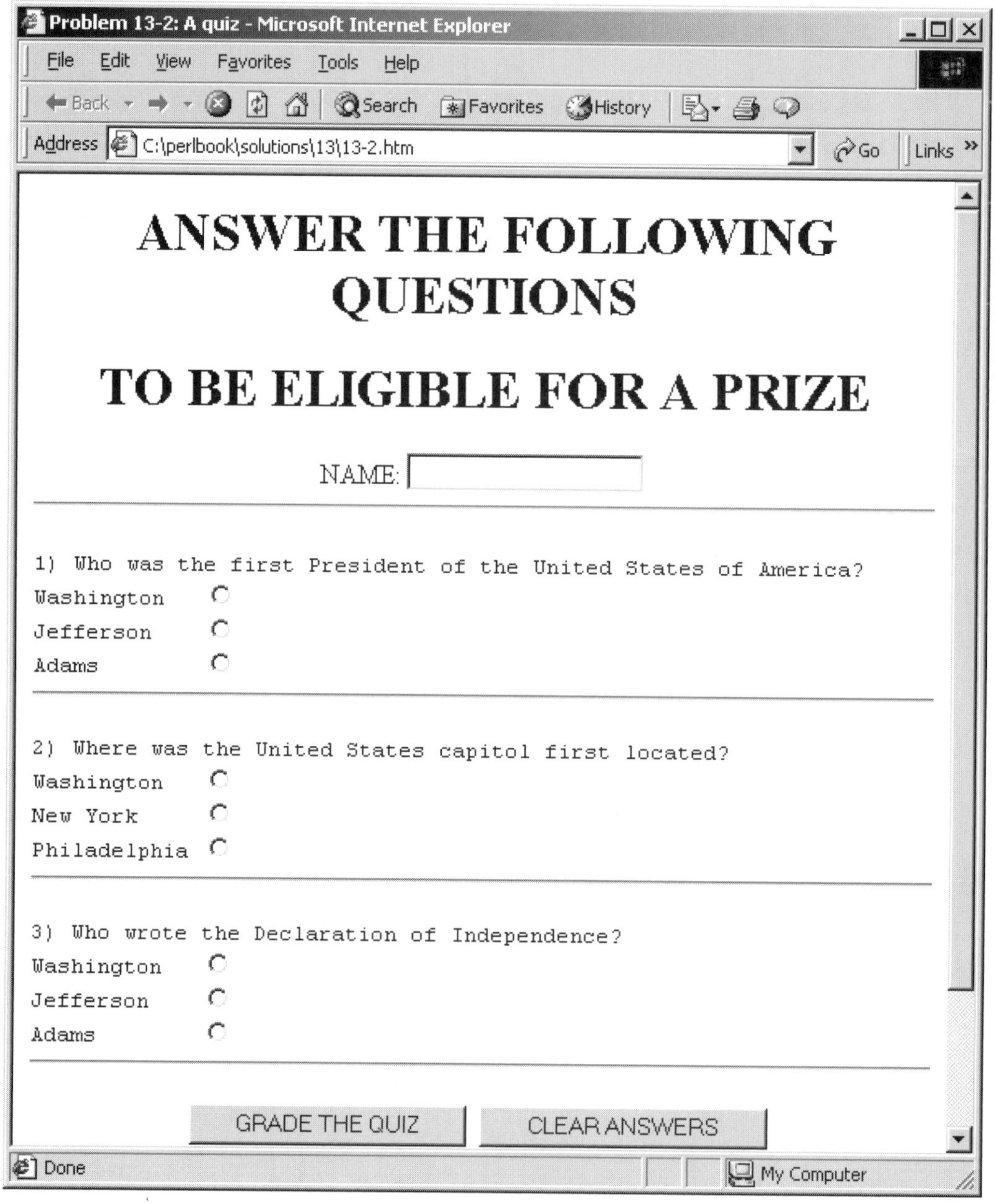

Figure 13.8   Form with quiz.

14

GRAPHICAL USER INTERFACES
WITH THE Tk.pm MODULE

We have seen a great deal of what Perl can do. We now want to switch the focus and see how Perl produces GUIs using the Tk.pm *module. This is a great undertaking as this is a vast body of knowledge. We will be demonstrating many* Tk *capabilities. All of the methods in this section take many options. We will only show a few for each and leave the rest for a book that specializes in writing GUIs in Perl.*

14.1 Introduction

The standard Perl distribution does not ship with the Tk module, so you will have to download it. Depending on which system you are using, the way in which you download the module will vary. On my Windows system, I used the ppm utility that comes with the ActiveState Perl distribution to download the Tk.pm module like this:

```
C> ppm
PPM interactive shell (2.1.2) - type 'help' for available commands
ppm> install package 'Tk?' (y/N): y
Installing Package Tk ...
D:\perl\bin\ptked
D:\perl\bin\ptked.bat
D:\perl\bin\ptksh
D:\perl\bin\ptksh.bat
D:\perl\bin\widget
D:\perl\bin\widget.bat
D:\perl\html\site\lib\Tk.html
D:\perl\html\site\lib\Tk\Adjuster.html
D:\perl\html\site\lib\Tk\Animation.html
D:\perl\html\site\lib\Tk\Button.html
D:\perl\html\site\lib\Tk\Canvas.html
D:\perl\html\site\lib\Tk\Checkbutton.htmlWriting
...
```

continued...

```
...
ppm> quit
Quit!
C>
```

14.1.1 Widgets

Tk is a Perl module that allows for the creation of GUIs. This module was originally written in conjunction with the Tcl ("tickle") scripting language and has a Motif/X-Windows look and feel. In a Tk application, a visual component is called a widget. Other systems refer to their components by different names. Visual Basic calls them controls, Java calls them components, and Motif calls them widgets as well. Here are a few examples of widgets:

- Buttons
- Checkbutton
- Labels
- Entry fields
- Scrollbars
- List boxes
- Canvases
- Menu buttons

The widget program that is delivered as part of the standard Tk module demonstrates many widget examples.

14.1.2 Event-driven programming

The programs we have seen thus far have typically been procedural in nature. These programs follow a logical path that is dictated by the data input to the program.

```
while(1)
{
    print "What is your name?   ";
    chomp($name = <STDIN>);
    print "Your name is $name!\n";
}
```

Event-driven programming executes a section of code only after a user has responded to a GUI widget such as a button or a checkbox. Then, the portion of the program that has been preset to respond to that code will get executed. Pseudo-code for an event-driven program is as follows:

```
initialize everything
while (1)
{
    read an event
    if (event is mouse movement)
          call mouse_movement_routine
    elsif (event is button click)
          call button_click_routine
    elsif (event is keyboard input)
          call keyboard_input_routine
    # ...
    # ...
    # etc.
    # etc.
}
```

The program runs forever, processing events as they happen. Tk also provides for the default processing of events so you do not have to write routines for every possible event.

14.1.3   A simple example

Here's the smallest possible GUI program. It simply places a window on the display and enters a main loop. All GUIs will have this humble beginning.

```
#!/usr/bin/perl
#
#    SimpleWin.pl
#
use Tk;
my $mw = MainWindow->new;
MainLoop;
```

The code simply opens up a window and enters an event handling loop. The GUI produced by this code is shown in Figure 14.1. The last line is important. It is responsible for displaying the GUI and entering the event handling loop.

You'll notice that the application displays a simple window with the default title SimpleWin. To provide your own title, you may add the following line just before the call to MainLoop:

```
$mw->title ("My Own Title!");
```

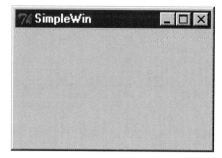

Figure 14.1   A simple window.

Built into this Window is a fully functioning GUI that responds the way that most GUIs will respond on your system. That is, you can close this window in the normal ways for your system. We can make this GUI a little nicer if we provide a Quit? button.

```perl
#!/usr/bin/perl
#
#    Button.pl
#
sub myfunc()
{
    exit(0);
}
use Tk;
my $mw = MainWindow->new;
$mw->title("My Application!");
$button = $mw->Button(-text           => "Quit?",
                      -command         => \&myfunc
                      );
$button -> pack;
MainLoop;
```

GUI produced by the above code is shown in Figure 14.2.

In this GUI, you can see that the text on the button is Quit? and the command to be executed when the user clicks the button is the subroutine named myfunc. This subroutine is an event handler. It will be executed when the user of this program presses the mouse button over the Quit? button. In this case, the subroutine simply causes the application to exit.

Figure 14.2   A simple button.

In the `Button` method, we have used a few pairs as parameters: the first pair specifies the text to be placed on the button; the second pair is a reference to a subroutine that will be called when the user clicks on this button. The `Button` method has many other parameters, some of which we will discuss later. It's not enough merely to create the button, however; it must be placed somewhere on the GUI. Where it is placed on the GUI is part of a larger topic called geometry management.

It should also be noted that there are many different styles of Tk programming. This is true even in the previous simple program. For example, we could have made the subroutine anonymous, and coded it as follows:

```
$mw->Button(-text       => "Quit?",
            -command    => sub {exit 0} ) ->pack;
```

Note that we called `pack` directly in the code above rather than on the returned reference from `$mw->Button`.

14.2 Geometry Management

When several widgets are displayed in the same window, a part of the software must be responsible for how the widgets are rendered with respect to one another. This is called geometry management. There are three flavors of geometry managers in the Tk module:

- pack()
- grid()
- place

14.2.1 pack

Only one geometry manager should be used per window. `pack()` is the most commonly used manager. It may be used with or without arguments. `pack()` allows you to control widget positioning, size, and spacing. Here's an example that shows the default placement of widgets when using `pack()` (see Figure 14.3). The code follows the display.

Figure 14.3 pack with defaults.

```perl
#!/usr/bin/perl
#
#   pack1.pl
#
use Tk;
sub openfun
{
        print "Open\n";
        $open++;
}
sub closefun
{
        print "Close\n";
        $close++;
}
sub exitfun
{
        print "Close: $close\n";
        print "Open:  $open\n";
        exit 0;
}
my $mw = MainWindow->new;
$mw->title ("Pack Example");
$mw->Button (    -text => "Open",
                 -command => \&openfun
             ) -> pack;

$mw->Button (    -text => "Close",
                 -command => \&closefun
             ) -> pack;

$mw->Button (    -text => "Exit",
                 -command => \&exitfun
             ) -> pack;
MainLoop;
```

If you do not like the default placement, you may place a widget against a specified side of the window by using the −side attribute. The default is 'top.'

```
-side => 'left' | 'right' | 'top' | 'bottom'
```

You can also place a widget so that it fills the available space in a specified direction. The default is 'none.'

```
-fill => 'none' | 'x' | 'y' | 'both'
```

You can then expand the widget to fill the available space in the window. The default is 0.

```
-expand => 0 | 1
```

The `anchor` attribute anchors a widget inside a window. The default is `center.'

```
-anchor => 'n'   | 'ne' | 'e' | 'se' | 's' | 'sw'
               | 'w' | 'nw' | 'center'
```

Here is the same application as shown previously, but packed against the left side of the window:

```
#!/usr/bin/perl
#
#        packleft.pl
#
use Tk;
sub openfun
{
        print "Open\n";
        $open++;
}
sub closefun
{
        print "Close\n";
        $close++;
}
sub exitfun
{
        print "Close: $close\n";
        print "Open:  $open\n";
        exit 0;
}
my $mw = MainWindow->new;
$mw->title ("Pack Example");
$mw->Button (    -text => "Open",
                 -command => \&openfun
            ) -> pack(-side => 'left');

$mw->Button (    -text => "Close",
                 -command => \&closefun
            ) -> pack(-side => 'left');

$mw->Button (    -text => "Exit",
                 -command => \&exitfun
            ) -> pack(-side => 'left');
MainLoop;
```

Figure 14.4 shows the rendering of the previous GUI.

Figure 14.4   pack with options.

14.2.2 grid

The grid() method is used to place widgets in rows and columns. Each call to grid() creates a new row. The first widget in a row invokes the grid() method. Remaining widgets for the row are grid() arguments. Various arguments control other positioning features. Here is the code that produces Figure 14.5:

```perl
#!/usr/bin/perl
#
#        grid1.pl
#
use Tk;
my $mw = MainWindow->new;
$button1 = $mw->Button(-text => "Open");
$button2 = $mw->Button(-text => "Close");
$button3 = $mw->Button(-text => "Save");
$button4 = $mw->Button(-text => "Exit");
$button1->grid ($button2, $button3, $button4);
$button5 = $mw->Button(-text => "Find");
$button6 = $mw->Button(-text => "Replace");
$button5->grid($button6, "-", "-", -sticky => "nsew");
MainLoop;
```

In the GUI above, the Replace button would have been rendered underneath the Close button, but each "-" specifies that the button should occupy an extra position. That button would have been centered within those three positions, except that the sticky option fills the entire set of positions as follows:

```perl
$button5->grid($button6, "-", "-", -sticky => "nsew");
```

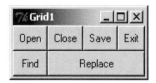

Figure 14.5   Using grid.

Note that the `sticky` parameter is with respect to directions such as north (n), south (s), east (e), and west (w).

14.2.3   `place`: **Absolute coordinates**

The `place` geometry manager allows you to specify absolute or relative x,y coordinates for a widget. The `Tk` coordinate system positions the point (0,0) at the upper left-hand corner of the window, with the x coordinate increasing to the right and the y coordinate increasing downward.

```perl
#!/usr/bin/perl
#
#   place1.pl
#
use Tk;
my $mw = MainWindow->new;
$button1=$mw->Button(-text=>'button1');
$button2=$mw->Button(-text=>'button2');
$button1->place(-x => 0, -y => 0);
$button2->place(-x => 20, -y => 17);
MainLoop;
```

Figure 14.6 is the GUI produced by the above code.

You can locate a widget anywhere in the window using the `-relx` and `-rely` options. When you use these parameters, Tk assumes the upper left corner to be (0,0) and the lower right corner to be (1,1). To place a widget in the center of the window, you can code:

```perl
$button1 = $mw->Button (text => 'button1');
$button1->place(-relx => 0.5, -rely => 0.5);
```

However, this will center the upper left corner point of the button rather than the button itself. You can fix this by changing the `anchor` position of the widget from the upper left-hand corner of the widget to the center of the widget (see Figure 14.7).

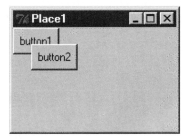

Figure 14.6   Using `grid`.

Figure 14.7   True centering.

```
$button1 = $mw->Button(text => 'button1');
$button1->place(-anchor   => 'center',
                -relx     => 0.5,
                -rely     => 0.5);
```

14.3 Buttons

The geometry management routines are in charge of placing widgets on a window. Thus far, we have only placed buttons on windows to illustrate some simple ideas. Before we take a look at some non-button widgets, let's take a closer look at some button issues.

14.3.1 Images/Bitmaps

It's typical for a button to display some instructional text. However, you can also place an image on a button if you think that is more informative. This is accomplished by using the Photo method:

```
#!/usr/lib/perl
#
#       image1.pl
#
use Tk;
sub display
{
        print "Print your message here\n";
```

continued...

```
}
my $mw = MainWindow->new;
$myImage = $mw->Photo (
                       -file => "thelogo.gif"
                      );
$button = $mw->Button (
                       -image => $myImage,
                       -command => \&display
                      ) -> pack;
MainLoop;
```

Figure 14.8 shows the rendering of the above code. If you click on the image, the `dis-play` method will be executed.

14.3.2   Button callbacks

A callback is the subroutine to be executed when a button is clicked (button with image shown in Figure 14.8). A callback can be defined as an anonymous subroutine, a reference to a subroutine, or an anonymous list. The last type is used if there is a need to pass arguments to the subroutine.

```
-command => sub { exit; }

-command => \&mySubroutine

-command => [ \&mySubroutine, $arg0, $arg1, $arg2 ];
```

14.3.3   The `Checkbutton` widget

A set of checkbuttons allow the user to select one or more choices from a list. See Figure 14.8.

```
$button1 = $mw->Checkbutton (-text => 'C++');
$button2 = $mw->Checkbutton (-text => 'Java');
$button3 = $mw->Checkbutton (-text => 'Perl');
```

Figure 14.8   A button with an image.

Figure 14.9   Checkbuttons.

To access the status of a Checkbutton widget, assign a variable to store the Checkbutton's status with the -variable option:

```
$button3 = $mw->Checkbutton (        -text => 'Perl',
                                     -variable => \$status
                        );
```

$status will contain the value 1 if the button is checked and the value 0 if it is unchecked. Callbacks can also be assigned with the −command method, which is executed whenever the checkbutton is selected. The GUI shown in Figure 14.10 contains a button and three checkbuttons. When each checkbutton is selected, a message is printed. When the List button is pressed, the list of selected courses is printed. Figure 14.10 is the rendering of the application.

Here is the code that produced it:

```
#!/usr/bin/perl
#
#         checkbutton1.pl
#
use Tk;
sub status
{
```

Figure 14.10   Button and checkboxes.

```
               print "Something selected or deselected\n";
               print "Press List button to see status\n";
}
sub list
{
               print "You have selected: ";
               print " C++ " if $cpp;
               print " Java " if $java;
               print " Perl " if $perl;
               print "\n";
}
my $mw = MainWindow->new;
$mw->Button       (
                           -text => 'List',
                           -command => \&list
                   ) -> pack;

$mw->Checkbutton (-text => 'C++',
                   -command => \&status,
                   -variable => \$cpp
                   ) -> pack;
$mw->Checkbutton (-text => 'Java',
                   -command => \&status,
                   -variable => \$java
                   ) -> pack;
$mw->Checkbutton (-text => 'Perl',
                   -command => \&status,
                   -variable => \$perl
                   ) -> pack;
MainLoop;
```

14.3.4 Radio buttons

Radio buttons can be mutually exclusive checkbuttons. The following example shows some radio buttons and how to make them mutually exclusive. We've also sneaked a `Label` widget into this GUI.

```
#!/usr/bin/perl
#
#         radiobutton1.pl
#
use Tk;
sub status
{
        %status = ( 1 => 'A',
                    2 => 'B',
                    3 => 'C'
                  );
```

continued...

```
            print "You have selected $status{$grade}\n";
}
my $mw = MainWindow->new;
$lab = $mw->Label (-text => "Select a Grade" ) ->pack;
$button1 = $mw->Radiobutton (-text => 'A',
                             -value => 1,
                             -command => \&status,
                             -variable => \$grade
                            ) ->pack;
$button2 = $mw->Radiobutton (-text => 'B',
                             -value => 2,
                             -command => \&status,
                             -variable => \$grade,
                            ) ->pack;
$button3 = $mw->Radiobutton (-text => 'C',
                             -value => 3,
                             -command => \&status,
                             -variable => \$grade
                            ) ->pack;
MainLoop;
```

Radio buttons are made mutually exclusive when the -variable option uses the same variable name for a set of radio buttons. The value of this variable is set to the value of the −value option for the selected radio button. For instance, in the previous example, $grade would be set to 3 if the C button was selected.

Callbacks can be assigned with the −command option. The display of the above code is shown in Figure 14.11.

14.4 Other Widgets

Thus far, we have concentrated on various types of buttons because they are the most popular widgets. Now we will look at other kinds of widgets.

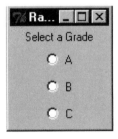

Figure 14.11   Mutually exclusive radio buttons.

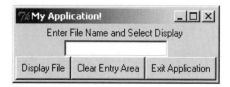

Figure 14.12   An `entry` widget.

14.4.1   The `Entry` widget

This widget is used to input a line of text. This is an important widget since it provides a simple way of getting input to your program. You can assign the text to a variable using:

```
$mainWindow->Entry( -textvariable => \$comments );
```

We might use this widget to get some information, such as a filename, from the user. Then, we could display the file within a GUI component such as a `text` widget. For now, we will display the file on the console. Later, when we have learned about other widgets, we can display the file in a text area. See Figure 14.12 for the rendering of this GUI.

The code producing this GUI will follow. When the user enters some data in the `entry` widget, the variable `$filename` contains this data. When the user selects the `Display File` button, the contents of this variable are opened as a file. The file is then displayed on the console. When the user selects the `Clear Entry Area` button, this variable is set to the empty string, thus clearing the `entry` widget's contents.

```perl
#!/usr/bin/perl
#
#   viewer.pl
#
use Tk;
sub display
{
    open(THISFILE, "< $filename") || die;
    print while(<THISFILE>);
    close(THISFILE);
}
sub clear
{
        $filename = "";
}
my $mw = MainWindow->new;
$mw->title ("My Viewer!");
$mw->Label (-text => 'Enter File Name and Select Display ') ->pack;
$mw->Entry ( -textvariable => \$filename) -> pack;
```

continued...

```
$mw->Button(      -text => "Display File",
                  -command => \&display
            ) -> pack(-side => 'left');
$mw->Button(      -text => "Clear Entry Area",
                  -command => \&clear
            ) -> pack(-side => 'left');
$mw->Button(      -text => "Exit Application",
                  -command => sub { exit }
            ) -> pack(-side => 'left');
MainLoop;
```

To hide the user's input to an entry widget, you would use the following code, which places an asterisk in the input entry rather than the character typed. Password fields would be handled this way.

```
$mainWindow->Entry(-textvariable=>\$comments,-show => '*');
```

14.4.2 List boxes

A list box is used to display a list of strings. To create a list box and display it, code it as follows:

```
$lis = $mainWindow->Listbox()->pack;
```

Use the insert method to add elements to the list. List elements can be added to the end of the list or inserted after a particular position. In the first example below, the items are added to the end of the list. The second example adds a few more items after the second entry.

```
$lis->insert('end', 'one', 'two', 'three', 'four', 'five');
$lis->insert(2, 'one', 'two', 'three', 'four', 'five');
```

The -selectmode => value option controls how many options can be selected at once. Here are a few values from which you may choose:

- single   Select one item at a time.
- multiple   Allows you to select more than one at a time.
- extended   Allows you to "drag" and select multiple items at a time.

Here are some methods that can be used with list boxes:

```
$lb->get(startindex [, endindex]);
```

retrieves the list of items between positions `startindex` and `endindex`. The second parameter is optional.

```
$lb->curselection();
```

retrieves a list of indexes of the items the user has selected.

```
$lb->delete (startindex [, endindex])
```

deletes the list of items from position `startindex` to `endindex`.

```
$lb->selectionSet (startindex [, endindex] )
```

selects the items from `startindex` to `endindex`.

```
$lb->selectionClear (startindex [, endindex])
```

clears the items from `startindex` to `endindex`.

```
$lb->size()
```

returns the number of items in the list box.

Here is an example list box application. It's a modification of the viewer application. When the program begins, the list box displays all the ordinary files in the current directory. The user can then select one to be displayed.

```perl
#!/usr/bin/perl
#
#         listfiles.pl
#
use Tk;
use Cwd;
sub display
{
        ($index) = $lis->curselection();        # assume 1
        ($file) = $lis->get($index);            # filename
        open(FILE, $file);
        print "about to print $file\n";
        sleep 2;
        print "$. $_" while(<FILE>);
        print "\nfinished printing $file\n";
        close(FILE);
```

continued...

```
}
my $mw = MainWindow->new;
$mw->title ("List Files");
$mw->Label (-text => "Select file\nFrom Listbox") ->pack;
$lis = $mw -> Listbox() -> pack;
opendir(THISDIR, ".");
@files = readdir(THISDIR);
$lis -> insert('end', grep(-f, @files));
$mw->Button(    -text => "Display Files",
                -command => \&display
           ) -> pack(-side => 'left');
$mw->Button(    -text => "Exit Application",
                -command => sub { exit }
           ) -> pack(-side => 'left');
MainLoop;
```

14.4.3 `text` widget

A `text` widget gives you a rectangular area in which to display text. It is created with:

```
$text = $mainWindow->Text->pack;
```

Once you have created this widget you may insert text with the `insert` method, which takes an index and a string. The index is the position at which to insert the string. There can be various first arguments, but the `end` index tells Perl to add the string to the end of the text.

```
$text->insert ("end", "Some sample text\n");
$text->insert ("end", "Add to end of sample\n");
```

You may also configure the text by using the `tagConfigure` method. This method creates a tag that represents some formatting capability. You can refer to this tag later with one or more inserts. Here are some examples that show various configuration tags:

```
$text->tagConfigure ('ulTag', -underline => 1)
$text->tagConfigure ('color', -foreground => 'red')
$text->tagConfigure ('font', -font => 16)
```

Now, any text that is to be inserted can refer back to this tag and get the accompanying style such as underlining, coloring, or font.

```
$text->insert ("end", "More text\n", 'ulTag');
$text->insert ("end", "Still more\n", 'color');
$text->insert ("end", "Still more\n", 'font');
```

Figure 14.13   A text widget

Figure 14.13 was produced with the following code.

```
#!/usr/bin/perl
#
#   text.pl
#
use Tk;
my $mainWindow = MainWindow->new;
$text = $mainWindow->Text->pack;
$text->tagConfigure ('ulTag', -underline => 1);
$text->tagConfigure ('color', -foreground => 'red');
$text->tagConfigure ('thefont', -font => 16);

$text->insert ("end", "Some sample text\n");
$text->insert ("end", "Add to end of sample\n");

$text->insert ("end", "More text\n", 'ulTag');
$text->insert ("end", "Still more\n", 'color');
$text->insert ("end", "Still more\n", 'thefont');
MainLoop;
```

14.4.4   Scrollbars

List boxes, text, and Entry widgets can also have scrollbars built around them. The most common way of creating a scrollbar is by using the Scrolled method when the parent window is created. The first argument to the Scrolled method specifies the type of widget to be created. The second argument specifies the placement of the scrollbars as follows:

- n   Above widget
- s   Below widget
- e   At the right of the widget
- w   At the left of the widget
- o   Only display scrollbar if necessary

To show you a GUI that has a few widgets with scrollbars, examine the following code and subsequent rendering in Figure 14.14:

```perl
#!/usr/bin/perl
#
#        scrolling.pl
#
use Tk;
$text = "Use the scrollbar to see all of this text.";
my $mainWindow = MainWindow->new;
$entry = $mainWindow->Scrolled('Entry',  -scrollbars => 's',
                                          -textvariable => \$text);
$list = $mainWindow->Scrolled('Listbox', -scrollbars => 'se');
$list -> insert("end",
                'Here is a listing of some great courses!',
                'With the best at the top!',
                '==================',
                'Augusta National',
                'Pebble Beach',
                'Pinehurst # 2',
                'St Andrews',
                'Royal Troon',
                'Oakmont',
                'Baltusrol',
                'Southern Hills'
                );
$entry->grid();
$list->grid();
MainLoop;
```

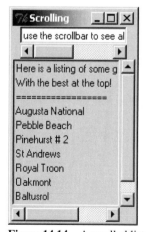

Figure 14.14   A scrolled list.

Figure 14.15   A dialog box.

14.4.5   Dialog boxes

In a few previous examples, whenever an `Exit` button was selected, the program was unconditionally terminated. A better approach would be to allow the user to confirm or deny this selection. This is where a dialog box is useful. See Figure 14.15.

A dialog box prompts the user for input and returns the string attached to the button selected by the user. A dialog box requires two steps: create the dialog box with the `Dialog` method and then display the dialog box with the `Show` method. The code below produces the rendering beneath it:

```
$d = $mw->Dialog(
        -text => "Really Wanna Quit?",
        -bitmap => "question",
        -buttons => ["Yes", "No", "Cancel"] );
$answer = $d->Show();
```

When the user selects `Yes`, `No`, or `Cancel`, the `$answer` variable contains the label on the button as a string. The GUI in Figure 14.16 allows a user to enter Perl expressions into an `Entry` widget. The user can then select a button to evaluate the expression, clear the `text` widget, or exit the application. If the user selects `Exit`, a dialog is presented when the following subroutine is executed:

```
sub quit
{
    $d = $mw->Dialog(
        -text => "Really Wanna Quit?",
        -bitmap => "question",
        -buttons => ["Yes", "No", "Cancel"] );
    $answer = $d->Show();
    exit if ($answer eq "Yes")
}
```

Here is the entire program:

```perl
#!/usr/bin/perl
#
#   dialog.pl
#
use Tk;
use Tk::Dialog;
my $mw = MainWindow->new;
sub trans
{
    ++$i;
    $text->insert ("end", "$i\t$comments");
    $text->insert ("end", " has the value ");
    $result = eval $comments;
    $ans = $@ if $@;
    $text->insert("end", "$result\n");
}
sub clear
{
    $i = 0;
    $text-> delete ("1.0", "end");
    $text->insert ("end", "Watch this window\n");
}
sub quit
{
    $d = $mw->Dialog(
        -text => "Really Wanna Quit?",
        -bitmap => "question",
        -buttons => ["Yes", "No", "Cancel"] );
    $answer = $d->Show();
    exit if ($answer eq "Yes")
}
$mw->title ("Calculator");
$text = $mw->Scrolled('Text', -scrollbars => 'se');
$text->insert ("end", "Watch this window\n");
$lab = $mw->Label (-text => 'Enter Expression and Select a Button');
$entry = $mw->Entry(-textvariable => \$comments);
$quit = $mw->Button(-text => "Quit",     -command=> \&quit);
$clear = $mw->Button(-text => "Clear", -command=> \&clear);
$calc = $mw->Button(-text=>"Calculate",-command=> \&trans);
$quit->grid($calc, $clear);
$lab->grid("-", "-",     -sticky => "news");
$entry->grid("-","-",    -sticky => "news");
$text -> grid("-", "-", -sticky => "news");
MainLoop;
```

This GUI is rendered in Figure 14.16. Each expression is entered into an Entry widget and then copied to a text widget when the user selects the Calculate button.

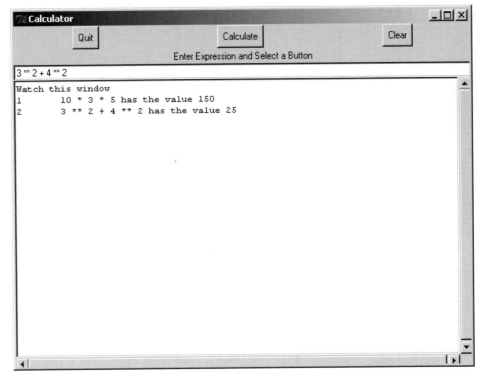

Figure 14.16   A complete GUI.

14.4.6 **Menus**

Sometimes a menu can provide an easier selection mechanism than a set of buttons or a list box. A menu may also be chosen because it takes up less real estate in the GUI than a set of buttons or a list of items. Additionally, you may want to use a menu to be consistent with other applications.

A menu is created with the `Menubutton` method. This method has ample arguments, the most important of which are the names of the menu items and the names of their respective callbacks. Remember that a callback is the function to be executed when a menu item is selected.

Here is the code and the rendering of an application with a menu (see Figure 14.17):

```perl
#!/usr/bin/perl
#
#    Menu1.pl
#
use Tk;
sub quit
{
                print "quit\n";        }
```

continued...

```
}
sub clear
{
                print "clear\n";
}
sub trans
{
                print "trans\n";
}
$mw = MainWindow->new;
$mb1 = $mw->Menubutton
    (
            -text => "File",
            -menuitems =>
            [
            ['command' => "Calculate", -command => \&trans ],
            ['command' => "Clear",     -command => \&clear ],
            ['command' => "Quit",      -command => \&quit ]
            ]
    );
$mb1 -> pack(-anchor => "nw");
MainLoop;
```

If you click the mouse on the `File` menu, you will see that the choices, `Calculate`, `Clear`, and `Quit` will drop down. If you select one of those choices, the particular callback that is registered with your choice will be executed.

Code such as `menu1.pl` could be added to the expression GUI seen previously so that the user would have the choice of interfacing with the application through the buttons or through the menu.

Of course, there can be more than one menu. Here is the code which produces an application with two menus. See Figure 14.18 for the rendering.

Figure 14.17   A menu.

```perl
#!/usr/bin/perl
#
#        menu2.pl
#
use Tk;
sub quit  { print "quit\n";   }
sub clear { print "clear\n";  }
sub trans { print "trans\n";  }
sub cut   { print "cut\n";    }
sub copy  { print "copy\n";   }
sub paste { print "paste\n";  }
$mw = MainWindow->new;
$mb1 = $mw->Menubutton
        (
          -text => "File",
          -menuitems =>
      [ [ 'command' => "Calculate",  -command => \&trans],
        [ 'command' => "Clear",  -command => \&clear  ],
        [ 'command' => "Quit",   -command => \&quit ]]
        );
$mb1 -> pack(-anchor => "nw");
$mb2 = $mw->Menubutton
        (
          -text => "Edit",
          -menuitems =>
          [ [ 'command' => "Cut",   -command => \&cut],
            [ 'command' => "Copy",   -command => \&copy  ],
            [ 'command' => "Paste",   -command => \&paste ] ]
        );
$mb1 -> pack(-side => "left", -anchor => "nw");
$mb2 -> pack(-side => "left", -anchor => "nw");
MainLoop;
```

Figure 14.18 A GUI with two menus.

14.5 Frames

Before we put the menu on the GUI for the expression evaluator, we need to know more about the frame widget. This widget makes it easier to design your overall GUI. A frame can be used as a placeholder on which you can add widgets. Rather than adding widgets to the main window, you can create several frames, add widgets to each frame, and then add the frames to the main window.

In the example that follows, there will be two frames attached to the main window. The top frame will have an Entry widget and three buttons. See Figure 14.19. The bottom frame will have a text widget and a few buttons. As each string is typed into the Entry widget and a particular button is pressed, the appropriate function labeled on the button will be performed on the string. The resultant string is shown in the Entry widget and recorded on the text widget.

The user may quit the application or clear the text as a function of the buttons in the bottom frame.

```perl
#!/usr/bin/perl
#
#          Frames.pl
#
use Tk;
my $mw = MainWindow->new;
$ct = 1;
sub clear
{   $text1->delete("1.0", "end");
    $ct = 1;
}
sub rev
{
    my $val = reverse($value);
    $text1->insert("end", "$ct\t$value: rev is: $val\n");
    $value = $val;
    $ct++;
}
sub len
{
    my $val = length($value);
    $text1->insert("end", "$ct\t$value: len is: $val\n");
    $value = $val;
    $ct++;
}
sub upcase
{
```

continued...

```
            my $val = uc($value);
            $text1 -> insert("end", "$ct\t$value: upc is: $val\n");
            $value = $val;
            $ct++;
}
$top = $mw->Frame(     -background =>   "red");
$bottom = $mw->Frame( -background => "blue");
$top->grid(-sticky => "news");

$bottom->grid;

$text1 = $bottom->Text( -background => "yellow");
$close = $bottom->Button(    -text => "close",
                             -command => sub { exit; });
$clear = $bottom->Button(    -text => "clear",
                             -command => \&clear);
$close->grid($clear);
$text1->grid("-");

$ent = $top ->Entry(-textvariable => \$value);

$rev = $top->Button(-text => "reverse", -command => \&rev);
$len = $top->Button(-text => "length",  -command => \&len);
$up = $top->Button(-text => "upper", -command => \&upcase);
$rev -> grid($len, $up, -sticky => "news");
$ent -> grid("-", "-");
MainLoop;
```

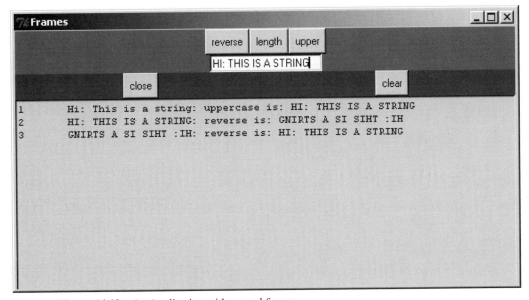

Figure 14.19   An Application with several frames.

Figure 14.20   Possible user information screen.

14.5.1   Top-level windows

A top-level window allows for the creation of additional "windows" in an application. These additional windows are standalone windows. They can be created as needed to fit whatever "screens" your application needs. Top-level windows are created with the Toplevel method.

Suppose your application needs to obtain some information about a user. You could make the following screen appear at the pressing of a button (see Figure 14.20).

The main screen would appear as shown in Figure 14.21. When the Next Screen button is pressed, the GUI in Figure 14.20 is displayed.

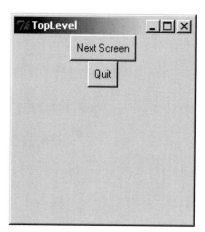

Figure 14.21   A top-level window.

Here is the code for the application depicted in Figure 14.21:

```perl
#!/usr/bin/perl
#
#  topLevel.pl
#
use Tk;
my $mw = MainWindow->new;
$mw->geometry("200x200");
$b1 = $mw->Button(    -text => "Next Screen",
                      -command => \&next) -> pack;
$b2 = $mw->Button(    -text => "Quit",
-command => sub { exit }) -> pack;
open(INFO, "> info");
MainLoop;
sub next
{
        if ( ! Exists($t) )# do not confuse with exists
        {
                $t=$mw->Toplevel();
                $t->geometry("150x150");
                $t->Label(-text => "Name") ->pack;
                $t->Entry(-textvariable =>\$name) -> pack;
                $t->Label(-text => "Age ") -> pack;
                $t->Entry(-textvariable =>\$age) -> pack;
                $t->Button( -text => "Save",
                            -command => \&save) -> pack;

        }
}
sub save
{
        print INFO "$name $age\n";
}
close(INFO);
```

Note that top-level windows, including `MainWindow`, have methods defined on them. We've shown the use of one of them, the `geometry` method, in the code above. This method allows you to specify the height and width of the window. You may also specify the placement of the upper left-hand pixel of the window. For example, the string in the geometry method:

```perl
$mw -> geometry("300x200+50+50");
```

specifies that the window will be 300 x 200 pixels and that the upper left-hand pixel will be at position 50,50 relative to the entire desktop.

14.6 Binding

Each widget defined in the Tk module has a well-defined set of events. You can also define your own event for a particular widget. Coupling an event with a widget is called binding. For example, if a user wanted to take some action whenever an item was selected in a list box or when a Return was pressed in an Entry widget, then you must define the binding. In the example below, whenever the left mouse button, Button-1, is pressed on a list box item, an event is generated. In the code below, the statement:

```
$list = $mw->Scrolled('Listbox')->pack;
$list->bind("<Button-1>", \&select);
```

specifies that when the left mouse button is pressed, the select subroutine should be called.

```
#!/usr/bin/perl
#
#        bind.pl
#
use Tk;
$mw = MainWindow ->new;
$list = $mw->Scrolled('Listbox')->pack;
$mw->Entry(width => 20, -textvariable => \$var)->pack;
$list->bind("<Button-1>", \&select);
opendir(THISDIR, ".");
@files = readdir THISDIR;
$list->insert ('end', @files);
MainLoop;

sub select

{        $x = $list -> curselection();
         $var = $list -> get($x)
}
```

The select subroutine will be called whenever the left mouse button is pressed while the pointer is in the listbox widget.

To bind the Return key in an Entry widget, you must code as follows:

```
$mw->Entry(-width => 20, -textvariable => \$var) -> pack;
$entry -> bind("<Return>", \&work);

sub work
{    # do something here
}
```

There are more bindings that can be made, for example you may want to bind certain keystrokes. Likewise, there are a plethora of other Tk topics. Please refer to any text that specifically addresses Tk issues.

Exercise

1. Write a file display program that looks like the one below (Figure 14.22) when it is started.

Figure 14.22   File display screen.

The `File` menu has two items: `Open` and `Exit`. When you select `Exit`, the application terminates; when you select `Open`, the top-level window shown in Figure 14.23 appears:

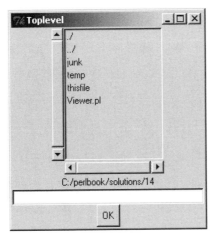

Figure 14.23   Current directory display.

The top-level window shows the current directory as a `label` widget and a list box that displays the files in the current directory. When a file is chosen from the list, the `Entry` widget displays the name of the file. When the `OK` button is clicked, the contents of the file are displayed in the main window.

15

ACCESSING REAL DATABASES IN PERL

Most computer software applications interface with databases sooner or later. Certainly, this is true of CGI applications. When we looked at CGI earlier, we used a flat file database. In this chapter, we will show the details of connecting to real databases such as Oracle and Sybase in Perl. However, rather than favoring a particular vendor, we will be using the MySQL database system, which can be downloaded at www.mysql.com. With this database, we can demonstrate the principles of accessing all databases in Perl, regardless of the vendor.

15.1 Introduction

If you want to test some of the programs in this section, there are a few Perl modules that you will need to download in addition to downloading the actual MySQL database program. In particular, you will need the DBI.pm and DBD-Mysql.pm modules. If you are using Windows and a Perl port from ActiveState, you can download these modules with the Perl Package Manager as follows:

```
C> ppm
PPM interactive shell (2.1.2) - type 'help' for available commands
ppm> install DBI
...
...
...
ppm> install DBD-MySQL
...
...
...
quit
C>
```

287

If you are using a Unix variant, then you will have to go to the CPAN site and download these modules.

15.1.1   What is DBI?

The database interface (DBI) module is a package that allows you to access relational databases from within a Perl script. It is the *de facto* standard for database access from Perl. DBI provides the means for writing code that is database vendor-independent. Databases accessible via DBI include:

- Informix
- Ingres
- Interbase
- MySQL
- Oracle
- Sybase

DBI also provides an interface for Open Database Connectivity (ODBC).

15.1.2   What is DBD?

The DBI module specifies the programming interface regardless of the actual database that is being used. In other words, when you want to make a database request from Perl, the Perl statement that you use is independent of the database being used. The DBI module funnels this request to a particular database driver (DBD) module. The DBD module takes the request and processes it, perhaps returning a result. Each database requires its own driver. In the Perl world, these drivers are contained in specialized modules with names such as DBD::Oracle, DBD::Sybase, DBD::MySQL, etc.

15.1.3   The DBI architecture

When you access a real database in Perl, there are certain levels of function calls that are hidden from you. Your Perl code calls a routine in the DBI module, which calls a routine in a DBD-specific module, which talks to the database. Figure 15.1 shows the various levels that funnel data in the DBI architecture:

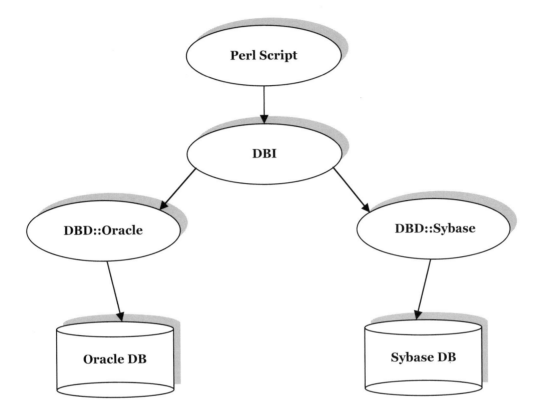

Figure 15.1   DBI Architecture

15.2 A Review of SQL and Relational Databases

Data in a relational database is stored in one or more related tables. A table is a collection of rows and columns. Each row is best thought of as a record. The record, or row, is divided into fields called columns.

When you download the MySQL database, you are given a database with a few tables. However, we created our own database, named `test`, with a table, named `Staff`. The `Staff` table is pictured on the next page (Table 15–1).

Table 15.1   Staff Table

item	name	age	dept.	city	years
1	Michael	56	Technical	Columbia	12
2	Susan	38	Finance	Columbia	6
3	Erin	28	Technical	Odenton	3
4	Sally	51	Courseware	Silver Spring	1
5	Patti	35	Instruction	Columbia	1
6	Bob	58	Marketing	Ft. Lauderdale	3
7	Kim	34	Marketing	Chicago	1
8	Roger	51	Instruction	Silver Spring	8
9	Alan	46	Instruction	Baltimore	6
10	Danko	38	Instruction	Columbia	7
11	Bob	51	Instruction	Columbia	4
12	Mike	55	Instruction	Columbia	1

The `Staff` table consists of 12 rows and 6 columns. Columns are sometimes referred to as fields.

15.2.1   Accessing a relational database

Accessing a relational database is done via the Structured Query Language, or SQL, which is pronounced "see-quel." SQL is the *de facto* standard database language so that regardless of whether you are using Oracle, Sybase, Access, MySQL, or some other database, all standard SQL commands should behave consistently. It should also be pointed out that each vendor typically adds its own set of commands, called extensions, to the base, standard SQL commands.

If you have MySQL installed and the `mysql` server started, then you can try some of the commands you see here. You can start the `mysql` client at your system prompt. The following line starts the `mysql` client with the `test` database; one of the tables is named `Staff`:

```
C> mysql test
Welcome to the MySQL monitor.  Commands end with a ;
  . .
  . .
mysql>
```

If you are using a database other than MySQL, you'll need to start that particular server and client. Once you have done this, you can enter any of the commands that you see below. If you've never written SQL code before, it's a good idea to see a few queries. When you later use Perl to make the same queries, you will see a striking similarity.

15.2.2   Retrieving data from a relational database

Retrievals are done with the `select` statement. Here are a few examples:

```
mysql> select name, age from Staff where city = "Columbia";
+---------+-----+
| name    | age |
+---------+-----+
| Michael |  56 |
| Susan   |  38 |
| Patti   |  35 |
| Danko   |  38 |
| Bob     |  51 |
| Mike    |  55 |
+---------+-----+
6 rows in set (0.00 sec)
```

The `select` statement is given a comma-separated list of field names. The `from` keyword is followed by the name of the table. The `where` keyword is followed by the selection criteria. Thus, the selection above yields the first name and age of all records that have Columbia as the `city` value. If you do not want to be selective, you may ask for all records using the `*` character.

```
mysql> select * from Staff;
+------+---------+-----+-------------+----------------+-------+
| item | name    | age | dept        | city           | years |
+------+---------+-----+-------------+----------------+-------+
| 0001 | Michael |  56 | Technical   | Columbia       |    12 |
| 0002 | Susan   |  38 | Finance     | Columbia       |    06 |
| 0003 | Erin    |  28 | Technical   | Odenton        |    03 |
| 0004 | Sally   |  51 | Courseware  | Silver Spring  |    01 |
| 0005 | Patti   |  35 | Instruction | Columbia       |    01 |
| 0006 | Bob     |  58 | Marketing   | Ft. Lauderdale |    03 |
| 0007 | Kim     |  34 | Marketing   | Chicago        |    01 |
| 0008 | Roger   |  51 | Instruction | Silver Spring  |    08 |
| 0009 | Alan    |  46 | Instruction | Baltimore      |    06 |
| 0010 | Danko   |  38 | Instruction | Columbia       |    07 |
| 0011 | Bob     |  51 | Instruction | Columbia       |    04 |
| 0012 | Mike    |  55 | Instruction | Columbia       |    01 |
+------+---------+-----+-------------+----------------+-------+
12 rows in set (0.00 sec)
```

15.2.3 Data modification commands

There are three types of data modification commands:

insert—Add new rows to a table:

```
insert into Staff values
(13, "Tom", 57, "Sales", "MD", 0);
```

update—Modify one or more columns of a table:

```
update Staff set City = "Baltimore", where item = 1;
```

delete—Delete rows from a table:

```
delete from Staff where item = 13;
```

There are also commands to return information about a database, such as the names of the tables and the names of the columns.

15.3 Accessing a Database from Perl

Now that we have seen several SQL commands, we will turn our attention to the database interface in Perl. To do this, we first have to learn about handles.

15.3.1 Database handles

Most database activity from a Perl script has to do with executing embedded SQL commands from within a script, just like most I/O in a Perl program has to do with reading and writing files. Of course, with a file, you must first create a filehandle to be able to perform reads and writes. With a database, you must first connect to it before you can execute statements against it.

Connecting to a database is a little more complex than opening a file because there are potentially more security issues involved. For example, most systems require a username and a password to gain access to the database.

A database handle is created when connectivity to a database is established. Multiple database handles may be created. This might be the strategy to use if you want to connect to more than one database from the same script. Although the syntax for the connection usually involves the DBD name, a username, and a password, it is the DBD name that will vary according to the database to which you wish to connect. For the MySQL database, the connection syntax is:

```
my $dbh = DBI->connect("dbi:mysql:test", $user, $password)
or die "Can't connect!";
```

The `connect` method returns a database handle, `$dbh`. The handle is actually an object on which you can execute methods to query the database.

15.3.2   Executing a query

Real databases normally give the user a shell interface and a graphical interface. In the shell interface, the user types SQL commands that are interpreted and then executed by the database engine, which in turn sends the output to the shell for display. This is what we have seen previously. In Perl, the situation is similar, although there is no shell. You simply prepare the statement, execute it, and the results are sent back to your program, where you can process the data any way that you wish. Here's a small example:

```
#!/usr/bin/perl
#
#   database1.pl
#
use DBI;
$user="";
$passwd="";
my $dbh = DBI->connect("dbi:mysql:test", $user, $password)
 or die "Can't connect!";
print "connected to mysql\n";
$sth = $dbh->prepare ("select * from staff;");
$sth->execute();
while (@r = $sth->fetchrow_array)
{
    printf "%3d  %-7s %3d %-13s%-15s%4d\n",
        $r[0], $r[1], $r[2], $r[3], $r[4], $r[5];
}
```

After the connection has been made, we use the `prepare` method to prepare a SQL statement. `prepare` returns a statement handle, `$sth`. The next step is to execute the statement with the `execute` method. At this point, we may retrieve the data in various ways. One way is with the method named `fetchrow_array`, which fetches a row of data. Here is the output of `database.pl`:

```
% database1.pl
connected to mysql
    1  Michael   56 Technical    Columbia           12
    2  Susan     38 Finance      Columbia            6
    3  Erin      28 Technical    Odenton             3
    4  Sally     51 Courseware   Silver Spring       1
    5  Patti     35 Instruction  Columbia            1
    6  Bob       58 Marketing    Ft. Lauderdale      3
    7  Kim       34 Marketing    Chicago             1
    8  Roger     51 Instruction  Silver Spring       8
    9  Alan      46 Instruction  Baltimore           6
   10  Danko     38 Instruction  Columbia            7
   11  Bob       51 Instruction  Columbia            4
   12  Mike      55 Instruction  Dallas              1
%
```

Using this method, the data is returned as an array, one row at a time, until no more rows are available. Data may also be retrieved with the code shown here:

```
while ($ar = $sth->fetchrow_arrayref)
{
    print $ar->[0], " ", $ar->[1], "etc!\n";
}
```

fetchrow_arrayref returns an array reference rather than the array itself. This method can help with performance since it does not have to allocate space for a new array for each row. Remember that the same array reference is used for every row, so you would have to copy the data to another location if you need it later. You may also retrieve data with the fetchrow_hashref method. You can then use hash notation to pick out the elements you need.

```
while ($hr = $sth->fetchrow_hashref)
{
    print $hr->{name}, " ", $hr->{age}, "!\n";
}
```

The hash keys are the column names in the database, and the hash values are the data returned from the database.

15.3.3   Binding output columns

The most efficient method of retrieving data from a database is to associate a Perl variable with a fetched value. This is accomplished by binding fields to variables. There are two ways to do this: The bind_col method allows you to pick and choose which fields to bind, while the bindcolumns method insists that every field be bound to a Perl variable:

```
$sth = $dbh->prepare ("select * from staff;");
$sth->execute();
#
#   bind whichever fields you might
#
$sth->bind_col (2, \$name);
$sth->bind_col (5, \$city);
while ($sth->fetch)
{
    print "$name\t$city";
}

$sth = $dbh->prepare ("select * from staff;");
$sth->execute();
#
#   must bind all fields
#
$sth->bind_columns(\$id, \$nm, \$age, \$job, \$city, \$yr);
while ($sth->fetch)
{
    print "$nm\t$city\n";
}
```

15.3.4   Accessing database metadata

In addition to the actual data stored in a table, there may sometimes be a need to recover data about a table. This kind of data is called metadata, that is, data about data. Several methods may be used to determine information about a table.

```
@tables = $dbh->tables()
```

returns an array of the tables in the database relative to the last table accessed.

```
$num = $sth->{NUM_OF_FIELDS}
```

returns the number of columns in this table.

```
$arrayref = $sth->{NAME}
```

is a reference to an array containing the field names returned by the SQL statement associated with the statement handle. To print these names, you can code as follows:

```
$i = 1;
foreach $ref (@$arrayref)
{
    print "Field $i is named $ref\n";
    $i++;
}
```

Note that statement handle attributes are available only after the `prepare()` and `execute()` methods have been executed. Here is a program that prints some metadata for the database we have been using. This is followed by a run of the program.

```
#!/usr/bin/perl
#
#   metadata.pl
#
use DBI;
$user="";
$passwd="";
my $dbh = DBI->connect("dbi:mysql:test", $user, $password)
                                    or die "Can't connect!";
print "connected to mysql\n";
$sth = $dbh->prepare ("select * from staff;");
$sth->execute();
@tables = $dbh -> tables();        # table names
$num = @tables;
$fields = $sth->{NUM_OF_FIELDS};  # number of fields
$fieldnames = $sth->{NAME};        # reference to field names
$fieldnames = join(" ", @$fieldnames);
print <<EOF;                        # print everything
There are $num tables in this database
They are: (@tables)
There are $fields fields in the 'shop' table
They are: ($fieldnames)
EOF


%
connected to mysql
There are 2 tables in this database
They are: (shop staff)
There are 6 fields in the 'staff' table
They are: (item name age dept city years)
%
```

15.3.5 Dynamic requests

metadata.pl is instructive, but it could be more robust. The program needs some variability; that is, a user should be able to select whatever criteria he or she wishes. Here is an example of interactive database processing:

```perl
#!/usr/bin/perl
#
#        interactive.pl
#
use DBI;
$user="";
$passwd="";
my $dbh = DBI->connect("DBI:mysql:test",
    $user, $password) or die "Can't connect!";
print "connected to mysql\n";
$sth = $dbh->prepare ("select * from staff;");
$sth -> execute();
$ref = $sth->{NAME};
print "Select fields from\n(@$ref)\n";
print "Enter quit to end selections\n";
print "Enter ONE field per line: ";
while($f = <STDIN>)
{
        chop($f);
        last if ( $f eq quit);
        $flag = 1;
        foreach $item (@$ref)
        {
                $flag = 0 if ( $item eq $f);
        }
        die "not a legal field\n" if ( $flag );
        $fields = $fields . $f . ",";
        print "Enter field ";
}
chop($fields);
print "Enter conditions? ";
chop($cn = <STDIN>);
$sth=$dbh->prepare("select $fields from Staff where $cn;");
$sth -> execute();
while (@data = $sth->fetchrow_array)
{
    print "@data\n";
}
$sth->finish;                           # administrative
$dbh->disconnect;                       # bookkeeping
```

interactive.pl displays all of the field names and asks the user to choose which ones to display.

```
$ref = $sth->{NAME};
print "Select fields from\n(@$ref)\n";
print "Enter quit to end selections\n";
print "Enter ONE field per line: ";
while($f = <STDIN>)
{
        chop($f);
        last if ( $f eq quit);
        $flag = 1;
        foreach $item (@$ref)
        {
                $flag = 0 if ( $item eq $f);
        }
        die "not a legal field\n" if ( $flag );
        $fields = $fields . $f . ",";
        print "Enter field ";
}
```

If the user selects an incorrect field, the program dies; otherwise, the program goes on and asks the user for a condition on the fields. Then, the statement is prepared and executed. Here is an example run of the program:

```
% interactive.pl
connected to mysql
Select fields from
(item name age dept city years)
Enter quit to end selections
Enter ONE field per line: name
Enter field age
Enter field city
Enter field quit
Enter conditions? age > 50
Michael 56 Columbia
Sally 51 Silver Spring
Bob 58 Ft. Lauderdale
Roger 51 Silver Spring
Bob 51 Columbia
Mike 55 Columbia
%
```

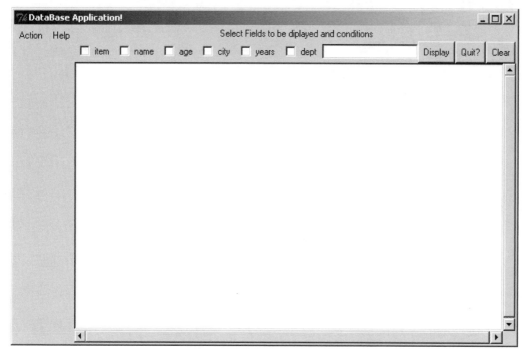

Figure 15.2 Tk-produced GUI.

15.4 Adding a Graphical Front-End

Interactive DBI applications always look more professional if there is a graphical front-end. Thus, our next example will use Tk to produce the GUI shown in Figure 15.2. The above figure shows an example of the front-end followed by the code that produced it.

The idea behind this GUI is simple. A user selects the desired checkboxes, which represent the fields to be displayed. In addition, the user can specify a condition. Then, when the Display button is clicked, the desired query is displayed. The Clear button clears the screen, and the Quit? button quits the application, after a confirm dialog box is displayed. The Action menu also allows you to quit the application or clear the text area.

Figure 15.3 shows the Dialog box after a query has been completed and the user has selected to quit the application.

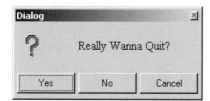

Figure 15.3 Confirming the Quit.

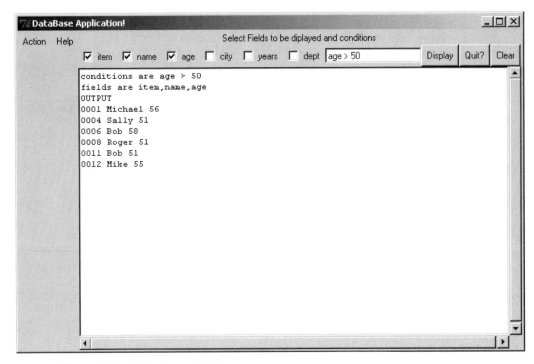

Figure 15.4   Displaying a selection.

Here's the code that produced Figure 15.4:

```perl
#!/usr/bin/perl
#
#   menudb.pl
#
use Tk;
require Tk::Dialog;
use DBI;
$user="";
$password="";
my $dbh = DBI->connect("DBI:mysql:test", $user, $password) or die
    "Can't connect to database!";
my $mw = MainWindow->new;

$mb1 = $mw->Menubutton(-tearoff => 0, -text => "Action",
   -menuitems =>[
                   ['command'=>"Quit", -command=>\&quit ],
                   ['command'=>"Clear",-command=> \&clear ]
                   ]
                   )->pack(-side =>"left",-anchor=>"nw" );

$mb2 = $mw->Menubutton(-tearoff => 0, -text => "Help",
```

continued...

```
                -menuitems =>[
                        ['command'=>"Help",-command => \&help ],
                        ['command'=>"About",-command=>\&about ]
                        ]
                        )->pack(-side=>"left",-anchor=>"nw");

$lab = $mw->Label (
-text=>'Select Fields and conditions')-> pack;
$text = $mw->Scrolled('Text',-scrollbars => 'se'
                        )->pack(-side=>'bottom',-fill => 'x');
$mw->title ("DataBase Application!");
$button1 = $mw->Checkbutton (   -text => 'item',
                                    -variable=>\$item)
                    -> pack(-side => 'left', -expand => 1);
$button2 = $mw->Checkbutton (-text => 'name',
 -variable => \$name)
                    -> pack(-side => 'left', -expand => 1);
$button3 = $mw->Checkbutton (-text => 'age',
                                -variable => \$age)
                    -> pack(-side => 'left', -expand => 1);
$button4 = $mw->Checkbutton (-text => 'city',
 -variable => \$city)
                    -> pack(-side => 'left', -expand => 1);
$button5 = $mw->Checkbutton (-text => 'years',
 -variable => \$years)
                    -> pack(-side => 'left', -expand => 1);
$button6 = $mw->Checkbutton (-text => 'dept',
 -variable => \$dept)
                    -> pack(-side => 'left', -expand => 1);

$textWidget = $mw->Entry(-textvariable => \$comments)
                    -> pack(-side => 'left');
$mw->Button(-text => "Display",-command => \&display)
  -> pack(-side => 'left', -expand => 1);
$mw->Button(-text => "Quit?", -command => \&quit)
  ->pack(-side => 'left', -expand => 1);
$mw->Button(-text => "Clear", -command => \&clear)
    ->pack(-side => 'left',  -expand => 1);
MainLoop;

sub help
{
    $d = $mw->Dialog(
            -text =>     "1. Very little help here!\n".
                         "2. Check desired fields\n" .
                         "3. Enter conditions to the " .
                         "   right of the checkboxes" .
                         "   examples:  age > 50\n" .
                         "            city = 'Columbia'\n".
                         '4.Bugs to: michael@trainingetc.com',
```

continued...

```perl
                  -buttons => ["OK"]);
        $answer = $d->Show();
}
sub about
{
    $d = $mw->Dialog(
        -text =>    "This App produced by M.S. " .
                    "As a rudimentary example of a Tk  " .
                    "Interface to DBI",
            -buttons => ["OK"]);
    $answer = $d->Show();
}
sub quit
{
    $d = $mw->Dialog(
        -text => "Really Wanna Quit?",
        -bitmap => "question",
        -buttons => ["Yes", "No", "Cancel"] );
    $answer = $d->Show();
    exit if ($answer eq "Yes")
}
sub clear
{
    $i = 0;
    $text-> delete ("1.0", "end");
    $text->insert ("end", "Watch this window\n");
}
sub display
{
    my ($command) = "";
    $command .= "item," if ( $item );
    $command .= "name," if ( $name );
    $command .= "age," if ( $age );
    $command .= "years," if ( $years );
    $command .= "city," if ( $city );
    $command .= "dept," if (  $dept );
    chop($command) if( length($command) > 0);
    $text->insert("end", "conditions are $comments\n");
    $text->insert("end", "fields are $command\n");
if ( length($comments) > 0)
{
        $sth = $dbh->prepare
        ("select $command from staff where $comments;");
}
else
{
        $sth = $dbh->prepare
        ("select $command from staff;");
}
$sth->execute();
```

continued...

```
$text-> insert("end", "OUTPUT\n");
while (@items = $sth->fetchrow_array)
{
        foreach $value (@items)
        {
                $text-> insert("end", "$value ");
        }
        $text-> insert("end", "\n");
}


}
```

15.5 Accessing a Real Database via a Web Form

This section discusses the inclusion of real databases with CGI applications. This is a simple idea. The user fills out an HTML form requesting information from a database or adding information to a database. A back-end Perl script simply processes these requests through the support provided by the DBI and DBD modules. Here is an example of a Web front-end to the previous Staff database.

First, we will show you the Web interface, that is, the fill-in form to the database query. When the user fills in this form, the back-end Perl script will process it. The processing is fairly simple, and is representative of how a query can be built from within a Perl script and then passed to the DBI methods. Here is the HTML file, database.htm, followed by its rendering:

```
<!—
    database.htm
    The HTML file
-->
<HTML>
<HEAD>
<TITLE>Database</TITLE>
</HEAD>
<BODY>
<CENTER><H1>Database Application</CENTER>
<CENTER>Using CGI and DBI</H1></CENTER>
<HR>
<CENTER><H2>Check field you wish to display</H2>
<FORM ACTION="http://localhost/cgi-bin/db.pl">
Item<INPUT TYPE=Checkbox NAME=Item>
```

continued...

```
Name<INPUT TYPE=Checkbox NAME=Name>
Age<INPUT TYPE=Checkbox NAME=Age>
Occ<INPUT TYPE=Checkbox NAME=Occ>
City<INPUT TYPE=Checkbox NAME=City>
Years<INPUT TYPE=Checkbox NAME=Years> 
Condition <INPUT TYPE=text NAME=Condition>
<BR>
<BR>
<CENTER><INPUT TYPE=submit VALUE="GET RECORDS">
<INPUT TYPE=reset VALUE="CLEAR FORM"></CENTER>
</FORM>
</BODY>
</HTML>
```

The HTML file above produces the fill-in form shown in Figure 15.5.

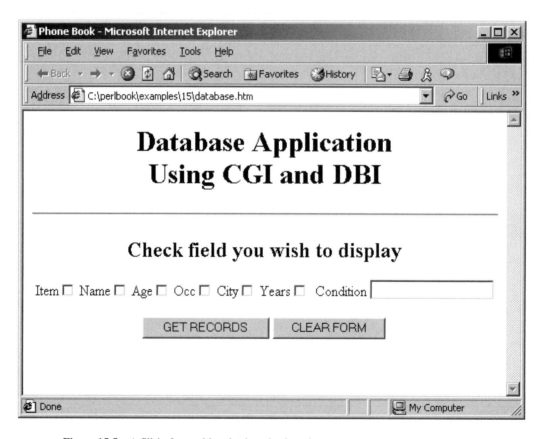

Figure 15.5 A fill-in form with a database back-end.

If the form is filled out as shown above, the `Name`, `Age`, and `City` for all records whose `Age > 50` are displayed.

The following Perl script is the CGI script that processes the form in Figure 15.5:

```perl
#!/usr/bin/perl
#
#   db.pl
#
use DBI;
use CGI;
CGI::ReadParse();
$user="";
$passwd="";
print "Content-Type: text/html\n\n";
my $dbh = DBI->connect("DBI:mysql:test",
    $user, $password) or die "Can't connect!";
$query .= "item,"     if  $in{Item};
$query .= "name,"     if  $in{Name};
$query .= "age,"      if  $in{Age};
$query .= "city,"     if  $in{City};
$query .= "dept,"     if  $in{Occ};
$query .= "years,"    if  $in{Years};
chop $query;

if ( $in{Condition} )
{
    $query = "select $query from Staff where $in{cond};";
}
else
{
    $query = "select $query from Staff;";
}
$sth = $dbh->prepare($query);
$sth -> execute();
print "<CENTER><H1>You have selected the following:";
print "<TABLE BORDER=1>";
$row = 1;
while (@data = $sth->fetchrow_array)
{
        print "<TR><TD>$row</TD><TD>@data</TD></TR>";
        $row++;
}
```

With the selections as shown in Figure 15.5, the output is displayed in Figure 15.6. (Note that you can make the output as pleasing as you wish. In this example, we simply printed a table of all the records that were selected.)

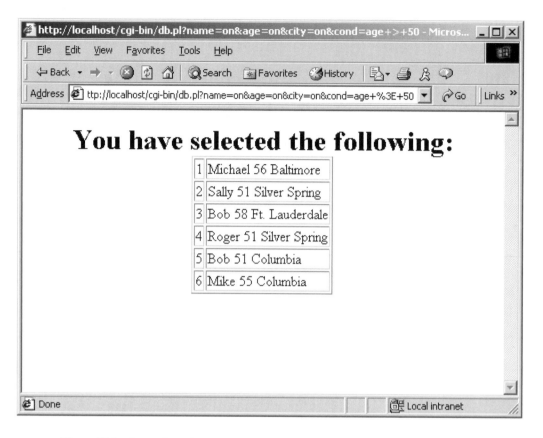

Figure 15.6   Output from the database back-end CGI script.

CHAPTER

16

DEBUGGING PERL SCRIPTS

Debugging a piece of software is a difficult task in any programming language. Some would say that it is even more difficult in Perl since the language is so permissive. This chapter gives the details of various ways in which you can effectively debug Perl programs.

16.1 Introduction

There are various ways of debugging Perl programs. One common technique is to use `print` statements profusely. Another technique is to use command-line switches that will give warnings about potential errors in Perl programs. Perl programmers also have at their disposal some Perl modules that can find program errors. Finally, there is the Perl debugger, a wonderful Perl program that can help find bugs when all else fails.

16.2 Using the `print` Function

It's always a good idea to strategically place a lot of calls to `print` functions in your programs so that you can see both the flow of control in your program and the values of key variables. Placing `print` function calls at the beginnings of subroutines can help in determining exactly what you have passed to the subroutines. Be careful about placing them at the end of subroutines, however. Notice the following function, which computes the length of the hypotenuse of a right triangle given the first two sides:

```
#!/usr/bin/perl
#
#   hypot.pl
#
sub hypot
{
        my ($side1, $side2, $hypot) = @_;
        $side1 *= $side1;
        $side2 *= $side2;
        $hypot = $side1 + $side2;
}
$first = 3;
$second = 4;
$hypot = hypot($first, $second);
print "$hypot\n";
```

It should be clear to the reader that the writer of this subroutine forgot to take the square root of $hypot just before the subroutine ended. It might not be as clear to the writer of this code, however. In an attempt to track down the bug, the writer might try to place a print function just before the subroutine returns.

```
sub hypot
{       my ($side1, $side2, $hypot) = @_;
        $side1 *= $side1;
        $side2 *= $side2;
        $hypot = $side1 + $side2;
        print "From hypot: Value = $hypot\n";
}
```

If you proceed as above, you will affect the return value from the subroutine. Recall that the return value from a subroutine is the value of the last statement evaluated inside the subroutine. In this case, it is the value of the print function. Even though it is rarely used, print will typically return the value 1. This isn't the world's greatest debugging tip, but it will save you once or twice now that you have seen this example.

16.2.1   The warn **function**

We have already given the details of the die function. Perl also contains the warn function, which behaves exactly like die except the program does not terminate. Whether you use die or warn is up to you. It strictly depends on the severity of the error you find.

When should you check for errors? That's also up to you, but there are a few cases when you absolutely should:

- check on the number of arguments to a script
- check on the status of the open or opendir function
- check on whether a user has input the desired type

isfound.pl is a program that should receive two arguments: a directory and a filename. The program then checks to see if this file is found in this directory. The beginning
of this program should make the tests recommended above.

```
die "usage directory file\n" if $#ARGV != 1;
die "first arg not a directory\n" if ! -d $ARGV[0];
opendir(DIR, $ARGV[0]) || die "can't open $ARGV[0]\n";
```

The entire program is shown next:

```
#!/usr/bin/perl
#
#       isfound.pl
#
#
#       Program Usage:
#       $ perl directory file
#
die "usage directory file\n" if $#ARGV != 1;
die "first arg not a directory\n" if ! -d $ARGV[0];
opendir(DIR, $ARGV[0]) || die "can't open $ARGV[0]\n";
@files = readdir(DIR);
if ( grep(/^$ARGV[1]$/, @files) )
{
        print "$ARGV[1] is found in $ARGV[0]\n";
}
else
{
        print "$ARGV[1] is NOT found in $ARGV[0]\n";
}
```

16.2.2   The eval function

Occasionally, you will have the need to build strings that contain Perl expressions or even
Perl programs. Once you have done this, you may also need to evaluate these strings. For
example, if you have code such as the following:

```
$b = 10;
$c = 20;
$str = '$var = $b + $c';
print eval $str;
print "$var\n";
```

It is clear that `str` will have the string `$var = $b + $c` as its contents. If you now print `$str`, then that string would be displayed. When Perl executes the statement:

```
print eval $str
```

the `eval` function evaluates the expression inside `$str` and hands the results to `print`. However, it also sets the variable `$var` to the value 30. Thus, the program has dynamically created a variable. If `eval` is handed a syntactically incorrect string, it sets the special variable `$@` to an error message. Here's a calculator that evaluates Perl expressions entered at the keyboard. Notice that the program uses `warn` instead of `die`.

```
#!/usr/bin/perl
#
#   calc.pl
#
while (1)
{
    print "Enter an expression ";
    chomp($expression = <STDIN>);
    last if $expression =~ /^quit$/;
    print eval $expression, "\n";
    warn $@ if $@;
}
% calc.pl
Enter an expression 2 + 3
5
Enter an expression 2 +
Syntax error at (eval 2) line 2 at EOF
Enter an expression $a = 10
10
Enter an expression $a + 5
15
Enter an expression quit
%
```

There's also a block form of `eval` that is used predominately for error checking. In the script `oops.pl`, the user enters two values. The program divides the first value by the second. If the division is by 0, `$@` is set and the block terminates, but the program doesn't. Even if a `die` is executed from an `eval` block, only the block is terminated, not the program.

```
#!/usr/bin/perl
#
#   oops.pl
#
print "Input numerator and denominator ";
```

continued...

```
chomp($_ = <STDIN>);
($a, $b) = split;
eval {
    $c = $a / $b;
    $c = $c * $c;
};
warn $@ if $@;
print '( $a / $b ) ** 2 is ', $c, "\n";
```

16.3 Command-Line Options

There are many options that you can use on the command line. Not all of them represent debugging tools, but the ones presented here represent some form of aid in finding bugs. You can see all of the options by using –h on the command line.

```
% perl -h
-c          check syntax only
-d          run program under debugger
-e          one line of program
-n          apply command to entire file
-v          print version
-w          enable many useful warnings (RECOMMENDED)
-x          strip off text before #!perl line
...
...
%
```

16.3.1   The –c option

When you run a Perl command with the –c option, Perl simply checks for syntax errors without actually running your script. Perl responds by either listing your syntax errors or by informing you that the syntax is okay. This option is very important for CGI scripts. When a CGI script contains a syntax error, the server sends the browser an error message, but it does not pertain to the syntax of the program. Thus, the only way you can see the syntax error is with the –c option.

16.3.2   The –e option

The –e option allows you to run a single Perl command from the command line. This may be useful in determining the results of a particular command without having to create a Perl file, change the mode if on Unix, and run it. Here are a few examples:

```
% perl -e 'print "hello";'
% perl -e 'print join("\n", @INC, "\n");'
```

Note here that in a DOS window, the outer quotes are double quotes rather than single quotes. This can make for a cumbersome command when you have to escape the double quotes inside a Perl command.

```
% perl -e "print 'hello';"
% perl -e "print join(\"\n\", @INC, \"\n\");"
```

You may also use multiple –e options on the same command line:

```
% perl -e 'print "hello";' -e 'print "bye";'
```

16.3.3   The –n option

The –n option allows you to apply a command to each line of a file. For example, to number lines for a file, you could use:

```
% perl -ne 'print "$. $_";' thisfile
```

16.3.4   The –v option

The –v option gives version information. The uppercase –V option gives more information, including the place where your libraries are kept.

```
% perl -v
This is perl, v5.6.0 built for MSWin32-x86-multi-thread
(with 1 registered patch, see perl -V for more detail)

Copyright 1987-2000, Larry Wall

... listing truncated here
```

16.3.5   The –w option

Without a doubt, the most useful debugging option is the –w option. This gives you various warnings about what may have gone wrong in your program. Here is a program that has potential errors in it:

```
#!/usr/bin/perl
#
#         minusw.pl
#
open(FILE, " input");
$inputln = <INPUT>;
print "$inputline\n";
$x = $x + 1;
print FILE "just printed line $x\n";
```

First we run the program and then we run it with the –w option:

```
% minusw.pl                             # gives no output


% perl -w minusw.pl
Name "main::inputln" used only once: possible typo at minusw.pl line
    6.
Name "main::INPUT" used only once: possible typo at
minusw.pl line 6.
Name "main::inputline" used only once: possible typo at
minusw.pl line 7.
Read on closed filehandle <INPUT> at minusw.pl line 6.
Use of uninitialized value at minusw.pl line 7.
Use of uninitialized value at minusw.pl line 8.
Filehandle main::FILE opened only for input at minusw.pl line 9.
%
```

The following various potential problems were found: For one, there are several instances where a symbol is used only once in the program. This does not have to be a bug in a program, but often it indicates a misspelling of a symbol name. In effect, this is a bug. Likewise, the –w option will warn about variables that are used before being initialized. Another bug caught in the above program is that the filehandle is used in the wrong context, that is, for output rather than input.

16.4 Executing Portions of Your Code

There are several techniques in Perl to comment away chunks of code.

16.4.1 The −x option

The −x option is used to prevent Perl from executing all lines above the #! line. Note the code below and see how it behaves when it is executed:

```
print "The lines above\n";
print "the #! line\n";
print "will not be executed\n";
print "if -x is given on the command line.\n";
#!/usr/bin/perl
#
#       minusx.pl
#
print "If -x is given, then you will only see\n";
print "these 2 lines.\n";


% minusx.pl
The lines above
the #! line
will not be executed
if -x is given on the command line.
If -x is given, then you will only see
these 2 lines.
%


% perl -x minusx.pl
If -x is given, then you will only see
these 2 lines.
%
```

If you decide to run the two examples above, the latter will work equally well on Windows or Unix. However, the former example will cause an error on Unix because on Unix systems, the top line must be the pathname to your Perl executable.

16.4.2 The __END__ word

Another way to prevent Perl from executing a portion of code is to use the __END__ directive. Whenever Perl detects this sequence of seven characters as a word by itself, it will not process any lines below and including that line. (Note: The first two and last two characters are the underscore character!)

```
#!/usr/bin/perl
#
#        end.pl
#
print "You should only see these\n";
print "three lines and not the ones\n";
print "below the __END__ line.\n";
__END__
print "You should not see these\n";
print "lines being executed.\n";

% end.pl
You should only see these
three lines and not the ones
below the __END__ line.
%
```

16.4.3 The DATA filehandle

It is a nice idea to be able to include the data for a program alongside the source code. This may be accomplished by simply entering your data below the __END__ line. This data may be read by using the special filehandle DATA. Here's a program to illustrate this technique:

```
#!/usr/bin/perl
#
#        data.pl
#
$chars = $words = 0;
while(<DATA>)
{
        $words += split;
        $chars += length;
}
print "CHARS: $chars\n";
print "WORDS: $words\n";
print "LINES: $.\n";
__END__
This is a small data file to illustrate
the DATA filehandle. This program counts the number
of lines, words, and characters in this file.
```

continued...

```
% data.pl
CHARS: 163
WORDS: 31
LINES: 3
%
```

16.4.4   Documenting Perl code

Somewhere in the software development cycle, there needs to be time for documentation. Programmers typically detest this work, and it is usually never done on time or as well as it ought to be.

In any event, documentation is traditionally kept separate from the actual code being documented. However, the current thinking in software development is to have the source code and documentation bundled into the same file. All Perl modules are packaged this way. When you write any OO modules, you ought to follow this convention. The documentation style in Perl has been given the name "plain old documentation," or POD. You can look in any Perl module bundled with the standard distribution to see these so-called POD files.

The motivation behind the documentation "language" was to facilitate the translation of the documentation into other formats such as HTML or Unix man pages. Several translation tools such as pod2html, pod2man, and pod2text are delivered with the standard Perl distribution.

Like HTML files, POD files use tags interspersed with text. Each tag defines a paragraph. Paragraphs must be separated from one another by at least one blank line. A POD tag is an equal sign, =, followed by one of several currently understood keywords, all of which are listed below:

```
head1, head2, item, over, back, cut, pod
```

The first two tags, head1 and head2, specify how far the text is to be moved over when one of the translation tools reads this file.

=item *	Identifies that a list will follow. Each item will have a *.
=over	Specifies that each item will be displayed four spaces to the right.
=back	Ends the list.
=cut	Allows you to intersperse documentation with code. Anything between =head and =cut will be treated as documentation.

You can take advantage of the =cut sequence to "comment out" sections of code inside Perl source files. Here's an example taken out of the IO.pm module, which comes from the standard Perl distribution. This module offers an OO alternative to handling I/O in a Perl program:

```
package IO;
=head1 NAME
IO - load various IO modules
=head1 SYNOPSIS

use IO;

=head1 DESCRIPTIONC
<IO> provides a simple mechanism to load some of the IO modules once.
Currently this includes:

        IO::Handle
        IO::Seekable
        IO::File
        IO::Pipe
        IO::Socket

For more information on any of these modules, please see their
    respective documentation.

=cut

use IO::Handle;
use IO::Seekable;
use IO::File;
use IO::Pipe;
use IO::Socket;
1;
```

All of the lines between the =head1 and the =cut are not processed by Perl, and as such can be considered comments. To see how documentation can be built from this module, use the pod2html tool to produce HTML from the file:

```
$ pod2html IO.pm > out.html
```

Now, load your browser with out.html. The results are depicted in Figure 16.1.

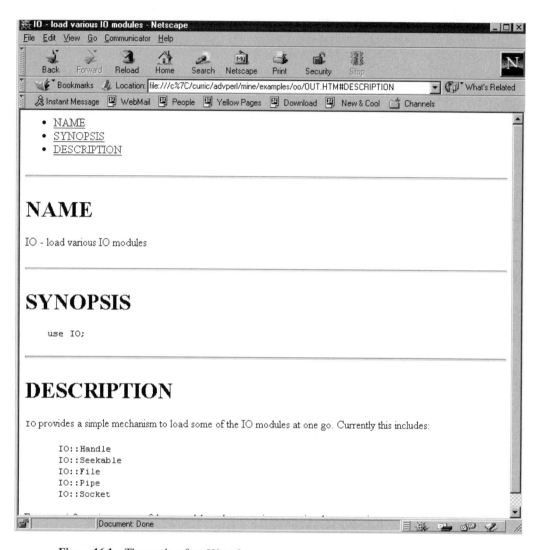

Figure 16.1   The results of `pod2html`.

16.5 Quoting

In languages like the Unix shells and Perl, there are many special characters. Quoting refers to the ways in which you can turn off the meaning of special characters. This can sometimes be confusing and can easily lead to bugs.

Within single quotes, everything except \\, which prints a \ and \ ', which prints a ', is taken literally. Within double quotes, scalar and array names are interpolated, as are escape sequences beginning with \, but everything else is taken literally. Thus, strings containing escape sequences such as \n and \t must be double quoted for interpretation.

Like the Unix shells, command substitution takes place within back quotes. Because of all the various quoting mechanisms, Perl allows alternative notations to lessen the possibility for potential errors. For example, suppose you wanted to print the eight characters below. Try it!

```
'$a'='5'
```

One way to do this is as follows:

```
print '\'$a\'=\'$b\'';
```

The `print` above uses the backslash character to turn off the special meaning of whatever character follows it. This solution is at best hard to follow and is certainly error-prone. There is another approach. Instead of using a pair of single quotes, you can use the q character and a pair of #'s to enclose whatever text you wish to compose. Using this technique, you could code:

```
print q#'$a'='$b'#;
```

In addition to the #'s, you may use any of the following:

```
print q#'$a'='$b'#;
print q!'$a'='$b'!;
print q('$a'='$b');
print q{'$a'='$b'};
```

Likewise, the double quote characters have another means of expression. The following are equivalent:

```
print "hello there";
print qq#hello there#;
print qq!hello there!;
print qq{hello there};
print qq(hello there);
```

Perl also allows a synonymous expression for back quotes:

```
$x = `ls`;
$x = qx#ls#;
$x = qw!ls!;
$x = {ls};
$x = (ls);
```

And finally, if you want a comma-free notation for array elements, you may use any of the following:

```
@e = qw(hello there folks);
@a = qw/hello there folks/;
@b = qw#hello there folks#;
@c = qw!hello there folks!;
@d = qw{hello there folks};
```

16.6 Useful Perl Modules

In addition to all of the debugging techniques that we have seen so far, there are also a few Perl modules that are helpful in debugging.

16.6.1 `strict.pm`

The `strict` module forces Perl programmers to conform to certain coding practices. There are three main categories enforced by the `strict` module: variables, subroutines, and references. If your program contains the line:

```
use strict;
```

then all three categories are enforced.

16.6.2 `strict vars`

To limit the capabilities of the `strict` module so that it just checks on variable use, you need to code:

```
use strict qw(vars);
```

In this case, Perl makes sure that your use of variables is limited to my variables or full package name variables. This virtually removes the chances of making the following error:

```
$mesgtxt = "start ";
$msgtext .= "middle";                    # wrong spelling
print "$msgtext\n";
```

If the above code had been written as:

```
use strict qw(vars);          # or use strict
$mesgtxt = "start ";
$msgtext .= "middle";         # wrong spelling
print "$msgtext\n";
```

then the above code would have yielded the following error message:

```
Global symbol $mesgtxt requires explicit package name at strict line 2
Global symbol $msgtext requires explicit package name at strict line 3
Global symbol $msgtext requires explicit package name at strict line 4
```

This error message will alert you to the fact that the first line of code has a misspelling in the variable name. The code should have been written as:

```
use strict qw(vars);          # or use strict
my $msgtext;
$msgtext = "start ";
$msgtext .= "middle";
print "$msgtext\n";
```

16.6.3 strict refs

One of the improvements in Perl 5 was the introduction of hard references.

```
$var = 20;            # a variable
$ref = \$var;         # a hard reference
print $$ref;          # access $var through reference
```

Prior to this, Perl references were known as soft references and were difficult to debug.

```
$var = 20;            # a variable
$ref = "var";         # store name of variable
print $ref;           # prints var
print $$ref;          # prints 20
```

In Perl, soft references can be made through more than one level, increasing the difficulty in debugging. If you code:

```
use strict qw(refs)       # or use strict
```

then soft references are prohibited.

16.6.4 `strict subs`

There are various rules about how to call a Perl subroutine. As long as a subroutine is declared before it is invoked, you may use any of the following. Suppose the function is named `square`.

```
sub square
{
        print "hello\n";
}
square;
&square;
square();
&square();
```

If the subroutine is defined beyond where the calls are made, then the first call above will fail. However, notice how the following example can introduce a bug in the program:

```
$r = compute;            # assign the string
print "$r\n";            # print the string
sub compute
{
    return 10;
}
$r = compute;            # execute the function
print "$r\n";            # print results of function call
```

Most subroutines are placed in libraries and imported through `use` or `require`, so the above can be thought of as bad programming style. Nevertheless, it can be avoided by using the following, which mandates that all functions be invoked with either `&` or `()`, unless they are predefined or they have already been seen:

```
use strict qw(subs);
```

Now any attempt to use an unquoted (bare) word will be flagged.

```
use strict qw(subs);
$result = sa;            # error, what's this?
$x = compute;            # error, what's this?
&compute;
compute();
&compute();
sub compute
{
        return 10;
}
```

16.6.5 `diagnostics.pm`

There is another module, `diagnostics`, which you can use to see various warnings. You can activate these warnings by coding the following in any of your Perl source files:
`use diagnostics:`

When you use this module, you will see warnings about the exact same things that the –w option gives you. The difference is that the diagnostics module gives you longer, more verbose information about your potential errors.

16.6.6 `Carp.pm`

Most Perl programmers use the `die` function when they catch an error for which there is no legitimate recovery and the `warn` function to catch an error for which there may be a recovery. `die` will terminate the program and `warn` will not. If `die` or `warn` is nested inside a function, then neither call will give you any information about the place from which this function was called. The `Carp` module provides some functions that give you this information. You can use `croak` instead of `die`, and you can use `carp` instead of `warn` to gain this extra information. In the following example, the program reports an error if a number passed to the function `isMultiple` is divisible by 10:

```
#!/usr/bin/perl
#
#   app.pl
#
use Carp;
sub isMultiple
{
     if ( $_[0] % 10 == 0)
     {
         croak "terminate: $_[0] is a multiple of 10\n";
     }
     return 0;
}
$result = isMultiple(101);
print "After the first call: result is $result\n";
$result = isMultiple(100);
print "After the second call: result is $result\n";

% app.pl
After the first call: result is 0
terminate: 100 is a multiple of 10
     main::isMultiple(100,10) called at app.pl line 17
%
```

16.7 The Perl Debugger

The Perl debugger is set in motion by the -d flag. It does not run as a separate program. To start the Perl debugger, type the following:

```
$ perl -d program.pl
```

You will see:

```
Loading DB routines from perl5db.pl version 1.07
Editor support available.

Enter h or `h h' for help.

main::(program1.pl:1):        $b = $a;
DB<1>
```

This tells you that you are debugging the script `program.pl` and that you are about to execute the following command from that script:

```
$b = $a;
```

Now you can start to enter debugger commands. The line:

```
DB<1>
```

is the debugger prompt. By entering the h command at this prompt, you will get a list of debugger commands. If you want a simple explanation of a specific command, simply enter:

```
h command_name
```

Here are some examples of debugger commands:

Set a breakpoint at line 25	b 25
Run the program to the breakpoint	r
Print a value type	print $val
Place debugger in trace mode	t
Print a data structure pointed to by $ref	x $ref
Single-step through the program	s
Step over subroutines	n

List lines min-max	`l min-max`
Quit the debugger	`q`

When you are ready to quit the debugger, enter q at the debugger prompt.

16.8   Useful Perl Functions

The last section in this chapter shows you how to use several functions that may be useful for a wide variety of problems. In some cases, they may help you debug a program, and in other cases, they may make it easier to solve a particular problem.

16.8.1   The `ord` function

To determine the numeric value of a character, use the ord function. Here's a program that produces a table of characters and associated numeric values for digits, uppercase characters, and lowercase characters:

```
#!/usr/bin/perl
#
#   table.pl
#
foreach $item ('0' .. '9', 'A' .. 'E', 'a' .. 'e')
{   print "$item => [", ord($item), "]\n";
}
% table.pl
0 => [48]
1 => [49]
2 => [50]
3 => [51]
4 => [52]
5 => [53]
6 => [54]
7 => [55]
8 => [56]
9 => [57]
A => [65]
B => [66]
C => [67]
D => [68]
E => [69]
a => [97]
b => [98]
c => [99]
d => [100]
e => [101]
%
```

Also, beware of the difference between the following two statements:

```
$a = '1' +  '2';                  # 3
$b = ord('1') + ord('2');         # 99
```

16.8.2 The `chr` function

`chr` takes a number and produces the character represented by the number. It's the exact inverse of `ord`.

```
#!/usr/bin/perl
#
#       chr.pl
#
foreach $number (48 .. 57, 65 .. 69, 97 .. 101)
{
        print chr($number), " => $number\n";
}




% chr.pl
0 => 48
1 => 49
2 => 50
3 => 51
4 => 52
5 => 53
6 => 54
7 => 55
8 => 56
9 => 57
A => 65
B => 66
C => 67
D => 68
E => 69
a => 97
b => 98
c => 99
d => 100
e => 101
%
```

16.8.3 The `hex` and `oct` functions

The `hex` function takes an argument that is interpreted as a hexadecimal string and returns the equivalent decimal value. In other words:

```
$a = hex(100);
print "$a\n";          # 256;
```

The `oct` function takes a string that is interpreted as an octal sequence and returns the equivalent decimal value:

```
$a = oct(100);
print "$a\n";          # 64
```

16.8.4 `pack` and `unpack`

Some applications require the preparation or reception of data that must be in a special format. Perl handles these situations by preparing this data with the `pack` function and reading this data with the `unpack` function. We've seen a few examples of these functions already. Now we will give several more.

`pack` takes a list of values and packs it into a binary structure according to a format string given as its first argument. It also returns the string containing that structure. The format string is a sequence of characters that gives the order and type of value.

`unpack` does the reverse. These two functions have a myriad of special uses in Perl. Here are a few examples of `pack`:

```
$fname = pack("cccc",77,73,75,69);
print "$fname\n";                              # prints MIKE
$fname = pack("c4",77,73,75,69);
print "$fname\n";                              # prints MIKE
$fname = pack("c4xc2",77,73,75,69, 83, ord("."));
print "$fname\n";                              # prints MIKE S.
```

Each format applies to the next value in the list. As you can see, `c4` is equivalent to `cccc`. An `x` places a null byte into the output string. We also used the `ord` function to place the value of the period into the `pack` function.

The above examples merely show how to use the `pack` function. The next example shows how to write a series of integers in binary to an external file. The program creates `$ARGV[0]` many random integers in the range 0 to 10000 and writes each one to a file. Of course, the file is not displayable as a text file. To display the values in the file, we need to use the `read` function to read each integer from the file. Then we use the `unpack` function to extract the integer into a Perl variable.

```perl
#!/usr/bin/perl
#
#        writeints.pl
#
die "need an argument\n" unless $#ARGV == 0;
die "arg 1 must be a number\n" unless $ARGV[0] =~ /^\d+$/;
open(BINARY, "+> binary") || die qq/can't open 'binary'\n/;
srand(time);
for ( $i = 0; $i < $ARGV[0]; $i++)
{
    $value = int (rand(10000));
    $int = pack("i", $value);      # signed integer value
    print "writing $value\n";
    print BINARY $int;
}
print "rewinding output file\n";
seek(BINARY,0,0);
print "reading values from file\n";
while(($x = read(BINARY, $var, 4)) > 0 )
{
    print "just read $x bytes: ";
    $value = unpack("i", $var);
    print "$value\n";
}
```

Here's an example of executing `writeints.pl`:

```
% writeints.pl 10
writing 1585
writing 5277
writing 6532
writing 3909
writing 8936
writing 5639
writing 5408
writing 5776
writing 2715
writing 1572
rewinding output file
reading values from file
just read 4 bytes: 1585
just read 4 bytes: 5277
just read 4 bytes: 6532
just read 4 bytes: 3909
just read 4 bytes: 8936
just read 4 bytes: 5639
just read 4 bytes: 5408
just read 4 bytes: 5776
just read 4 bytes: 2715
just read 4 bytes: 1572
%
```

Here's another example. This one uses the `B32` format to express an integer as a bitstream.

```perl
#!/usr/bin/perl
#
#   bits.pl
#
for ($i = 1; $i <= 31; $i++)
{
    $str = unpack("B32", pack("N", $i));
    print substr($str, 25,8), "\n";
}

% bits.pl
0000001
0000010
0000011
0000100
0000101
0000110
0000111
0001000
0001001
0001010
0001011
0001100
0001101
0001110
0001111
0010000
0010001
0010010
0010011
0010100
0010101
0010110
0010111
0011000
0011001
%
```

INDEX

E

N

O

P

S

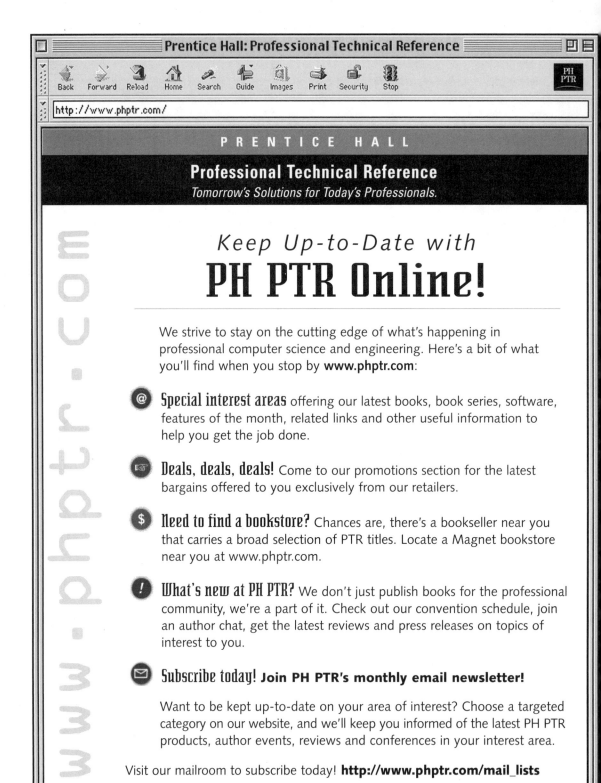